HOLT *Traditions*

Sixth Course

ANSWER KEY
Language and Sentence Skills Practice
Support for *Warriner's Handbook*

▶ **Lesson Worksheets**
▶ **Chapter Reviews**
▶ **"Choices" Activities**
▶ **Literary Models**
▶ **Proofreading Applications**

FOR
■ **Grammar**
■ **Usage**
■ **Mechanics**
■ **Sentences**

HOLT, RINEHART AND WINSTON

ISBN 978-0-55-400191-3
ISBN 0-55-400191-8

3 4 5 6   1689   13 12 11 10
4500237054

Contents

iii

Contents

Contents

Chapter 7

CLEAR REFERENCE:
PRONOUNS AND ANTECEDENTS

Chapter 8

USING VERBS CORRECTLY:
PRINCIPAL PARTS, TENSE, VOICE, MOOD

Chapter 9

USING MODIFIERS CORRECTLY:
FORMS AND USES OF ADJECTIVES AND ADVERBS;
COMPARISON

Contents

Chapter 10

PLACEMENT OF MODIFIERS:
MISPLACED AND DANGLING MODIFIERS

Chapter 11

A GLOSSARY OF USAGE:
COMMON USAGE PROBLEMS

Chapter 12

CAPITALIZATION:
STANDARD USES OF CAPITAL LETTERS

Contents

Contents

Chapter 16

CORRECTING COMMON ERRORS:
KEY LANGUAGE SKILLS REVIEW

Chapter 17

WRITING CLEAR SENTENCES

Contents

Chapter 1: The Parts of Speech, pp. 1–27

Choices: Exploring Parts of Speech, p. 1

Choices activities are designed to extend and enrich students' understanding of grammar, usage, and mechanics and to take learners beyond traditional classroom instruction. To use the Choices worksheet, have each student pick an activity that interests him or her. In some cases, you may wish to assign an activity to a particular student or group of students. You may also want to request that students get your approval for the activities they choose. Establish guidelines for what constitutes successful completion of an activity. Then, help students plan how they will share their work with the rest of the class.

Choices activities can be scored with a pass-fail grade or treated as bonus-point projects. Those activities that require students to research or create a certain number of items might be graded in a traditional manner.

Common, Proper, Concrete, and Abstract Nouns, p. 2

EXERCISE

1. My <u>father</u> [C] believes <u>sunshine</u> [C] can make you smart.
2. The <u>cowboys</u> [C] took the <u>horses</u> [C] to the <u>creek</u> [C] just past <u>Razzleberry Hill</u>.
3. <u>Jon</u> [C] did not have the <u>strength</u> [A] to close the <u>window</u>.
4. I learned to speak <u>Portuguese</u> from my <u>teacher</u> [C], <u>Dr. Tihonen</u>.
5. That's a good <u>thought</u> [A], <u>Jacob</u>, but I don't have any plastic <u>bags</u> [C].
6. From the <u>house</u> [C], you can see both the <u>waterfall</u> and the <u>stream</u>.
7. It's not about how you hit the <u>baseball</u> [C]; it's about your mental <u>attitude</u> [A].
8. The <u>province</u> [C] finally won its <u>independence</u> [A].
9. It takes <u>patience</u> [A] to learn the <u>guitar</u> [C].

10. <u>Farley</u> [C], <u>Jack</u> [C], and I paddled our <u>canoes</u> [C] down the <u>Colorado River</u>.
11. Moving to <u>Pittsburgh</u> caused me a lot of <u>heartache</u> [A].
12. Why don't you take off your <u>shoes</u> [C] and rest your <u>feet</u> [C], <u>Lucy</u>?
13. That <u>student</u> [C] has great <u>ambition</u> [A].
14. Our <u>homework</u> [C] is due <u>tomorrow</u> [A].
15. My <u>brother</u> [C] is a <u>surgeon</u> [C] in <u>Houston</u> [C].
16. <u>Robby</u> [C] is an excellent saxophone <u>player</u> [C].
17. I wish everyone could enjoy the <u>love</u> [A] of a loyal <u>pet</u> [C].
18. <u>Paul</u> [C] thought the <u>play</u> [C] was about <u>forgiveness</u> [A].
19. The <u>hippopotamus</u> [C] rested in the cool <u>water</u> [C].
20. Let's not listen to that <u>CD</u> [C] right now.

Collective and Compound Nouns, p. 3

EXERCISE

Compound nouns may vary depending on dictionary used.

1. On our way to the <u>Museum of Fine Arts</u>, the bus began to overheat.
2. Our <u>bus driver</u>, <u>Mr. Peterson</u>, said we had to pull over to the <u>wayside</u>.
3. One <u>group</u> of students wandered down to see the pond.
4. There was a mother duck with a <u>brood</u> of ducklings.
5. "Look," I said, "a <u>fleet</u> of ducks!"
6. "Silly!" said Lynn. "It's called a <u>flock</u> of ducks."
7. "But they float around like ships," I said. "Maybe we should call them a <u>crew</u>."
8. A few people from the <u>class</u> fed the <u>flock</u> with bread from our <u>lunchboxes</u>.

9. Lynn got too close to the <u>waterside</u> and almost fell in.

10. Some of our <u>classmates</u> walked to the other side of the lake.

11. A <u>group</u> of boys began throwing a <u>football</u>.

12. Some students in the <u>choir</u> decided to practice a song.

13. I'm not in the <u>choir</u>; I'm in the <u>band</u>.

14. The teacher used a <u>cell phone</u> to call the school.

15. After the radiator was fixed, the <u>crowd</u> got back on the bus.

16. When I bent down to retie my <u>shoelace</u>, I noticed a baby duck under the seat.

17. We coaxed the bird back to the duck pond, where its <u>family</u> was waiting.

18. As we drove off, the entire <u>class</u> waved <u>goodbye</u> to the <u>flock</u> through the rear window.

19. I was happy that our <u>group</u> was finally on its way to the museum.

20. However, when we got there, there was a sign on the museum door: "Museum closed due to <u>floodwater</u>."

Pronouns and Antecedents, p. 4

EXERCISE *Possessive pronouns in items 9, 17, and 19 may be identified as adjectives.*

1. <u>Uncle Andrew</u> is in this picture; <u>he</u> is on the far left.

2. When <u>Clara</u> was a little girl, <u>she</u> wanted to be an artist.

3. The <u>dishes</u> are in the dishwasher because <u>they</u> are dirty.

4. <u>Mary</u> drove here <u>herself</u>.

5. <u>Clifford</u> will have to hurry; <u>he</u> is late.

6. Where is the <u>screwdriver</u>? <u>It</u> was here a minute ago.

7. Tell <u>George</u> the blue umbrella is for <u>him</u>.

8. <u>Tori</u> is leaving. Will Ed go with <u>her</u>?

9. <u>Andrea</u> had something in <u>her</u> eye.

10. The <u>sign</u> was so small <u>it</u> could not be seen from the road.

11. Dad went with <u>him</u> when <u>Sven</u> took the driving test.

12. <u>Tom</u> built the shed <u>himself</u>.

13. <u>Seth</u> said, "<u>I</u> intend to be president of the class."

14. The <u>students</u> painted the mural <u>themselves</u>.

15. The <u>clock</u> needs to be wound because <u>it</u> has stopped.

16. As <u>they</u> entered the pep rally, <u>Carl</u> and <u>Christopher</u> announced loudly, "The wrestling team has arrived!"

17. <u>Louie</u> and <u>Rachel</u> are tired of <u>their</u> toys.

18. Ms. Young told <u>Jamie</u>, "<u>You</u> were the student voted most likely to succeed."

19. Is <u>Sergio</u> at <u>his</u> job?

20. The factory <u>workers</u> and the <u>managers</u> are happy <u>they</u> get along so well.

Personal, Reflexive, and Intensive Pronouns, p. 5

EXERCISE *Possessive pronouns in items 5, 6, 7, 8, 10, 11, 12, 14, 17, and 20 may be identified as adjectives.*

1. <u>They</u> rode the <u>train</u> west for as far as <u>it</u> would carry <u>them</u>.

2. <u>We</u> thought this house was <u>hers</u>.

3. <u>He</u> convinced <u>himself</u> to finish the chores.

4. <u>They</u> <u>themselves</u> made the waffles.

5. I found her house all by myself. (P, P, R)

6. Our greatest challenge is ahead of us. (P, P)

7. His sister went with him to find your dog. (P, P, P)

8. I wrote myself a note about their party. (P, R, P)

9. You could paint the room yourself. (P, I)

10. She is my favorite designer. (P, P)

11. The puppy chased its tail until it tired itself out. (P, P, R)

12. Her grandparents live next door to you, don't they? (P, P, P)

13. You may help yourself to the buffet. (P, R)

14. It was so cold that we could see our breath. (P, P, P)

15. She fixed the leaking faucet herself. (P, I)

16. The scientists themselves could not figure out the problem. (I)

17. You and your friends should join us. (P, P, P)

18. We are not planning to see the movie ourselves. (P, I)

19. If she said we would not finish the race, then she does not know us well. (P, P, P, P)

20. Monica herself was there to meet us when we dragged ourselves off the plane after the longest flight of our lives. (I, P, P, R, P)

Demonstrative, Interrogative, and Relative Pronouns, p. 6

EXERCISE

1. "We must discover the culprit who is guilty of this crime." (R)

2. "The shoehorn was last seen near a window, which has been broken." (R)

3. "Which is the window that was broken?" asked Ann, the housekeeper. (I, R)

4. "This must be the one," said Harold, the butler. (D)

5. Harold pointed to a window, which had been shattered. (R)

6. "What are the marks on the ground outside the window?" asked Ann. (I)

7. "Those are footprints," replied the great detective. (D)

8. "They belong to someone whose boots are very large." (R)

9. "Who has boots as big as the footprints?" asked Ann, looking at the butler's feet. (I)

10. "What are you implying?" demanded the butler. (I)

11. "The thief must have large feet. That's all," said Ann, looking down at her small shoes. (D)

12. "These are certainly the footprints of the thief," said the great detective. (D)

13. "However, those were not necessarily the boots of the thief." (D)

14. "What do you mean?" they both asked. (I)

15. "There is one thing that you are forgetting," said the great detective. "Small feet can fit into large boots, too." (R)

16. "That is silly," said Ann. (D)

17. "Why would someone who had small feet wear large boots?" (R)

18. "What could be a better way of disguising your footprints than using someone else's shoes?" (I)

19. "That is right," said the butler. "A pair of my boots is missing." (D)

20. "This is the thief!" cried the great detective, pointing at Ann, the small-footed housekeeper. (D)

Indefinite Pronouns, p. 7

EXERCISE A

1. one's; nothing
2. anyone
3. Someone
4. Few
5. most
6. Many
7. one
8. most
9. anyone
10. most

EXERCISE B

Answers may vary.

11. Some
12. Many
13. No one
14. everything
15. each

Adjectives and the Words They Modify, p. 8

EXERCISE

1. Larry brought four suitcases on vacation.
2. I enjoyed the scary movie we saw yesterday.
3. Will we have enough soup for everyone?
4. The dry leaves crunched underfoot.
5. The first time I saw snow, I was in New Mexico.
6. The young skater was surrounded by many admirers.
7. There is less need for caution now.
8. All students must go to the new auditorium.
9. Sunny weather makes me smile.
10. I don't need those notes anymore.
11. We will need some fennel for this recipe.
12. The red wagon is rusting in the rain.
13. The second door on the left is the bathroom.
14. Several children in the group are afraid of clowns.
15. Chloe had three tests on the same day.
16. After the storm, we found the hungry dogs hiding in an old shed.

17. You must have more courage than I do.
18. They made a lemon glaze for the short-bread cookies.
19. This song has twelve verses.
20. The club has little money, so I don't think we can afford an end-of-the-year trip.

Adjective or Pronoun? p. 9

EXERCISE A

1. *P* Few would spend so *A* few hours studying.
2. *A* Which review sheet is *P* which?
3. *A* These notes are better, so we should study *P* these.
4. *A* Any way of remembering these dates would help; can you think of *P* any?
5. *P* This is how I remember *A* this fact.

EXERCISE B

6. Few—P
7. those—A
8. Several—A
9. Some—P
10. that—P
11. Either—A
12. many—P
13. such—A
14. which—P
15. either—P

Adjective or Noun? p. 10

EXERCISE

1. restaurant—A
2. cat ran—N; cat door—A
3. fudge—A
4. pride—N
5. bedroom—A
6. bulldozer—N
7. mountain—N
8. travel—A

HOLT HANDBOOK | Sixth Course

9. vacation—A
10. town—N; harvest—A
11. boy—N
12. mandolin—A
13. Apricots—N; peaches—N
14. toenail—A
15. neighbor—N; beekeeper—N; yard —A
16. store—N; plant—A
17. computer—N
18. Birthday—A; table—N
19. picnic—N; egg—A; paper—A; plastic—A
20. garden—N

Main Verbs and Helping Verbs, p. 11

EXERCISE

1. Sir Ernest Shackleton, who <u>was</u> the leader of the expedition, <u>was</u> a seasoned explorer who <u>had been</u> on two expeditions to Antarctica.

2. Shackleton and his team <u>were planning</u> a trip across the continent on foot.

3. The trip <u>was delayed</u> first at South Georgia Island, which <u>is</u> near Antarctica.

4. None of the whalers on the island <u>could remember</u> a time when the ice conditions <u>had been</u> as bad.

5. The whalers advised Shackleton that he <u>should wait</u> at least a month and perhaps <u>should</u> even <u>wait</u> another season.

6. After a month's delay, the *Endurance* <u>was continuing</u> south when the ship <u>ran</u> into ice about 80 miles from its destination.

7. The men <u>could</u> not <u>free</u> their ship from the ice.

8. They <u>were</u> slowly <u>being carried</u> farther and farther from land, as the ice pack <u>was drifting</u> with the current.

9. Since they <u>could</u> not <u>sail</u> again until the spring, Shackleton and his men <u>settled in</u> for the winter.

10. It <u>was</u> boring for the men that winter, but at least they <u>had</u> good shelter and enough food.

Action Verbs, p. 12

EXERCISE

1. I <u>know</u> about every book in that series. [M over know]

2. I <u>doubt</u> the accuracy of that statement. [M over doubt]

3. Herman <u>rides</u> the bus every day. [P over rides]

4. I <u>think</u> I <u>understand</u> this assignment. [M over think, M over understand]

5. You <u>will find</u> your keys on the hall table. [P over find]

6. We <u>should drive</u> to the beach. [P over drive]

7. He <u>thought</u> we <u>were arriving</u> at noon. [M over thought, P over arriving]

8. They <u>have solved</u> the problem. [M over solved]

9. We <u>baked</u> gingerbread cookies. [P over baked]

10. <u>Consider</u> the risks before you <u>start</u> your own business. [M over Consider, P over start]

11. Who <u>will open</u> this jar for me? [P over open]

12. The pie <u>cooled</u> on the windowsill. [P over cooled]

13. She <u>runs</u> like the wind. [P over runs]

14. I <u>wonder</u> if it <u>will rain</u>. [M over wonder, P over rain]

15. <u>Think</u> of the possibilities! [M over Think]

16. Elizabeth <u>told</u> us about it. [P over told]

17. Harry <u>will go</u> first today. [P over go]

18. I usually <u>exercise</u> for an hour. [P over exercise]

19. He <u>says</u> he <u>can estimate</u> the number of people who <u>will vote</u>. [M over says, M over estimate, P over vote]

20. I <u>suppose</u>[M] the meeting <u>will begin</u>[P] on time.

Linking Verbs, p. 13
EXERCISE

1. is
2. appeared
3. seems
4. are
5. have been
6. looks
7. could be
8. felt
9. were
10. would be
11. became
12. was
13. is
14. could be
15. Is
16. smelled
17. grow
18. is
19. tastes
20. sounds

Transitive and Intransitive Verbs, p. 14
EXERCISE

1. I <u>play</u> the character of Regan in our school's production of Shakespeare's tragedy.
2. We <u>rehearse</u> every weeknight.
3. Fortunately, I <u>can memorize</u> lines fairly quickly.
4. My friend Robert <u>plays</u> the character Kent.
5. He always <u>arrives</u> early for rehearsal.
6. The last school play <u>was</u> *Waiting for Godot* by Samuel Beckett.
7. I <u>was</u> not in that play, but I <u>helped</u> the set designers on the weekends.
8. One day I <u>would like</u> to act in a big Broadway musical.
9. I <u>can sing</u> enthusiastically.
10. My mother <u>sings</u> beautifully.
11. She <u>has</u> perfect pitch.
12. She <u>sang</u> in jazz clubs.
13. It <u>was</u> at a performance that she <u>met</u> my father, a piano player.
14. He <u>can</u> really <u>tickle</u> the ivories!
15. They <u>help</u> with tips about show business.

16. Sometimes my mother and I <u>sing</u> a duet while my father <u>plays</u> the piano.
17. "Music <u>comes</u> from the heart, not the head," my dad <u>says</u>.
18. Of course, there <u>is</u> no music in *King Lear*, but I <u>enjoy</u> my part a lot.
19. The next production <u>will be</u> *Romeo and Juliet*.
20. I<u>'ll be</u> auditioning for the part of Juliet.

Adverbs and the Words They Modify, p. 15
EXERCISE A

1. Considering that this video game is <u>fairly</u> old, it has <u>surprisingly</u> good graphics.
2. Is that the <u>surpassingly</u> lovely princess I have to rescue?
3. That was an <u>unusually</u> friendly gnome.
4. My character in the game is an <u>exceptionally</u> skilled archer.
5. At the archery tournament, I shot my arrow <u>almost</u> <u>exactly</u> in the center of the target.
6. I think a goblin is lurking <u>nearby</u>.
7. The castle's towers loom <u>ominously</u> over the <u>treacherously</u> swampy landscape.
8. <u>Rather</u> <u>reluctantly</u>, the gatekeeper let me into the city.
9. My sister mastered this game <u>quickly</u>.
10. The <u>continually</u> elusive high score escaped me <u>again</u>.

EXERCISE B
Answers will vary.

11. enthusiastically
12. fervently
13. quickly
14. more
15. Finally

Noun or Adverb? p. 16
EXERCISE

1. <u>yesterday</u>—ADV

2. uptown—ADV

3. uptown—N

4. downtown—ADV

5. Downtown—N

6. home—N

7. home—ADV

8. today—ADV

9. today—N

10. tomorrow—ADV

11. Tomorrow—N

12. upstate—ADV

13. upstate—N

14. First—ADV

15. first—N

16. Sunday—N

17. Sunday—ADV

18. then—ADV

19. then—N

20. Wednesday—N

The Preposition, p. 17
EXERCISE

1. underneath
2. behind
3. in
4. at
5. on; without
6. of; onto
7. beside
8. on
9. out
10. At; like

11. about
12. as; as
13. on
14. off
15. in
16. without
17. into; of
18. to
19. from; of
20. for

Adverb or Preposition? p. 18
EXERCISE

1. After going inside *ADV*, I realized there was no more room for food inside *PREP* the refrigerator.
2. By *PREP* ourselves, we watched the cars go by *ADV*.
3. The game is over *ADV*, over *PREP* there.
4. Get off *PREP* the court, but don't run off *ADV*.

5. We must surround that building because the fugitive is within *ADV*, still within *PREP* our reach.
6. Before you go out *PREP* the door, tell me if we are going out *ADV* tonight.
7. If the show is going to go on *ADV*, we have to be on *PREP* time.
8. You can't go across *PREP* this mountain range in your car, because there is no good road to take you across *ADV*.
9. After he climbed down *PREP* the telephone pole, he sat down *ADV* on the ground.
10. When you go outside *ADV*, see if there are any snowdrifts outside *PREP* our fence.
11. We left Ted behind *ADV* when we went behind *PREP* the curtain.
12. I cooked the roast throughout *PREP* the afternoon, until it was well-done throughout *ADV*.
13. They walked around *PREP* the park because they like to walk around *ADV*.
14. Carry on without *PREP* fear, and don't worry that you will have to go without *ADV*.
15. Above all *PREP*, we noticed the helicopter hovering above *ADV*.
16. Let's climb up *ADV*, because the best view is from up *PREP* this hill.
17. Along *PREP* the side of the road, a dog was ambling along *ADV*.
18. In *PREP* 1997, my grandmother moved in *ADV*.
19. After reading a book about *PREP* exotic locations, we decided to travel about *ADV*.
20. Past *PREP* ninety, and still charming, the man lifted his hat whenever a lady walked past *ADV*.

The Conjunction, p. 19
EXERCISE

1. Not only; but also

2. and

3. While

4. Since

5. Not only; but also

6. Since

7. and

8. If

9. While

10. though; and

11. either; or

12. and

13. or

14. because

15. Although

16. While

17. and

18. than

19. Whether; or

20. After

The Interjection, p. 20

EXERCISE

1. Oh

2. ouch

3. Uh-oh

4. Well

5. My

6. Oh

7. Oops

8. Wow

9. well

10. Aha

11. Yes

12. No

13. Sure

14. Hey

15. Yippee

16. hey

17. Well

18. Aha

19. oops

20. Phew

Determining Parts of Speech, p. 21

EXERCISE A

1. Wow—INT

2. Every—ADJ

3. first—ADJ

4. and—CON

5. by—PREP

6. sure—ADJ

7. Although—CON

8. rather—ADV

9. represents—V

10. several—PRO

EXERCISE B *The possessive pronoun in item 13 may be identified as an adjective.*

11. opens; moves (*verb*)

12. senior; advertising (*adjective*)

13. their; it; many (*pronoun*)

14. Then; faster; longer; often (*adverb*)

15. mid-March; work (*noun*)

Review A: Parts of Speech, p. 22

EXERCISE

1. As we drew near the light *(N)* at the end of the road, a light *(ADJ)* rain was falling.

2. The bird-watcher saw the woodpecker hop off *(PREP)* the wooden fence and fly off *(ADV)*.

3. After *(CON)* the play had become a success, the director made dinner for the cast and crew after *(PREP)* a performance.

4. The gardener plants *(V)* seeds in the spring and harvests the plants *(N)* in the fall.

5. According to the school's monthly *(ADJ)* newsletter, an open meeting of the debate club is held monthly *(ADV)*.

6. When the fire alarms sound *(V)*, you cannot hear the sound *(N)* of anything else.

7. This *(PRO)* indicates that you do not understand this *(ADJ)* grammatical concept very well.

8. The kite flew high *(ADV)* until its string got caught in the high *(ADJ)* branches of a cottonwood tree.

9. Before *(CON)* the arena's gates opened, you were standing before *(PREP)* us in the waiting line.

10. Telephone *(V)* me when your telephone *(N)* is repaired.

11. Aretha walked along *(ADV)* with us as we enjoyed our hike along *(PREP)* the river.

12. If you won't climb up *(PREP)* the ladder, then I will have to climb up *(ADV)*.

13. This *(PRO)* is the first time I have read this *(ADJ)* book.

14. After *(CON)* I left the room, I remembered my promise to stay after *(PREP)* class.

15. I will sled *(V)* down the hill, and then you can use my sled *(N)*.

16. Scientists must fully understand the effect *(N)* before they can effect *(V)* a correction.

17. Well *(INT)*, I believe my watch just fell down the well *(N)*.

18. Those *(PRO)* are the costumes worn by those *(ADJ)* actors.

19. The new assistant *(N)* reports directly to the assistant *(ADJ)* principal.

20. Put that down *(ADV)*; it's an antique down *(ADJ)* pillow, and you could damage it.

Review B: Parts of Speech, p. 23

EXERCISE A

1. As; and *(conjunction)*
2. Anyone; who *(pronoun)*
3. one *(adjective)*
4. accounts *(verb)*
5. of *(preposition)*
6. calculator; capabilities *(noun)*
7. With; of *(preposition)*
8. remarkably *(adverb)*
9. Everyone *(pronoun)*
10. already; perhaps *(adverb)*

EXERCISE B

11. computer —N
12. works—V
13. tirelessly—ADV
14. In—PREP
15. computer —ADJ
16. He—PRO
17. and—CON
18. someday—ADV

19. Wow—INT
20. that—PRO

Review C: Parts of Speech, p. 24

EXERCISE

1. consul—N
2. in—PREP
3. He—PRO
4. shrewdly—ADV
5. English—ADJ
6. published—V
7. book—N
8. One—ADJ
9. while—CON
10. between—PREP
11. outside—ADJ
12. besides—PREP
13. hilly—ADJ
14. Hawthorne—N
15. it—PRO
16. dangerously—ADV
17. became—V
18. bordered—V
19. Ouch—INT
20. about—PREP

Literary Model: Poetry, pp. 25–26

EXERCISE A

1. lovers—used as noun in line 2

   love—used as noun in line 2; used as verb in line 1

2. line 3: shield—noun; shield—verb

   line 5: grieve—verb; grievances—noun

   line 6: love—noun; love—noun

   line 7: alters—verb; alteration—noun

3. -ance(s); -tion

EXERCISE B

Answers will vary.

   Audiences in Shakespeare's day enjoyed puns and other kinds of word play. Using varied forms of the same word within a line or a passage probably received the same kind of appreciation as the use of a pun or a riddle. Both kinds of word play would have required wit on the part of the poet or writer and, on the part of readers or listeners, an interest in embracing the fun of such word play.

EXERCISE C

Answers will vary.

Take on life as a conqueror, and you may only conquer happiness;

In your search for success, search with grace;

Please yourself by enjoying the pleasure of others;

Assurance you give others will assure you of this:

You cannot claim contentment if cynicism has a claim on you.

If life is a dance, be a dancer divine.

EXERCISE D

Answers will vary.

You probably wouldn't see an extended series of word play lines like this, but one or two lines such as these might show up in a speech or possibly a commercial since repetition helps to reinforce ideas and causes them to stay in the memory more easily.

Writing Application: Description, p. 27

Writing Applications are designed to provide students immediate composition practice in using key concepts taught in each chapter of the *Language and Sentence Skills Practice* booklet. You may wish to evaluate student responses to these assignments as you do any other writing that students produce. To save grading time, however, you may want to use the following scoring rubric.

Scoring Rubric

Well-chosen, sensory modifiers bring the description to life.

| 1 | 2 | 3 | 4 | 5 |

The paragraphs are organized either spatially or chronologically.

| 1 | 2 | 3 | 4 | 5 |

A single tradition is discussed.

| 1 | 2 | 3 | 4 | 5 |

The assignment is relatively free of errors in spelling and punctuation.

| 1 | 2 | 3 | 4 | 5 |

Total Score _____

5 = highest; 1 = lowest

Chapter 2: The Parts of a Sentence, pp. 28–52

Choices: Investigating Sentences, p. 28

Choices activities are designed to extend and enrich students' understanding of grammar, usage, and mechanics and to take learners beyond traditional classroom instruction. To use the Choices worksheet, have each student pick an activity that interests him or her. In some cases, you may wish to assign an activity to a particular student or group of students. You may also want to request that students get your approval for the activities they choose. Establish guidelines for what constitutes successful completion of an activity. Then, help students plan how they will share their work with the rest of the class.

Choices activities can be scored with a pass-fail grade or treated as bonus-point projects. Those activities that require students to research or create a certain number of items might be graded in a traditional manner.

Sentences and Sentence Fragments, p. 29

EXERCISE

Answers may vary.

1. S—Oraibi is one of the oldest continually inhabited villages in America.
2. S—According to the guide's lecture, the Hopi reservation is surrounded by the Navajo reservation.
3. She gave us a remarkable description about the life of the Hopi people.
4. Eleven villages by the canyon are situated near several massive stone mesas.
5. The mesas are found on the protected Hopi reservation in the beautiful Arizona desert.
6. S—Tewa, Sichomovi, and Walpi are three villages atop the mesa.
7. S—Breathtaking cliff-side stone houses they are.
8. The villages are also called "pueblos."
9. S—Are some villages known for pottery?
10. What a pleasant visit we had to this ancient reservation, a sight to behold.

Subjects and Predicates, p. 30

EXERCISE

1. The four-star general examined the maps and other strategic information.
2. The writer will strive to be more thorough and accurate in her work.
3. Was Carla at the bowling alley or the movie theater?
4. The skilled guide dog waited attentively for the traffic light to change.
5. Along the winding road through the woods, we made our way to the cabin.
6. Was the jewel heist at the department store the top story on the evening news?
7. Under the current policy, soft drinks and snacks are not permitted in Ms. Garcia's classroom.
8. The search turned up nothing but a pencil and sixty-five cents in change.
9. Did Perry get on the subway at 96th Street and Broadway?
10. The girls' gymnastics squad at my high school is training for the district championship.
11. At the top of the page, the writer listed the sources that he had used.
12. After storing our backpacks in the cabin, we sat and watched the sun set over the water.
13. The tiny restaurant, tucked in the corner of the square, had only sandwiches on the menu.
14. The movie starred two mermaids, an alien, and a lovable dog named Ralph.

15. Under the neon sign, <u>the portrait artist</u> **S** waited for another customer.

16. Just beyond the train station and the infor- **P** mation booth, Adam <u>found the youth hostel</u>.

17. Is <u>this</u> it? **S**

18. The tour bus <u>will be making another stop</u> **P** <u>soon</u>.

19. Three books, a coffee mug, slippers, a chess set, and a toothbrush <u>were all he owned</u>. **S**

20. <u>The actors dressed as pirates</u> exited the stage.

Simple and Complete Subjects, p. 31
EXERCISE

1. <u>Regular exercise</u> helps prevent certain diseases.

2. <u>People in excellent health</u> also feel better emotionally.

3. <u>Sedentary people</u> risk developing health problems.

4. <u>Sensible, safe, low-impact exercise</u> is ideal.

5. <u>The capacity of the lungs to take in air</u> can be increased.

6. With exercise, <u>a person's muscles</u> can grow stronger.

7. <u>A consistent exercise regimen</u> helps people stay in shape.

8. <u>Top athletes</u> pay close attention to their exercise routines.

9. <u>Everyone, not just top athletes</u>, needs to be physically active.

10. <u>Even the best-conditioned athletes</u> should stretch before a workout.

11. <u>Proper, careful stretching</u> helps prevent injuries.

12. <u>People young and old</u> need to exercise each day.

13. Do <u>your high school classmates</u> exercise?

14. <u>Even simple, everyday activities like climb- ing stairs</u> are good for you.

15. <u>Low-impact workouts</u> include walking, swimming, and cycling.

16. <u>People with health conditions</u> should talk to their doctors first.

17. <u>Your doctor or physical therapist</u> may be able to design an exercise program just for you.

18. <u>Some daily form of exercise</u> can improve your endurance.

19. <u>The flow of oxygen to the heart</u> can be increased.

20. What a difference <u>a little exercise</u> can make!

Simple and Complete Predicates, p. 32
EXERCISE

1. Gary, Joan, and Lisa <u>want their own company</u>.

2. This new museum <u>will certainly attract more visitors</u>.

3. <u>Will</u> they <u>do more research into the pro- posed ecology initiative</u>?

4. I <u>was born in the small California coastal town of Mendocino</u>.

5. The perfect sandwich <u>needs mustard and mayonnaise on two slices of rye bread</u>.

6. An innovative, unusual work of art <u>can provoke thought</u>.

7. <u>Is</u> the science project <u>focusing on the latest developments in energy conservation</u>?

8. Phillip <u>does not give in easily</u>.

9. In the morning, the tour group will begin a train trip through Mexico's Copper Canyon.

10. The antique lamp seems dignified and grand.

11. Can you see the playing field from the upper level of the stadium?

12. Carpeting is needed only in the cabin's bedrooms and hallway.

13. The black mastiff in the backyard is running along the fence.

14. We bought these tasty apricots at the store.

15. After midnight, the moon crept out from behind the clouds.

16. Truck drivers travel long distances with their payloads.

17. The delivery from the sporting goods store was late as always.

18. Among the professor's many reference books were ten dictionaries for ten different languages.

19. Next to my cat sat a tiny stuffed mouse.

20. When will the ceremony in the school auditorium end?

Complete and Simple Subjects and Predicates, p. 33 *In item 13, students need not identify* book club *as a compound noun in this exercise.*

EXERCISE

1. Before the tenth century, not many foreigners had visited Iceland.

2. One of the early Norse settlers was Eric the Red.

3. A kind of parliament, the Althing was established in 930.

4. The island nation had much turmoil in its early days.

5. The stories of early Icelanders are recorded in long narratives called *sagas*.

6. One famous saga is called the *Laxdaela Saga*.

7. Pirates from other countries often raided the coastal towns.

8. In the late 1800s, a measure of stability returned to the island.

9. For centuries, the small nation of Iceland remained under the Danish crown.

10. During World War II, the Allied forces sent troops to Iceland in case of a German attack.

11. Toward the end of the war came an almost unanimous Icelandic vote for independence from Denmark.

12. The people of Iceland, nearly all highly literate, are some of the world's most avid readers.

13. The oldest book club in Iceland was founded in 1816.

14. The fishing industry is one of Iceland's most important.

15. Only about one fourth of the island is suitable for human habitation.

16. Many of Iceland's two hundred volcanoes are active to this day.

17. In 1963, a new island was formed by volcanoes off the southern coast.

18. The island was named Surtsey after Sutur, the god of fire in Icelandic mythology.

19. Deep canyons, called *fjords*, cut into the island's coasts.

20. The island's residents sometimes keep warm in the natural hot springs.

Compound Subjects and Verbs A, p. 34

EXERCISE A

1. <u>Chocolate</u> and <u>strawberry</u> <u>are</u> the two flavors available.

2. <u>Jim</u>, his <u>sister</u>, <u>Louise</u>, and <u>I</u> <u>went</u> to the Grand Canyon.

3. Will the <u>Cougars</u> or the <u>Rockets</u> <u>win</u> the regional championship?

4. <u>Jennifer</u> and <u>Amy</u> <u>took</u> the couch, the bookshelf, and the floor lamp.

5. <u>Carter</u> and his <u>dog</u> <u>swam</u> across the lake.

6. My <u>ankle</u> and <u>knee</u> <u>ache</u> because of the workout.

7. The <u>reporter</u> and his <u>editor</u> <u>discussed</u> the committee's findings.

8. <u>Wind</u> and <u>rain</u>, not to mention hail, <u>made</u> the trip hazardous.

9. In the meantime, <u>Kenny</u> and <u>I</u> <u>put</u> on our hats and boots.

10. <u>Eugene</u>, <u>Noah</u>, <u>Harold</u>, <u>Louis</u>, <u>Glen</u>, and <u>Paul</u> <u>slept</u> on the bus.

EXERCISE B

11. The quarterback <u>passed</u> the football and <u>ran</u> for more than 200 yards.

12. <u>Can</u> your cat <u>meow</u> and <u>purr</u> at the same time?

13. Carla <u>took</u> the money and <u>flew</u> to Hawaii for a much-needed vacation.

14. Kelly <u>will study</u> and <u>memorize</u> the material.

15. My brother <u>found</u> an old radio and <u>donated</u> it to the Salvation Army.

Compound Subjects and Verbs B, p. 35

EXERCISE

1. <u>Did</u> <u>you</u> and <u>Carla</u> <u>fly</u> or <u>drive</u> to New Mexico?

2. <u>Bob</u> and his <u>father</u> <u>ate</u> heartily and <u>enjoyed</u> themselves at the Thanksgiving dinner.

3. <u>Sally</u> and <u>I</u> <u>knocked</u> on the door and <u>called</u> through the window.

4. <u>Paper clips</u> and <u>rubber bands</u> <u>bind</u> and <u>organize</u> my documents and notes.

5. <u>He</u> or <u>she</u> <u>should</u> not <u>add</u> or <u>delete</u> any information in this typing exercise.

6. When did <u>James</u> and <u>Brooke</u> <u>win</u> the tennis match and <u>advance</u> to the next level?

7. Before the game, the <u>coach</u> and the <u>players</u> <u>stretched</u> and <u>waited</u> in the locker room.

8. <u>Gabe</u>, <u>Rochine</u>, and the other club <u>members</u> <u>planned</u> and <u>organized</u> the awards ceremony.

9. Would <u>you</u> and your <u>brother</u> rather <u>prepare</u> lunch or <u>wash</u> the dishes?

10. In the triathlon, professional <u>athletes</u> and novice <u>competitors</u> <u>run</u>, <u>bike</u>, and <u>swim</u>.

11. My <u>brother</u> and my <u>father</u> both <u>went</u> to Yale and <u>studied</u> architecture.

12. <u>Violet</u> and <u>sage</u> <u>are</u> my favorite colors and <u>appear</u> in most of my artwork.

13. My <u>cousin</u> and <u>I</u> mostly <u>slept</u> and <u>watched</u> TV.

14. From the top of the volcano, <u>lava</u> and <u>ash</u> <u>surged</u> and <u>threatened</u> the campers.

15. <u>Jake</u> and <u>I</u> <u>found</u> the fossil and <u>gave</u> it to the geology teacher.

16. <u>Jennifer</u>, <u>Darla</u>, <u>Sandi</u>, and <u>Ben</u> <u>are competing</u> and <u>have been selected</u> as our four finalists.

17. In the gymnasium, retired <u>teachers</u> and former <u>students</u> <u>congregated</u> and <u>conversed</u>.

18. Both <u>Wyoming</u> and <u>Idaho</u> <u>have</u> rugged terrain and <u>are</u> great camping destinations.

19. The <u>employees</u> and <u>volunteers</u> <u>must wipe</u> and <u>polish</u> every single statue in the exhibit.

20. Will <u>you</u> and your twin <u>brother</u> please <u>be</u> quiet during the movie or <u>go</u> outside to play?

Finding Subjects in Sentences, p. 36

EXERCISE

1. A partial <u>eclipse</u> *(what)* of the moon will take place tonight.

2. You—Who

3. What year did your <u>cousin</u> *(who)* buy his new computer?

4. A <u>panel</u> *(who)* of experts oversaw the research.

5. From the crashing waves came a veteran <u>surfer</u>. *(who)*

6. Are these two coffee <u>mugs</u> *(what)* clean?

7. My <u>house</u> *(what)* is on Far West Boulevard.

8. Under the tree behind the house was Kerry's missing <u>bicycle</u>. *(what)*

9. As for the old tenement building, several influential council <u>members</u> *(who)* want it destroyed.

10. You—Who

11. Many classic <u>lunchboxes</u> *(what)* from the '60s are now very valuable.

12. Before the meeting, however, <u>no one</u> *(who)* on the team had met the volunteers.

13. During the first part of the century, my <u>great-grandmother</u> *(who)* on my mother's side worked as a nurse.

14. The <u>condition</u> *(what)* of the garment was very poor.

15. Last winter, my <u>brothers</u> *(who)* made several huge snowmen.

16. Here is your new semester class <u>schedule</u>. *(what)*

17. Are these <u>books</u> *(what)* on the front shelf for sale?

18. Last night at the track meet, <u>Amy</u> *(who)* got a first-place trophy.

19. According to the legend in the fairy tale book, the brave and honest <u>knight</u> *(who)* triumphed.

20. <u>Growing</u> *(what)* three inches in one year is no surprise for Tom.

Complements, p. 37

EXERCISE

1. Managing money and being financially responsible are challenging <u>goals</u>. *(C)*

2. Courage under stress is <u>essential</u> for an emergency-rescue worker.

3. Rafael considered <u>carefully</u> *(A)* his choices of universities to attend in the fall.

4. The journalist's reasons were <u>many</u> *(C)* for keeping his inside sources confidential.

5. Did Mariah speak <u>calmly</u> *(A)* during the debate round?

6. The Koran is the sacred scripture of the Muslim <u>faith</u>. *(OP)*

7. The list of prizes for the geography quiz show seems quite <u>impressive</u>. *(C)*

8. They sent <u>me</u> *(C)* the information in the mail.

9. My favorite documentary show on <u>PBS</u> *(OP)* starts at eight o'clock in the evening.

10. I think I drew the peach <u>accurately</u> *(A)* in my still-life drawing class.

11. It seems that the trouble with the <u>car</u> *(OP)* is the transmission.

12. Did she throw the ball <u>perfectly</u> *(A)* into the hoop in the last quarter of the game?

13. Through the front <u>door</u> *(OP)* the hornets flew in a whirlwind.

14. I gave my CD player to Ralph's *[OP]* <u>sister</u> to use during her bus trip.
15. My mom bought contact *[C]* <u>lenses</u> for me when I joined the basketball team.
16. I left the faucet running in the upstairs *[OP]* <u>bathtub</u> this morning!
17. Why not take the blank computer *[C]* <u>disk</u> with you to school?
18. The judge declared her *[C]* <u>candidacy</u> for state office.
19. Your dad seems *[C]* <u>happy</u> that he won the amateur golf tournament.
20. Until recently, Joe drove his *[C]* <u>truck</u> to Philadelphia at the end of each month.

Direct Objects, p. 38

EXERCISE

1. John Le Carré writes suspenseful spy *[what]* <u>stories</u> about international intrigue.
2. You are eating a nutritious *[what]* <u>meal</u> this morning.
3. Elizabeth sold me her *[what]* <u>computer</u> for a very reasonable price.
4. Ramón entertained *[who]* <u>Sam</u> and *[who]* <u>me</u> with an account of his vacation.
5. Andrés Segovia transcribed *[what]* <u>pages</u> of classical music for the guitar.
6. After a lengthy campaign process, the students elected *[who]* <u>Miguel</u>.
7. Doing word puzzles makes *[who]* <u>Tien</u> and his *[who]* <u>grandfather</u> happy.
8. Ms. Hamilton appointed *[who]* <u>Bill</u> and *[who]* <u>me</u>.
9. You may pick up an information *[what]* <u>sheet</u> at the front desk.
10. Open this *[what]* <u>envelope</u> and please read *[what]* <u>it</u> to me.

11. Ted and I will carry the *[what]* <u>tent</u> during the weekend camping trip.
12. Before the storm, we all filled *[what]* <u>sandbags</u>.
13. Please sign your *[what]* <u>name</u> at the bottom of the registration form.
14. Lindsey received her pilot's *[what]* <u>license</u> last year.
15. Miss Webber has canceled the *[what]* <u>meeting</u> of the student dance committee.
16. Karen left her *[what]* <u>coat</u> in Mr. Singh's restaurant the other night.
17. Did Tina and Tranh finish Ms. Yanez's *[what]* <u>homework</u>?
18. A robin has built its *[what]* <u>nest</u> on the stone ledge outside my window.
19. Unfortunately, I have lost my mother's car *[what]* <u>keys</u> again!
20. The flamenco dancer from Paraguay practiced his dance *[what]* <u>steps</u> last night before the show.

Indirect Objects, p. 39

EXERCISE

1. Would you lend <u>me</u> your (umbrella)?
2. I sent <u>Bill</u> and <u>Norine</u> a (card) for their anniversary.
3. At Thanksgiving, I gave my <u>aunt</u> a (basket) of fruit and some (flowers).
4. Please lend <u>Allison</u> your (sheet music) for that chorus.
5. Did Mr. Terry write <u>you</u> a dramatic (role) in the school play?
6. Maria taught her family's <u>dogs</u> some clever (tricks).
7. I am sure we can find <u>Al</u> a tennis (racket).

8. Raul assigned <u>me</u> the (role) of secretary.

9. Derrick offered the <u>three</u> of us (tickets) to the school concert.

10. After three months of procrastination, Lani finally sent <u>Janet</u> a (letter).

11. I picked my <u>mom</u> a (bouquet) of flowers for her birthday.

12. The chef offered <u>everyone</u> (bread), (cheese), and (fruit) after dinner.

13. Worrying about his college entrance exam gave <u>Arthur</u> (headaches).

14. Can you and your sister show <u>Dora</u> the right (bus)?

15. Clara built her older sister's <u>children</u> a (treehouse) in the backyard.

16. Samuel gave our hiking <u>group</u> detailed (directions) to the campsite.

17. The judges awarded <u>Tina</u> the first-place (prize) in the spelling competition even though she could not attend the (ceremony).

18. My veterinarian gave my <u>cat</u> a fuzzy new (toy).

19. His adventure in Mr. McGregor's garden taught <u>Peter Rabbit</u> a (lesson).

20. Ilse brought our entire <u>family</u> some Christmas (gifts) from Germany.

Objective Complements, p. 40
EXERCISE

1. I find his collection of antiques <u>outstanding</u>.

2. Would you call her actions <u>heroic</u> or <u>foolish</u>?

3. Her dazzling performance as Joan of Arc rendered the audience <u>speechless</u>.

4. We must consider the defendants <u>innocent</u> unless we can prove them <u>otherwise</u>.

5. The novelist made his villain <u>dynamic</u> and <u>enigmatic</u>.

6. In his recommendation, Mr. Gatwood, my English teacher, called me <u>hard-working</u> and <u>conscientious</u>.

7. Hillary painted her clay sculpture <u>indigo</u>, <u>tangerine</u>, and bright <u>green</u>.

8. The governor named Lisa her personal <u>assistant</u> during the campaign.

9. I found the story of the Trail of Tears <u>sad</u> and <u>moving</u>.

10. Will they elect Jeffrey <u>treasurer</u> for a second term?

11. We consider Terence's behavior <u>authentic</u> and <u>inspiring</u>.

12. I find cooking, which is one of my favorite hobbies, <u>challenging</u> and <u>creative</u>.

13. The critics called her performance <u>spontaneous</u> and <u>funny</u>.

14. I made the chili mildly <u>spicy</u> just for you.

15. That conversation made me <u>happy</u> about my choice of university.

16. After his comedy routine in the cafeteria, we voted Charlie class <u>clown</u>.

17. The court's ruling rendered that law virtually <u>unenforceable</u>.

18. I found that kind of glue <u>ineffective</u> for building model airplanes.

19. Do you think this gift <u>appropriate</u> for a graduation party?

20. Most of the viewers found the global-travel series <u>fascinating</u> and <u>informative</u>.

Complements, p. 41
EXERCISE

1. I find these <u>stories</u> (fascinating).

2. She told <u>me</u> <u>one</u> about the blue-ringed octopus.

3. She called the small <u>creature</u> (“dangerous.”)

4. The poison from a tiny, blue-ringed octopus could kill a <u>person</u>.

5. My mom gave <u>me</u> a <u>book</u> with more interesting animal trivia.

6. Some hummingbirds beat their <u>wings</u> eighty times a second.

7. A 4,000-pound hippopotamus can outrun a <u>human</u>.

8. A python in Indonesia once ate a fourteen-year-old <u>boy</u>.

9. Scientists consider the <u>whale shark</u> the largest (fish) in the world.

10. Experts gave the world's biggest <u>frog</u> the <u>name</u> “Goliath.”

11. The hefty amphibian tips the <u>scales</u> at about seven pounds.

12. My husky cat Shadow gives <u>Goliath</u> a <u>challenge</u>, though.

13. My mom calls <u>Shadow</u> a “big but agile” (kitty.)

14. We usually feed <u>him</u> special dry cat <u>food</u> or <u>tuna</u>.

15. We consider <u>Shadow</u> a beloved and valued (member) of the family.

16. Sometimes I walk my big <u>kitty</u> on a generous leash.

17. He's not happy about the leash, but he accepts <u>it</u>.

18. I gave my dearest <u>friend</u>, Kim, a tiny <u>kitten</u> for her most recent birthday.

19. Much to my dismay, she named the feisty <u>tabby</u> (Torvald).

20. What <u>name</u> would you give a <u>cat</u>?

Predicate Nominatives, p. 42
EXERCISE

1. Troy is a <u>carpenter</u> of the highest level.

2. Laura will be <u>captain</u> and <u>manager</u> of the team while I am away.

3. Who was the <u>President</u> of the United States in 1916?

4. The things that got us through the competition were <u>hope</u> and hard <u>work</u>.

5. This is a <u>mystery</u> to me!

6. The first ones in line were <u>Bill</u>, <u>Grace</u>, and <u>Albert</u>.

7. That noise must have been the <u>wind</u> whipping at the shutters.

8. Is Kevin a <u>drummer</u>, <u>guitarist</u>, and <u>vocalist</u>?

9. My uncle is the <u>principal</u> of a high school in Georgia.

10. My favorite places to go on vacation are <u>Virginia Beach</u> and <u>Martha's Vineyard</u>.

11. This is the <u>way</u> home from the stadium.

12. Our dog Cora is a <u>mother</u> of five puppies.

13. The winner of the chess tournament was <u>she</u>.

14. The eldest of our three parrots is <u>Edgar</u>.

15. The book we found on the bench is <u>hers</u>.

16. The only thing I want for my birthday is <u>that</u>.

17. The solution to this plant's problem is better <u>security</u>.

18. She became the new <u>district attorney</u> for the southern district.

19. One hindrance to completing the project was the dean's <u>opposition</u>.

20. This is the last <u>exercise</u> we have to complete.

Predicate Adjectives, p. 43
EXERCISE

1. The sidewalk is always <u>slippery</u> right after a rain shower.

2. The darkness was <u>impenetrable</u> but oddly <u>comforting</u>.

3. The soil was too <u>chalky</u> to grow the crops we wanted.

4. The solution to Jake's problem was <u>obvious</u> to me.

5. It was <u>foggy</u> outside earlier, but now it is <u>fine</u>.

6. Astonished by the news of the election, Milly and I were absolutely <u>ecstatic</u>.

7. This puzzle is <u>difficult</u> to solve.

8. <u>High</u>, <u>clear</u>, and <u>beautiful</u> was her singing voice.

9. It is <u>dark</u> in the basement, so we should bring our flashlights.

10. Were you <u>happy</u> about the good fortune you had?

11. Our cat was <u>tired</u> and <u>listless</u> after the surgery.

12. My new dress is black-and-white <u>striped</u> and <u>long</u>.

13. My, how <u>cheery</u> Mr. Morris seems today!

14. <u>Fragile</u> and <u>helpless</u> were the newly hatched chicks.

15. These confetti eggs certainly are <u>delicate</u> and <u>colorful</u>!

16. Mike's story about his photo safari in Africa was quite <u>captivating</u> and <u>inspiring</u>.

17. The melted wax for the art project was <u>sticky</u> and <u>gooey</u>.

18. It is <u>refreshing</u> to go for a swim on such a hot and humid afternoon.

19. The librarian said that the old textbook is <u>excellent</u> and <u>thorough</u> as a reference.

20. Their negligence in this case was not <u>surprising</u>, considering their busy schedules.

Predicate Nominatives and Adjectives, p. 44
EXERCISE

1. In 1776, Patrick Henry became the first <u>governor</u> of Virginia.

2. The Wren Building is the oldest <u>building</u> on campus.

3. The gust of wind felt <u>icy</u> against our unprotected faces.

4. Geographically, Alaska is the largest <u>state</u> in the United States.

5. Tony must have been <u>nervous</u> before that interview.

6. Willis appeared <u>disoriented</u> and <u>dazed</u> when he walked into the room.

7. The bite of a tarantula can be <u>painful</u>.

8. The next captain of our soccer team will be either <u>Julia</u> or <u>I</u>.

9. This year, Mr. Pinkham's sociology course is my favorite <u>class</u>.

10. How <u>delicious</u> this soup tastes!

11. Suddenly I was the <u>center</u> of attention.

12. For me, acting is <u>exciting</u> and <u>fulfilling</u>.

13. On our soccer team, Alex always seems most <u>daring</u>.

14. Is she a crossing <u>guard</u>?

15. Sandy and Dave were <u>lucky</u> and <u>grateful</u> this time.

16. This after-school job is a great <u>responsibility</u>.

17. Are you <u>excited</u> about something?

18. This folder is too <u>flimsy</u>; a sturdy one would be <u>better</u>.

19. I may be <u>shy</u>, but I am not <u>frightened</u>.

20. Such lively cities are <u>New York</u> and <u>New Orleans</u>.

Parts of a Sentence, p. 45

EXERCISE

1. My sister won a <u>Fulbright</u> [DO] when she graduated from college.

2. She was the only Fulbright <u>winner</u> [PN] at her school.

3. For one year, the <u>program</u> [S] allowed her to live and study in Germany.

4. She studied European <u>history</u> [DO] at a university in Marburg.

5. She tells <u>everyone</u> [IO] she meets that she loved it.

6. She found the city of Marburg <u>charming</u> [OC].

7. The U.S. Congress <u>started</u> [V] the program in 1946.

8. It helps promote cultural <u>exchange</u> [DO] and mutual <u>understanding</u> [DO] between the United States and other nations.

9. <u>Thousands</u> [S] of Americans have studied in more than one hundred nations thanks to the Fulbright.

10. J. William Fulbright was the <u>senator</u> [PN] who sponsored the legislation.

11. He was <u>popular</u> [PA] in his home state of Arkansas.

12. He gave the <u>nation</u> [IO] a great gift.

13. My sister considers the German language somewhat <u>guttural</u> [OC].

14. The Spanish language is very <u>beautiful</u> [PA] to my ear.

15. "Educational <u>exchange</u> [S] can turn nations into people."

16. My sister told <u>me</u> [IO] that quote is from Senator Fulbright.

17. The program <u>sponsors</u> [V] students, artists, and professionals.

18. It is <u>interesting</u> [PA] to learn about other countries.

19. Someday, I will be a <u>world traveler</u> [PN].

20. Are <u>you</u> [S] going to apply for a Fulbright?

Review A: Fragments and Complete Sentences, p. 46

EXERCISE

Answers will vary.

1. F—I was late for the plane to Chicago.

2. S

3. F—Of course now the meeting in Chicago is about a new toothpaste for whiter teeth.

4. S

5. F—Eight dollars is too much for a hamburger!

6. F—While waiting at my gate, I saw an old friend from high school.

7. S

8. F—We rode in a rented limousine with the sunroof and the windows heavily tinted.

9. F—Matching my vest to her dress color and all of that fuss wasn't really necessary.

10. S

Review B: Sentence Parts, p. 47

EXERCISE

1. Nazi Germany had threatened an armed <u>invasion</u> [DO] of Czechoslovakia.

2. Hitler wanted the <u>Sudetenland</u> [DO], a highly industrialized region of Czechoslovakia.

3. The Sudetenland was the <u>land</u> [PN] near the border of Germany and Czechoslovakia.

4. The unification of the German people under one flag was the excuse *(PN)* presented by Hitler for this demand.

5. The majority of the inhabitants of the Sudetenland were Germans *(PN)*.

6. Hitler considered the Sudetenland *(DO)* part *(OC)* of Germany.

7. France and Britain were uneasy *(PA)* about Nazi Germany's demands for territory.

8. However, the French and the British remembered vividly the terrible destruction *(DO)* of World War I.

9. Therefore, they made the annexation *(DO)* of the Sudetenland possible *(OC)*.

10. British Prime Minister Neville Chamberlain and French Premier Édouard Daladier met Hitler *(DO)* in Munich and gave him *(IO)* everything *(DO)* he wanted.

11. Hitler gave them *(IO)* his word *(DO)* that Germany's aggressive expansion would cease.

12. Within a few months, however, German troops occupied the rest *(DO)* of Czechoslovakia.

13. Poland's treatment at the hands of the Nazis was similar *(PA)*.

14. On September 1, 1939, Nazi Germany invaded Poland *(DO)*.

15. The German "blitzkrieg" strategy left Poland *(IO)* little chance *(DO)*.

16. The country's flat terrain made the Germans' new tactic *(DO)* very successful *(OC)*.

17. The German tactic dealt the Poles *(IO)* an overwhelming defeat *(DO)*.

18. The Germans and their ally the Soviet Union divided Poland *(DO)* between them.

19. Hitler's Germany scored important early victories *(DO)* against the Czechs and the Poles.

20. War between Germany on one side and Britain and France on the other soon became inevitable *(PA)*.

Review C: Sentence Parts, p. 48

EXERCISE

1. Aaron Copland is my favorite composer *(PN)*.

2. One of Copland's highest achievements, *Appalachian Spring*, is a ballet *(PN)*.

3. The versatile Copland *(S)* wrote songs in many styles.

4. Last week I bought *(V)* a Philip Glass CD.

5. A serious composer, Glass has also written TV jingles *(DO)* and film scores.

6. My friend Lenny told me *(IO)* Glass's music is very hypnotic.

7. Glass is more popular *(PA)* than many of his contemporaries.

8. Glass's style *(S)* is usually referred to as "minimalism."

9. Along with Robert Wilson, Glass produced *(V)* the four-hour opera *Einstein on the Beach*.

10. As a would-be composer, I consider his music inspiring *(OC)*.

11. Right now, I *(S)* am taking guitar lessons and listening to different styles of music.

12. I enjoy classical music, rock, and jazz *(DO)*.

13. My guitar teacher gave me *(IO)* a book about scales and chords.

14. I hope *(V)* to memorize all the scales by the end of the year.

15. Judging by the complexity of the fingering patterns, this *(S)* is going to be a difficult task.

16. It should be less *difficult* [PA] than learning the violin!

17. My grandfather was a *violinist* [PN].

18. I *think* [V] my love of music comes from him.

19. Thinking about him keeps me *enthusiastic* [OC] about learning guitar.

20. *Music* [S] has helped me become a more well-rounded human being.

Review D: Sentence Parts, p. 49

EXERCISE A

1. S	**3.** S	**5.** S
2. F	**4.** F	

EXERCISE B

6. The *drive* [SS] from here to Phoenix *is* [SP] long and desolate.

7. *Did* [SP] the *truck* [SS] *arrive* [SP] at the depot?

8. *We* [SS] *moved* [SP] across the bridge to the other side of town last year.

9. *Many* [SS] of the builders who worked on the project *became* [SP] ill.

10. *Kayaking* [SS] *is* [SP] an immensely enjoyable sport.

EXERCISE C

11. People from the neighboring village gave *Lewis* [IO] some corn and water.

12. Out of the cave came a giant *bear* [S] with a steady gaze and quick gait.

13. All of the pilots *were trained* [V] on flight simulators.

14. A triple play in baseball is a very rare *feat* [PN].

15. My dog is much *smarter* [PA] than most animals.

16. Eddie's *plan* [S] simply will take some hard work.

17. We received eight *dollars* [DO] for mowing Mr. Crabtree's backyard.

18. The doctor's poor handwriting made the prescription *indecipherable* [OC].

19. The brother of the former president *sings* [V] at special occasions.

20. The top surgeon at our local hospital is also an excellent *singer* [PN].

Literary Model: Metaphors in Poetry, pp. 50–51

EXERCISE A

1. *Responses may vary slightly.*

. . . It's a naked (child) against a hungry wolf;

It's (playing bowls) upon a splitting wreck;

It's (walking) on a string across a gulf

With millstones fore-and-aft about your neck;

But the thing is daily done by many and many a one;

And we fall, face forward, fighting, on the deck.

2. *Responses may vary. A sample response is given.*

Each of the clauses begins with the contraction *It's.* Two of the sentences use a gerund phrase as their complement.

EXERCISE B

Responses will vary. A sample response is given.

1. In these metaphors, the poet describes the daily life of a person with a low-paying job. These metaphors usually allude to a commonly known expression. The metaphor in the first line compares the danger of such poverty to the threat of a hungry wolf. In other words, a poor employee is as able to confront these perils just about as well as a naked child could face a vicious animal.

In the second metaphor, the poet places the image of a sinking ship before the reader's eyes. As a sinking ship is doomed, so the person playing the game of bowls is doomed to lose the game and may even lose his or her life.

In the third line, the poet possibly alludes to the saying, "Living on a shoestring allowance," a phrase that refers to having an amount of money sufficient only to purchase a single shoestring. The other picture the metaphor evokes is that of a highwire circus performer, a person who walks a tightrope.

The fourth line extends the description by referring to millstones. Here the poet is alluding to another familiar saying, "having a millstone around one's neck." This phrase refers to a situation in which a person has an unbearable burden weighing him or her down. The low-wage earner walks a tightrope while being weighed down by the debts of the past and the perils of the future—millstones.

2. With each metaphor, the poet draws closer to describing *It* by comparing *It* to something else. To make these comparisons, the author uses predicate nominatives. The first metaphor uses a noun to describe a state of being. The next two metaphors use gerunds to describe ongoing actions.

EXERCISE C

Responses will vary. A sample response is given.

It's reading between
from beginning to end;
It's whistling while
thinking of an inkling
on a lark in a dark park;
It's the bark with a bite
with no fight in sight
that lights my mind like
a kite out of time.

EXERCISE D

Responses will vary. A sample response is given.

1. The predicate nominative *bark* alludes to the saying "there's no bite in his bark," an expression referring to meaningless, seemingly threatening, noise. This noise—poetry—does have a bite, which is its point. There is "no fight in sight" because the struggle is an internal one. Rather than being based on hostility, this struggle leads to consciousness or creation.

2. I tried to describe the process that can lead to inspiration or sudden understanding.

Writing Application: Interview, p. 52

Writing Applications are designed to provide students immediate composition practice in using key concepts taught in each chapter of the *Language and Sentence Skills Practice* booklet. You may wish to evaluate student responses to these assignments as you do any other writing that students produce. To save grading time, however, you may want to use the following scoring rubric.

Scoring Rubric

Simple elements have been combined to avoid choppiness and wordiness.

| 1 | 2 | 3 | 4 | 5 |

Both quoted and paraphrased materials are included in the profile.

| 1 | 2 | 3 | 4 | 5 |

The profile adequately describes a typical work day.

| 1 | 2 | 3 | 4 | 5 |

The assignment is relatively free of errors in usage and mechanics.

| 1 | 2 | 3 | 4 | 5 |

Total Score _____

5 = highest; 1 = lowest

Chapter 3: The Phrase, pp. 53–78

Choices: Investigating Phrases, p. 53

Choices activities are designed to extend and enrich students' understanding of grammar, usage, and mechanics and to take learners beyond traditional classroom instruction. To use the Choices worksheet, have each student pick an activity that interests him or her. In some cases, you may wish to assign an activity to a particular student or group of students. You may also want to request that students get your approval for the activities that they choose. Establish guidelines for what constitutes successful completion of an activity. Then, help students plan how they will share their work with the rest of the class.

Choices activities can be scored with a pass-fail grade or treated as bonus-point projects. Those activities that require students to research or create a certain number of items might be graded in a traditional manner.

Identifying Phrases, p. 54

EXERCISE A

1. NP	6. NP
2. P	7. P
3. NP	8. NP
4. P	9. P
5. P	10. P

EXERCISE B

Responses will vary. Sample responses are given.

11. <u>Wanting to help</u>, we rushed toward the burning bridge.

12. The chipmunk quickly ran <u>behind the tree trunk</u>.

13. I have promised Laura <u>to help her with her homework</u>.

14. That old convertible, <u>the black one by the fence</u>, could run if we replaced its transmission.

15. <u>Hitting a home run</u> is more difficult than it looks.

Prepositional Phrases, p. 55

EXERCISE A

1. Many people used to believe that camels stored water <u>in their humps</u>.

2. <u>In 1954</u> a research team set out to study the camel's water-storing capacities.

3. The results <u>of their research</u> indicated, surprisingly, that a camel does not actually store extra water.

4. *none*

5. Human beings and many other animals must depend <u>on an evaporation process</u> to keep their body temperatures constant.

6. When a horse is hot, it perspires, and the evaporation <u>of this water</u> cools its body.

7. *none*

8. Therefore, a camel rarely needs to expend precious water <u>on any cooling system</u>.

9. <u>During a long, hot day</u>, a camel's temperature may rise ten degrees, but the animal does not suffer any ill effects.

10. Can you imagine having a temperature <u>of 108 degrees</u> and feeling healthy?

EXERCISE B

Responses will vary. Sample responses are given.

11. Empty the flour into an airtight canister.
12. Set the cinnamon on the spice rack.
13. Store the detergent beneath the sink.
14. Place the split peas upon the lowest shelf.
15. Stash the vitamins inside the medicine cabinet.

The Adjective Phrase, p. 56

EXERCISE A

1. I remember Grandmother when I smell freshly baked (bread) with butter.

2. The (aroma) of my grandmother's baking was often strong.

3. When I was young, Grandmother let me help make soft (rolls) with butter.

4. She made (breads) such as wheat rolls and cranberry muffins.

5. Grandfather would say that his (favorite) of all the rolls was the batch I had helped to make.

6. I remember the (tickle) of flour and baking powder when I breathed it in.

7. My grandmother would say that I was the "best (baker) of the bunch."

8. Now, years later, the (smell) of rising bread brings back these memories.

9. I can almost see Grandmother wearing her (dress) with the roses.

10. Whenever I get the chance, I bake (one) of Grandmother's specialties.

EXERCISE B
Responses will vary. Sample responses are given.
11. The trail led to a hilltop above the town.
12. Giuli could see the town in the valley.
13. Lights within the town were flickering.
14. The setting sun illuminated the horizon across the valley.
15. Giuli rested and watched the meadow by the river.

The Adverb Phrase, p. 57
EXERCISE A
1. Some (work) at fast food restaurants, while others work outdoors.
2. One important skill students (learn) at part-time jobs is communication.
3. Students (can earn) extra cash and experience at a part-time job.
4. Those who (contribute) to a savings account regularly can watch their money grow quickly.

5. Throughout the nation, many teens (have) career-related part-time jobs.

6. Students (may find) career-related jobs in a vocational catalogue.

7. Students (can check) with their guidance counselors, who will help them investigate possibilities.

8. A student who wants to study veterinary medicine (could work) for a local veterinarian.

9. Students who hope to practice law someday (could volunteer) at the attorney general's office.

10. Any part-time job can be (helpful) for the future.

EXERCISE B
Responses will vary. Sample responses are given.
11. Did you ask Cooper to help us during the party?
12. Call your cousin on the telephone.
13. Drew pitched the ball across the field.
14. We saw the fire trucks near the old warehouses.
15. I tried with all my strength.

Identifying Adjective and Adverb Phrases, p. 58
EXERCISE A
1. *ADJ*—The ice on the plane's wings made the mechanics uneasy.
2. *ADV*—Ariadne spoke with great confidence and enthusiasm about her favorite subject, fishing.
3. *ADV*—Throughout the school year, Ms. Cruz has tracked the students' progress.
4. *ADV*—Is Mr. Toyoda still active in local politics?
5. *ADJ*—A large group of uniformed six-year-olds descended upon the shrine.

6. Golf balls have changed a lot <u>over the years</u>. (*adverb*)

7. The earliest balls were made <u>of wood</u>. (*adverb*)

8. The first big breakthrough <u>in golf balls</u> was the "feathery" ball. (*adjective*)

9. This ball debuted <u>in the early seventeenth century</u>. (*adverb*)

10. "Featheries" were tightly stuffed, as you might guess, <u>with feathers that had been boiled</u>. (*adverb*)

11. <u>By the mid-nineteenth century</u>, the gutta-percha ball was being used. (*adverb*)

12. Gutta-percha is a latex <u>of several South American and South Pacific island trees</u>. (*adjective*)

13. Gutta-percha balls, unfortunately, were hard, brittle, and difficult to get <u>into the air</u>. (*adverb*)

14. The rubber ball, which was invented early <u>in the twentieth century</u>, provided better control. (*adverb*)

15. <u>Because of the rubber ball</u>, many more people began playing golf. (*adverb*)

The Participle, p. 59
EXERCISE A

1. Working as a children's photographer is a *present* <u>challenging</u> job.

2. On some <u>charmed</u> *past* days, all the children who come in for pictures are happy and cooperative.

3. Their faces light up when I show them a *Past* <u>stuffed</u> animal, and the pictures are keepers.

4. Their <u>delighted</u> *past* parents happily order photos for family and friends.

5. On the <u>frustrating</u> *present* days, however, the children cry and complain.

6. My <u>annoyed</u> *past* assistant tempts them with promises of a treat after the photo session.

7. Sometimes this bribery calms a <u>crying</u> *present* child.

8. Sometimes the <u>despairing</u> *present* parents must take the child home without having pictures made.

9. I remind them that another day will be the perfect time to photograph their <u>fussing</u> *present* baby.

10. In the end, this <u>rewarding</u> *present* job never ceases to surprise me!

EXERCISE B

11. Sean ignored the ∧ passengers in the backseat. (*fidget*) *fidgeting*

12. He carefully checked the ∧ traffic behind him. (*adjust*) *adjusting*

13. "Let the fire truck pass," came an ∧ word from one of the passengers. (*advise*) *advising*

14. With ∧ lights, the fire truck drove past. (*flash*) *flashing*

15. Finally, Sean merged slowly into the ∧ traffic. (*congest*) *congested*

The Participial Phrase, p. 60
EXERCISE A

1. <u>Located an hour or so from Austin, Texas</u>, the (domes) of Enchanted Rock are batholiths, underground rock formations that erosion has slowly revealed.

2. Many years ago, (Tonkawas) <u>living nearby</u> said that a pale man had been swallowed by the rock and reborn as rock.

3. Ghostly lights sometimes flicker from the domes' surfaces—the pale (man) weaving enchantments, said the Tonkawa.

4. Today, visitors know that the lights come from water (puddles) reflecting moonlight.

5. Hiking the path to the summit, (I) am struck by the beauty of the rock.

EXERCISE B

6. The clock striking the hour of noon, I thought that a brisk walk would be pleasant.

7. I bundled up and left the house, our excited dog straining at the leash.

8. The walk began beautifully, snow crunching underfoot.

9. We crossed the stream, the water rushing with new-melted snow.

10. Back at home, I relaxed by the fire, my hot chocolate steaming deliciously.

Participles and Participial Phrases, p. 61

EXERCISE A

1. wilting
2. Humming
3. sweetened
4. sweltering
5. refreshing

EXERCISE B

6. Clearing his throat, the tenor began his rehearsal.

7. The weary hikers spent the next night at a cabin stocked with food and blankets.

8. Moving with grace and stealth, the Siamese cat was stalking the mouse.

9. The sandwiches, shared with the children on the playground, provided a moment of peace for the teacher.

10. Checking her hair in the mirror, the actor practiced the first lines of her speech.

11. Repaired just weeks before, the radiator had developed yet another leak.

12. The German shepherd lying by that man's feet is a guide dog.

13. The head coach, discussing the call with the official, remained calm.

14. Ms. Ortiz whispered something to the lady sitting next to her.

15. The blankets piled on the bed are clean.

The Gerund, p. 62

EXERCISE A

1. Choosing from among many refreshing activities can be difficult. [S]

2. Some people enjoy gardening. [DO]

3. Others combine relaxation and health improvement by exercising. [OP]

4. Still others would far rather give playing chess their attention. [IO]

5. Reading continues to hold its own among leisure activities. [S]

6. Since somebody has to make dinner anyway, one favorite hobby is cooking. [PN]

7. There will always be those who prefer watching television. [DO]

8. Chatting on the phone is a very popular activity, especially with cell phone use on the rise. [S]

9. Simply enjoying conversation together is a critical part of most families' days. [S]

10. Whatever people choose to do, developing a hobby can ease the day's stress, both physically and mentally. [S]

Responses will vary. Sample responses are given.

11. Megan and I enjoy running.

12. I gave singing the song my best effort.

13. Dividing the pie into eight slices was easy.

14. We got help with designing our landscape.

15. The most challenging task was inventing a new fuel system.

The Gerund Phrase, p. 63
EXERCISE A

1. At the founding of the Academy of Motion Picture Arts and Sciences in 1927, *[OP]* Hollywood began to consider how to reward excellence.

2. Staying abreast of cinematic developments *[S]* is challenging, and the number of annual awards has fluctuated throughout the years since 1929.

3. The Oscar statuette was cast in bronze and gold-plated for many years, but World War II brought on the waning of U.S. metal *[DO]* supplies, so for a time the figure was made of plaster that was painted gold.

4. Today the technique used to make the statuette is covering a britannium base with *[PN]* gold plating.

5. Untold numbers of Americans have given the fateful ripping of each envelope their *[IO]* full attention.

EXERCISE B
Responses will vary. Sample responses are given.

6. The child enjoys applying colorful finger paints to the paper.

7. The key to my success is focusing on the task at hand.

8. My uncle, a meteorologist, makes a living by predicting the weather.

9. Borrowing my sister's clothes is rarely permitted.

10. Flinging the seeds in a wide arc is the best way to plant them.

Gerunds and Gerund Phrases, p. 64
EXERCISE A

1. *PN*—One of the most exciting experiences my family ever had was adopting my baby brother.

2. *S*—Translating from Chinese to English is a rare and valuable skill.

3. *OP*—The coach was praised for treating each of her players with respect.

4. *DO*—Emilio taught Cajun cooking in an adult education class.

5. *IO*—Tanya, a conscientious person, gives caring for her new puppy top priority.

EXERCISE B
Responses will vary. Sample responses are given.

6. Painting a still life is the assignment in art class today.

7. An annoying habit of some people is complaining on a regular basis.

8. I tried swimming in the public pool, but the pool was too crowded.

9. I prepared for next month's shopping trip by saving all the money I earned.

10. The babysitter gave caring for the infant her undivided attention.

Identifying Participial and Gerund Phrases, p. 65
EXERCISE A

1. Some tasks, such as putting away clutter, *[gerund phrase]* involve much walking from room to room.

2. Using the recycling bin judiciously, you can *[participial phrase]* make your way through the piles of paper that have been collecting for weeks.

3. It's easy to place the dishes into the patiently *[participial phrase]* waiting dishwasher.

4. Who wants to undertake the tedious task of ironing all the cotton clothes? *[gerund phrase]*

5. Personally, I've always found <u>folding warm</u> *gerund phrase* <u>towels</u> to be a soothing task.

6. One good way to pass the time pleasantly while working is <u>listening to good music</u>. *gerund phrase*

7. <u>Working together</u>, two people can quickly get the trash gathered and put out. *participial phrase*

8. Two people <u>cleaning the bathroom</u>, however, soon run out of room! *participial phrase*

9. Cleaning experts agree that <u>vacuuming the floors</u> is a task best left till last. *gerund phrase*

10. After <u>cleaning the house</u>, I'm going out for dinner! *gerund phrase*

EXERCISE B
Responses will vary. Sample responses are given.

11. Thriving after spring rains, the garden looked beautiful.

12. I regretted arguing with Marta.

13. Permitting the cat to walk on the kitchen counters is not a good idea.

14. Josh and Tameka, concentrating on their homework, did not hear the doorbell.

15. In the middle of the night, I heard the dog whining to go outside.

The Infinitive, p. 66
EXERCISE A

1. At the party, the toddler wanted <u>to eat</u> first. *N*

2. The large dog needs <u>to go</u> to the vet for shots. *N*

3. <u>To have finished</u> early would have required more help. *N*

4. Call me if you have any questions <u>to ask</u>. *ADJ*

5. Was Pauli really prepared <u>to leave</u>? *ADV*

EXERCISE B
Responses will vary. Sample responses are given.

6. We waited to see the sunset.

7. The garden pests to find are aphids.

8. To nurture a pet is a wonderful skill for a child to learn.

9. The clue to investigate is the muddy footprint beside the broken window.

10. The dog decided to crawl beneath the bushes and rest in their shade.

11. Remember to give the signal at 3:05.

12. When I play basketball, I play to win.

13. The experiment to begin next is described in Chapter 12.

14. To have gone to the dance would have been fun.

15. To have been recognized would have spoiled the surprise.

The Infinitive Phrase, p. 67
EXERCISE

1. For many decades, farmers have continued <u>to use artificial pesticides on their crops</u>. *N*

2. However, recent concerns about toxicity have convinced many farmers that they should seek ways <u>to avoid the use of such pesticides</u>. *ADJ*

3. <u>To think of organic farming as a recent idea</u>, however, is incorrect. *N*

4. In the 1930s, a British agri-scientist, Sir Albert Howard, presented the world with a new farming method <u>to examine for possible use</u>. *ADJ*

5. He developed a system of farming in which wastes were used <u>to fertilize crops</u>. *ADV*

6. Manure, compost, straw, and organic waste from crops work <u>to improve soil conditions for growing plants</u>. *ADV*

7. Eager <u>to improve nutrition without reducing crop yields</u>, some farmers choose organic methods. *ADV*

8. Rotating crops, releasing insect predators, and sowing pest-resistant plants are options <u>to employ for pest control</u>. *ADJ*

9. To improve sustainable agriculture *(N)* is one of the goals of organic farming.

10. More and more people are beginning to buy and enjoy organic foods *(N)* each year.

Infinitives and Infinitive Phrases, p. 68

EXERCISE A

1. *N*—To go to law school is Mai's goal.

2. *ADV*—Chucha is happy to be part of the Zuni ceremony.

3. *none*

4. *none*

5. *N*—The seamstress likes to see the needle-work done by her talented son.

6. *ADV*—Because of the howling wind and creaking shutters, Jamila was unable to sleep.

7. *ADJ*—The player to emulate is Manuel.

8. *N*—Halfway across the rock face, Nina began to lose her footing.

9. *ADV*—If you ask me, this little gray kitten should be eager to go home with you.

10. *N*—Chantel and Ricki have both offered to help with the park cleanup.

EXERCISE B

Responses will vary. Sample responses are given.

11. One of my favorite pastimes is to dream about my future.

12. Place the bruised apples over there; these are the ones to keep.

13. I will be happy to travel with you this summer.

14. Wise people have learned to listen with an open mind.

15. Are you ready to leave?

Identifying Prepositional and Verbal Phrases, p. 69

EXERCISE

[1] Considered *(PART)* by many the best jazz impro-viser, Yardbird Parker played alto sax, composed music, and originated bebop, [2] regarded as *(PART)* the pace-setting jazz style [3] of the mid-twenti-eth century *(PREP)*. Parker collaborated [4] with Dizzy Gillespie *(PREP)* [5] to define jazz *(INF)* [6] for two decades *(PREP)*. [7] Listening to swing music *(GER)* in the 1930s moved Parker [8] toward his own new style *(PREP)*. He also gained experience [9] playing with various bands *(PART)*. However, [10] to follow their own musi-cal ideas *(INF)*, he and Gillespie founded their own ensemble [11] in 1945 *(PREP)*. Parker incorporated many musical voices [12] into his music *(PREP)*, [13] from African-American folk songs *(PREP)* [14] to mod-ern concert music *(PREP)*. His style, [15] punctuated by quick tempos *(PART)* and [16] accented by sudden pauses and endings *(PART)*, became the root style [17] of many subsequent jazz musicians *(PREP)*. Sadly, Parker's death [18] at the young age *(PREP)* [19] of thirty-four *(PREP)* ended a career [20] of remarkable music-making *(PREP)*.

The Appositive, p. 70

EXERCISE A

1. Civic, one example, reads the same no mat-ter which end of the word you begin with.

2. *Desserts stress Ed* and *Sit on a potato pan, Otis!* are amusing examples real gems, of sentence-length palindromes.

3. The word *palindrome* comes from Greek and means "running back again."

4. Palindromes are little word games now but once had deeper significance to a supersti-tious people, the Romans.

5. They inscribed palindromes on decorative charms—amulets—to ward off harm.

EXERCISE B

Responses will vary. Sample responses are given.

6. She worked as a legal assistant at the company <u>Mercer and Morgan</u> to save money for the down payment.

7. The car's color, <u>blue</u>, is one of my favorites.

8. Maya will take her driver's test tomorrow, <u>Wednesday</u>, in the morning.

9. If she passes, she plans to drive her new car to a special place, <u>the beach</u>.

10. Her friend <u>Melinda</u> will go with her.

The Appositive Phrase, p. 71

EXERCISE A

1. (Volunteers), <u>excited children and experienced adults</u>, gathered for a day of cleaning cages, stocking supplies, and visiting with the animals.

2. Each animal would be kept here until those special (people,) <u>its new family</u>, chose it.

3. We called on my particular (friend) at the Haven, <u>a playful Irish Setter named Redbeard</u>.

4. Most (Irish Setters), <u>slightly nervous dogs</u>, calm down once they get to know people.

5. Some animals needed medical (attention,) <u>a healing touch from our veterinary volunteers</u>.

6. Generous (donors,) <u>financial supporters without whom the Haven would have to close</u>, provide for each pet to be spayed or neutered.

7. Still, now and then we take in a litter of bright-eyed (kittens,) <u>mischievous balls of fur</u>.

8. We keep the kittens till each finds just (what it needs,) <u>a loving and safe home</u>.

9. Some volunteers foster animals in their own (houses) <u>temporary homes-away-from-home</u>.

10. I often wish I could keep every animal I foster, but my (landlord,) <u>the man with the deciding vote in the matter</u>, would not approve!

EXERCISE B

Responses will vary. Sample responses are given.

11. Though a phone call is nice, receiving written thanks, <u>a thank-you note</u>, means more.

12. Also, unlike a phone call, <u>spoken thanks</u>, one can read a thank-you note again later.

13. It's all too easy to take a friend, <u>a trusted companion</u>, for granted.

14. Thank-you notes, <u>written messages of gratitude</u>, say the words that sometimes don't get past our lips.

15. There are bad habits and good habits, and writing thank-you notes, <u>an easy task</u>, is definitely one of the latter!

Appositives and Appositive Phrases, p. 72

EXERCISE A

1. We finally convinced Rashard's friend <u>Casey</u> to join the team.

2. Yori's letter, <u>a poem about our friendship</u>, made my birthday unforgettable.

3. Charlie Belliveau, <u>the high school custodian</u>, convinced a boy not to quit school, and that boy eventually became the mayor of our city.

4. Without Blair, <u>the housekeeper</u>, nobody in that family would know how to get through their days.

5. Those overalls, <u>my favorites</u>, have been mended and patched dozens of times.

6. This grandfather clock, <u>an oak masterpiece of handiwork</u>, is an antique.

7. My cousin <u>Amanda</u> is a veterinarian who works at a wildlife park.

8. <u>A hardy perennial</u>, the grape hyacinth comes from a bulb that is planted in the fall and blooms in the spring.

9. The party, <u>a celebration of my friend's eighteenth birthday</u>, was held at a local swimming pool.

10. Lanelle's favorite song, "<u>Moondance</u>," is a jazz rock tune sung by Van Morrison.

EXERCISE B
Responses will vary. Sample responses are given.

11. mortar boards with dangling tassels

12. a deep, midnight blue

13. a challenging, liberal arts college

14. two professors from the local college

15. carefully planned rituals

Review A: Phrases, p. 73
EXERCISE A

1. California, <u>a state famous for its natural beauty</u>, takes great pride in its flowers. *APP*

2. If you want <u>to see the world's greatest flower show</u>, watch the annual New Year's Day parade in Pasadena. *INF*

3. <u>Watching this parade</u> is one way that many people start the new year. *GER*

4. Some enthusiasts take up vantage spots <u>along the parade route</u> the day before New Year's. *PREP*

5. <u>Bearing thousands of flowers on a framework of wooden braces and wire netting</u>, a large float may take many weeks to design and build. *PART*

6. One float featured an artificial tree <u>decorated with approximately 40,000 orchids</u>. *PART*

7. The task of providing the flowers for the decoration of the floats falls <u>on the shoulders of local florists and nursery workers</u>. *PREP*

8. Even in the balmy climate of southern California, one major problem is <u>having enough flowers in bloom at the right time</u>. *GER*

9. Hundreds of thousands of people wait for hours <u>to enjoy this beautiful spectacle</u>. *INF*

10. The pageant, <u>the result of many months of cooperative effort</u>, is well worth seeing. *APP*

EXERCISE B

11. These two periods, <u>separated by a thousand years</u>, are known for their strong leaders. *PART*

12. Hammurabi, as king of Babylon, did not wish <u>to maintain an uneasy peace with unfriendly neighboring rivals</u>. *INF*

13. <u>The author of a famous code of laws</u>, Hammurabi was an outstanding king. *APP*

14. More than a thousand years after Hammurabi's reign, Nebuchadnezzar, <u>another great Babylonian leader</u>, came to power. *APP*

15. One of Nebuchadnezzar's greatest achievements was <u>overseeing the reconstruction of the city of Babylon</u>. *GER*

Review B: Phrases, p. 74
EXERCISE A

1. <u>Smiling broadly</u>, Anthony showed us the sizable amount of interest he had earned on his savings account. *PART*

2. The librarian, <u>asked about enjoyable fitness activities</u>, recommended the new book about taĭ chi. *PART*

3. Gabriel García Márquez, <u>the brilliant Colombian novelist</u>, was awarded the Nobel Prize in literature in 1982. *APP*

4. Donya wants to ride her bicycle from Washington, D.C., to Seattle, Washington. *(PREP)* *(INF)*

5. Kai's ambition is to drive a tractor-trailer. *(INF)*

6. Marnie made an appointment to audition for a part in the play this morning. *(INF)*

7. Many of us in biology class have mixed emotions about dissecting frogs. *(PREP)*

8. Moving their vehicles to the right, all of the drivers let the ambulance pass. *(PART)*

9. My cousin, who is hard of hearing, prefers watching closed-captioned television programs. *(GER)*

10. My friends Alecca and Leon sent me a postcard from Rome. *(APP)*

Exercise B
Responses will vary. Sample responses are given.

11. Revising the essay carefully, Darnell worked for several hours.

12. I refuse to consider dropping out of the race!

13. Joking with my friends is how I relax during lunch period.

14. The small spark, fanned by a gentle breeze, grew to a roaring flame.

15. As I grew older, I learned not to abhor broccoli and other vegetables.

16. I gave standing on the ladder my complete attention.

17. Speaking with enthusiasm, Gina described her role in the play.

18. The information to write on your test is your name, the date, and your teacher's name.

19. Don't leave before explaining where you're going.

20. Understanding my command, the dog lifted a paw to shake hands.

Review C: Phrases, p. 75
Exercise

I was camping [1] in the Guadalupe Mountains *(PREP)* last spring. I'd heard the stories that campers tell, [2] tall tales aggrandizing each camper's own bravery, *(APP)* I figured. Mountain lions and whole packs [3] of bears *(PREP)* starred [4] in these exaggerated stories, *(PREP)* so I ignored them as I huffed [5] up the path. *(PREP)* [6] Exhausted in every muscle, *(PART)* I tossed down my gear and set up camp. [7] Sleeping deeply and soundly *(GER)* was the main thing [8] on my mind, *(PREP)* and [9] having dismissed the bear scare stories, *(PART)* I neglected [10] to hang my pack *(INF)* [11] from a rope *(PREP)* [12] over a tree branch, *(PREP)* as one is supposed to do if bears might be around. I fell asleep right away, but minutes later, or so it seemed, I woke [13] to hear a snuffling, grunting, scratching noise *(INF)* [14] near my tent flap. *(PREP)* Adrenaline flooded my system as I regretted not listening [15] to the more experienced campers' stories. *(PREP)* However, I had heard how [16] to protect myself: *(INF)* I charged up my camera flash, leapt [17] through the tent door, *(PREP)* and, aiming at the bear, set off the flash. Then I scrambled back [18] into the tent *(PREP)* and listened hopefully as the confused bear loped off [19] through the woods. *(PREP)* I learned something that night: Skip the camera if you like, but never go camping [20] without the camera flash! *(PREP)*

Literary Model: Poetry, pp. 76–77
Exercise A
1. a. of you; for it
   b. of you; To Canterbury; to journey's end; from the days; of old; for it
   c. on the outward trip; on the homeward way; upon the way; at once; without another word

2. a. to make things slip
   b. for what we spend; to what you've heard

EXERCISE B

Responses will vary. A sample response is given.

Since every prepositional phrase begins with a preposition and concludes with an object, there is a brief tone of finality every time such a phrase ends. The prepositional phrases also fit neatly into the iambic pentameter of the poem. Usually, the preposition is unaccented and its object is accented.

EXERCISE C

Responses will vary. A sample response is given.

On our last trip together, the path is so long

Through the towns, on the highways, to the
    green water's brink.

Let us then in rich unison join in bright song

Of those popular tunes that caused us to think,

Or to revel in our youth or our choice.

May those without shyness soon start us in
    tunes

As each one to the chorus of top-tens adds
    voice,

Till our merry bus driver spots seagulls and
    dunes.

EXERCISE D

Responses will vary. Sample responses are given.

1. Of those popular tunes that caused us to think,

2. Through the towns, on the highways, to the green water's brink.

Writing Application: Informational Presentation, p. 78

Writing Applications are designed to provide students immediate composition practice in using key concepts taught in each chapter of the *Language and Sentence Skills Practice* booklet. You may wish to evaluate student responses to these assignments as you do any other writing that students produce. To save grading time, however, you may want to use the following scoring rubric.

Scoring Rubric

The speech uses at least two present and two past participial phrases.

| 1 | 2 | 3 | 4 | 5 |

The tone is appropriate for a spoken presentation to high school students.

| 1 | 2 | 3 | 4 | 5 |

The speech includes adequate information about the organization or activity.

| 1 | 2 | 3 | 4 | 5 |

The assignment is relatively free of errors in usage and mechanics.

| 1 | 2 | 3 | 4 | 5 |

Total Score _____

5 = highest; 1 = lowest

Chapter 4: The Clause, pp. 79–102

Choices: Exploring Clauses, p. 79

Choices activities are designed to extend and enrich students' understanding of grammar, usage, and mechanics and to take learners beyond traditional classroom instruction. To use the Choices worksheet, have each student pick an activity that interests him or her. In some cases, you may wish to assign an activity to a particular student or group of students. You may also want to request that students get your approval for the activities they choose. Establish guidelines for what constitutes successful completion of an activity. Then, help students plan how they will share their work with the rest of the class.

Choices activities can be scored with a pass-fail grade or treated as bonus-point projects. Those activities that require students to research or create a certain number of items might be graded in a traditional manner.

Identifying Clauses, p. 80

EXERCISE

1. the dog prefers the marigold patch

2. sleeping in the bushes by the front door
   not a clause

3. where the dog buries its bones

4. the afternoon sun winks through the pear tree's branches

5. the shadows dance and play on the dog's gold fur

6. known to many in the neighborhood *not a clause*

7. the birds splash in the birdbath

8. because the dog keeps an eye on them

9. the dog would never chase or bite them

10. if it sees a cat

The Independent Clause, p. 81

EXERCISE A

1. The wait staff wear brightly embroidered clothing.

2. Stuffed jalapeños make an excellent appetizer, but the black bean nachos are good, too.

3. I sometimes eat chips and salsa before the entrée arrives.

4. Fern likes enchiladas, but I like tacos.

5. I always leave a good tip, for the wait staff are attentive and quick.

6. The pico de gallo stings my mouth a bit, but it tastes good.

7. Is Mexican food your favorite, or do you prefer Italian?

8. Some people prefer bland foods.

9. I enjoy the soothing atmosphere and the delicious food.

10. I don't particularly like, on the other hand, the arrival of the bill.

EXERCISE B

Answers will vary. Sample responses are given.

11. On Thanksgiving Day, roast turkey is the only meal for me.

12. Grits are my favorite breakfast, but restaurants around here often do not have them.

13. Whenever I smell baked apples, I think of my grandmother.

14. A little salsa improves just about everything.

15. Just the smell of hot popcorn makes me happy.

The Subordinate Clause, p. 82

EXERCISE

Answers will vary. Sample responses are given.

1. Do you know anyone who purchased tickets to the figure-skating contest?

2. I saw Tom there while we waited in line.

3. I asked the clerk if there were still six seats together.

Language and Sentence Skills Practice Answer Key

4. He told me that the semifinals were not sold out yet.

5. We talked to Tom until we paid for our seats.

6. He asked me which events were scheduled for Monday.

7. We wondered if there were front-row seats, as if we could afford front-row seats.

8. The price, which included backstage passes, was astronomical!

9. Whoever wants to learn to skate should talk to my sister; she is giving lessons.

10. We usually make a point of attending because we enjoy the competition so much.

Independent and Subordinate Clauses, p. 83
EXERCISE

1. SC	6. SC
2. SC	7. SC
3. IC	8. SC
4. SC	9. SC
5. IC	10. SC

The Adjective Clause, p. 84
EXERCISE A

1. Sri Lanka is an island (nation) that lies off the coast of the southern tip of India.

2. This (island), which was formerly called Ceylon, is famous for its tea.

3. It is a (country) where both the land and the people present dramatic contrasts.

4. (Mount Pidurutalagala), which rises to a height of 8,281 feet (2,524 meters), stands in contrast to the coastal lowlands.

5. The teachings of the principal religion, Buddhism, contrast with the civil (war) that has ravaged the country in recent years.

EXERCISE B

6. It is futile to worry about (things) that are in the past.

7. Chinua Achebe is a Nigerian (author) whose books I enjoy.

8. I hardly recognized the (house) where I had spent my childhood.

9. The red (maple) that grows in our backyard turns a beautiful shade of red in the autumn.

10. The 1960s was an (era) when many young people debated government policies.

11. Astronomy is a (subject) that I would like to study in more depth.

12. The Shang people of ancient China imported (jade), which they laboriously carved into objects of exquisite beauty.

13. The (rain forests) where the cockatoos live are being destroyed.

14. Felicia explained the (terminology) that the programmers had used in the manual.

15. (Thailand), which provides the world with much of its rice and teak, is one of the largest countries in Southeast Asia.

Relative Pronouns, p. 85
EXERCISE A

1. (Taste buds), which help make the sense of taste possible, are located on the tongue.

2. Each taste bud is made of fifty to seventy (cells) that are arranged in clusters called papillae.

3. The different (tastes) *DO* that you experience come from the interplay between food, your taste buds, and your brain.

4. The tip of the tongue is the (spot) *ADV* where we taste sweetness.

5. Have you ever experienced a (time) *OP* during which your sense of taste wasn't functioning properly?

EXERCISE B

6. Susan is a (girl) *S* who always tries to focus on the positive aspects of a difficult situation.

7. The (field) *ADV* where I used to play soccer is now a shopping mall.

8. (Kelly,) *N* whose poem was published, was asked to recite it during graduation.

9. Henry found it difficult to think of a (time) *ADV* when cars didn't exist.

10. The toddler accidentally dropped the large (tumbler) *DO* of water that his mother gave him.

11. (People) *S* who are allergic to aspirin are usually able to take aspirin substitutes.

12. Helen decided to give the books to the (person) *S* who asked her first.

13. The baseball (league) *OP* in which Shelly plays is hosting a tournament this weekend.

14. The store, the (site) *ADV* where an infamous robbery took place, is located across the street.

15. Jennifer is a smart and friendly (student) *DO* whom many people simply call "Jen."

Essential and Nonessential Clauses, p. 86

EXERCISE

1. Tim is one friend *E* on whom I know I can always count.

2. Call out the numbers *E* that you draw from the basket.

3. The women *E* whose opinions I've always valued are talking with each other by the door. [or, *NE* whose opinions I've always valued.]

4. The students are busily decorating the room *E* in which the school dance is to be held.

5. Mrs. Tate, *N* whom I admire, always offers constructive criticism.

6. The house *E* where we will meet has a blue car in the driveway.

7. One speaker, *N* who seemed rather nervous, provided thorough information about the task of seeking scholarships.

8. Fifteen repetitions with each arm is the number *E* that my coach recommends.

9. She's a clever girl *E* who can figure out solutions to many problems.

10. I'm allergic to Bermuda grass, *N* which is planted all around my neighborhood.

The Noun Clause, p. 87

EXERCISE

1. You can discuss your report with *OP* whichever teacher is available.

2. A little praise from time to time is *PN* what most children need.

3. The mayor will give *IO* whoever passes the finish line first a key to the city.

4. The teacher said *DO* that this little chunk of granite is over four billion years old.

5. *S* What happened to the fabled city of Atlantis remains a mystery.

6. We will donate *DO* whatever we do not need to the Salvation Army.

7. The committee's decision was *PN* that solar power cells should be installed.

8. Deke expounded his weird theories to *OP* whoever would listen to them.

9. Marie Curie discovered *DO* that radium is an element.

10. *S* How whales hunt by means of echolocation will be our subject for today.

The Adverb Clause, p. 88

EXERCISE A

1. After I eat lunch, I (will clean) my room.

2. This hat is (prettier) than that one is.

3. When you get home, please (clean) your room.

4. Do you really watch tennis on TV (more) than you watch basketball?

5. George Bernard Shaw (did) not (write) a play until he was thirty-five years old.

6. Karen (makes) friends wherever she goes.

7. If you like the music of Mozart, you (will love) Beethoven's first symphony.

8. (Don't open) that present early unless you want to ruin the surprise.

9. Because Keith was born in Tokyo, his parents (gave) him a Japanese middle name.

10. Provided that you complete the training, you (can start) work next week.

EXERCISE B
Answers will vary. Sample responses are given.

11. If you wash the dishes, I'll dry them.

12. We waited as long as we could.

13. Because they are so rare, emeralds are quite valuable.

14. There will be no vote unless two thirds of the members are present.

15. While the dump truck backed up, the workers took their places.

Subordinating Conjunctions, p. 89
EXERCISE

1. (Although) many teens work during high school, they usually earn only a modest amount of money. *under what conditions*

2. However, they will have to start paying income taxes (as soon as) they begin to work.
   when

3. (Whether) teens know it or not, the practice of taxing income in the United States goes back to the Civil War. *under what conditions*

4. In 1873, the federal income tax ceased, (until) President Grover Cleveland reinstated it in 1894. *when*

5. (Because) the Supreme Court declared the personal income tax unconstitutional, those who supported the tax had to alter the Constitution. *why*

6. This they did in 1913 (when) the Sixteenth Amendment was ratified.
   when

7. (Provided that) a citizen made at least $3,000 a year, he or she was required to pay tax.
   under what conditions

8. (When) World War II ended, the minimum tax rate was 23 percent, and the maximum tax rate was 94 percent. *when*

9. (So that) they can raise revenue for schools and roads, some states also have a personal income tax. *why*

10. (Since) we have to work to pay for food, rent, clothing, and school, we will all end up paying taxes at some point!
    why

The Elliptical Clause, p. 90
EXERCISE A
Some answers may vary. Sample responses are given.

1. they were

2. you see

3. you are

4. he likes reading

5. you are

EXERCISE B

6. Unless ~~they are~~ frightened of clowns, children generally enjoy circuses.

7. While ~~you are~~ turning off the lights, check the doors, too.

8. I usually listen to the radio while ~~I am~~ studying.

9. Do you like chocolate as much as ~~you like~~ vanilla?

10. Jacob is taller than the other players ~~are tall~~.

Identifying Adjective and Adverb Clauses, p. 91

EXERCISE

1. _ADV_ <u>Although some people have had access to the Internet for only a short time</u>, its beginnings can be traced back to the 1960s.

2. The Internet, _ADJ_ <u>which is a network connecting many computers using a common communications protocol</u>, was once used mostly by academics.

3. The ARPAnet, _ADJ_ <u>which was established in 1969</u>, was the predecessor of the Internet.

4. ARPAnet is an acronym _ADJ_ <u>that stands for Advanced Research Projects Agency Network</u>.

5. The Department of Defense established ARPAnet _ADV_ <u>when they wanted to connect computers at military installations and universities</u>.

6. Later, in 1974, the Xerox Corporation adapted the communications network for use in its business _ADV_ <u>because it could inexpensively send information throughout the company</u>.

7. The people at Xerox, _ADJ_ <u>who called their adaptation an Ethernet</u>, cut the cost of installation with new wiring techniques.

8. _ADV_ <u>Although such communication nets were once used only by military personnel, academics, and business people</u>, today anyone can use the Internet.

9. _ADV_ <u>Provided that you have a library card</u>, you can access the Internet at many public libraries.

10. You can even go to an Internet café and have a snack _ADV_ <u>while you browse the World Wide Web</u>.

Identifying and Classifying Subordinate Clauses A, p. 92

EXERCISE A

1. The American bittern, a member of the heron family, is a bird _ADJ_ <u>that practices ventriloquism</u>.

2. The call of the bittern should be familiar to anyone _ADJ_ <u>who has ever explored a marshland</u>.

3. _ADV_ <u>Although the bittern's call is easy to identify</u>, the source of the sound is usually hard to locate.

4. _N_ <u>Whoever tries to spot a bittern or find its nest</u> may have a difficult job.

5. The call seems to come from one location _ADV_ <u>while the bird is actually somewhere else</u>.

6. Bird experts tell us _N_ <u>that the bittern also uses protective coloration</u>.

7. _ADV_ <u>When a bittern is alarmed</u>, it stands motionless and points its bill upward.

8. Its neck, _ADJ_ <u>which is marked with a vertical black stripe</u>, then fades in with the marsh reeds.

9. The nest _ADJ_ <u>in which the bittern lays its eggs</u> is also difficult to spot.

10. _ADV_ <u>Since the nest is made of reeds</u>, it is easily mistaken for a tangled patch of marsh grass.

Answers will vary. Sample responses are given.

11. Because camouflage enables birds to blend in with their surroundings, it protects them from predators.

12. Birds that blend in to their surroundings may be difficult for predators to see.

13. Hunters wear camouflage clothing while they are hunting.

14. Fashion designers who use camouflage colors know that the mystique of the military is attractive to many buyers.

15. People who wear "cammies" aren't seeking protection from anything!

Identifying and Classifying Subordinate Clauses B, p. 93

EXERCISE

1. The fact is <u>that Monopoly was invented during the financially difficult years of the Depression.</u> *PN*

2. Clarence B. Darrow, <u>who invented the game,</u> didn't succeed with it at first. *ADJ*

3. Darrow invented the game <u>while he dreamed of real fame and fortune.</u> *ADV*

4. The game was rejected by one company <u>because it had "fifty-two design errors."</u> *ADV*

5. <u>That the first company refused the game</u> did not deter Darrow. *S*

6. <u>As soon as he had sold 5,000 handmade sets,</u> however, game companies began to take interest. *ADV*

7. It's not hard to understand <u>why Monopoly was the bestselling game in 1935.</u> *DO*

8. Since then, an estimated 500 million people <u>who enjoy games</u> have played it. *ADJ*

9. You might not know <u>that one Monopoly game lasted seventy straight days!</u> *DO*

10. Monopoly terms have entered popular conversation, <u>so that trademark protection of the tokens, cards, and game board corners has become necessary.</u> *ADV*

Sentences Classified According to Structure, p. 94

EXERCISE

1. S	6. CD
2. CX	7. CX
3. CX	8. CD-CX
4. CX	9. CD
5. CD-CX	10. S

Sentences Classified According to Purpose, p. 95

EXERCISE

Some answers may vary.

1. I once rode a roller coaster that flipped the riders upside down and then ran around a steel loop. *dec.*

2. What a strange feeling that was! *exc.*

3. I expected my sandals to fly off and land on people in line below us. *dec.*

4. Have you ever ridden a coaster in which the riders must stand up? *int.*

5. No, this will be my first ride on a stand-up roller coaster. *dec.*

6. Be sure to secure all loose items in your pockets before boarding the ride. *imp.*

7. Don't forget to scream on the way down the hill! *imp.*

8. I much prefer calmer rides. *dec.*

9. How do you feel about those water rides that soak you to the bone? *int.*

10. What a relief it is to cool off on a hot day! *exc.*

Review A: Clauses, p. 96

EXERCISE

1. S—ADV
2. S—ADJ
3. I
4. I
5. I
6. S–ADJ
7. S—ADV
8. S—N
9. I
10. S—ADV
11. S—ADJ
12. S—N
13. S—ADJ
14. S—ADJ
15. S—ADV
16. S—N
17. S—ADJ
18. I
19. S—ADJ
20. I

Review B: Clauses, p. 97

EXERCISE

1. Do you know who George Sand was? *(N over "who George Sand was")*

2. I learned that she was born Amandine Aurore Lucie Dupin. *(N over "that she was born")*

3. *None*

4. When people choose pseudonyms, they do so for a variety of reasons. *(ADV over "When people choose pseudonyms")*

5. A pseudonym, or fictitious name, is not always one that conceals a person's identity. *(ADJ over "that conceals a person's identity")*

6. After all, nearly everyone knows who Mark Twain was. *(N over "who Mark Twain was")*

7. That he was really Samuel Langhorne Clemens is not a matter of great significance. *(N over "That he was really Samuel Langhorne Clemens")*

8. Some writers may conceal their gender, though, as Mary Ann Evans did by assuming the name George Eliot. *(ADV over "as Mary Ann Evans did")*

9. A modern writer who has done the same without a pseudonym is P. D. James. *(ADJ over "who has done the same")*

10. When men write romantic fiction, they sometimes assume a woman's name. *(ADV over "When men write romantic fiction")*

11. *None*

12. Cary Grant, who grew up as Archibald Leach, was one such entertainer. *(ADJ over "who grew up as Archibald")*

13. Another was Henry John Deutschendorf, Jr., better known as John Denver, a singer whose pseudonym comes from the name of a city. *(ADJ over "whose pseudonym comes from the name of a city")*

14. *None*

15. Whenever a sports star has a hard-to-pronounce name, the athlete may feel some pressure to change it to something easier. *(ADV over "Whenever a sports star has a hard-to-pronounce name")*

16. Even some avid baseball fans may not know who Aloysius Szymanski was. *(N over "who Aloysius Szymanski was")*

17. He was the great Hall of Fame outfielder Al Simmons, a player who also had a well-known nickname, "Bucketfoot Al." *(ADJ over "who also had a well-known nickname")*

18. There are "ordinary" people, too, with names they wish to change. *(ADJ over "they wish to change")*

19. Supposedly, a man by the name of Messerschmitt, living in England during World War II, asked to change his name because Messerschmitt was the name of a German airplane. *(ADV over "because Messerschmitt was the name of a German airplane")*

20. *None*

Review C: Sentences Classified According to Structure, p. 98

EXERCISE A

___CX___ 1. Cattle raisers have long used the technique of crossbreeding to produce animals that combine the best qualities of two different breeds.

___CD___ 2. The Hereford breed, for instance, originated in England in the eighteenth century; it was a cross between native Herefordshire cattle and cattle from the Netherlands.

_S_ **3.** More recently, American breeders have crossed Herefords and Brahmans in order to produce a breed called Brafords.

_CD_ **4.** The Hereford is a beef breed originally from England, and the Brahman, a breed native to India, is a type noted for its resistance to heat and to disease.

_CD-CX_ **5.** One of the most unusual animals that American breeders have produced is the cattalo; it is a cross between a buffalo and a cow.

EXERCISE B

6. CX

7. CD-CX

8. CX

9. S

10. CD

Review D: Sentences Classified According to Purpose, p. 99

EXERCISE

1. For instance, the word *panorama*, <u>which names a type of painting invented in 1787</u>, comes from two Greek words.

___*dec.*___

2. *Pan* in Greek means "all," and *horama* means "a view" and comes from the Greek word *horan*, "to see." *dec.—no clause*

3. Have you ever seen a panorama <u>that depicts a famous place or event?</u>

___*int.*___

4. In the nineteenth century, panoramas as large as three hundred feet long and fifty feet tall were popular. *dec.—no clause*

5. Hold on to the rails <u>if you ever see a "cyclorama," a panorama that revolves on rollers.</u>

___*imp.*___

6. Speaking of odd words, consider the word *farb.* *imp.—no clause*

7. Reenactors recreating historical battles and former ways of life use this word to describe people <u>whose costumes are not historically accurate.</u> ___*dec.*___

8. After all, would a Civil War soldier have worn sunglasses or carried a cellphone? *int.—no clause*

9. Perhaps this word comes from the German word for color, *farbe*, <u>because inauthentic costumes are often much more brightly colored than the more accurate dull-colored ones.</u> ___*dec.*___

10. What a sight it is to see a Civil War wife cooking in a microwave run by a generator! *exc.—no clause*

Literary Model: Narrative, pp. 100–101

EXERCISE A

1. This clause is an ___*adjective*___ modifying the word ___*one*___.

2. This clause is an ___*adverb*___ modifying the word ___*are*___.

3. This clause is an ___*adjective*___ modifying the word ___*philosophy*___.

4. This clause is an ___*adverb*___ modifying the word *would have been*.

EXERCISE B

1. In the revision, the clause functions as the direct object of the verb *asked*.

2. The clause is used as an adverb explaining *why*; its subordinating conjunction is *so that*.

EXERCISE C

Answers will vary. A sample response is given.

By leaving out the subordinate clauses, the reader misses the idea that cowardice or carelessness might be the cause of some ignorance.

Also, the important idea of supernatural enthusiasm is lost. Consequently, the passage loses some of its depth and significance.

EXERCISE D
Answers will vary. A sample response is given.

Upon high school graduation, two of my friends and I hope to rent an apartment together and work <u>while we attend community college classes</u>. <u>So that self-sufficiency becomes a reality as soon as possible</u>, we plan to learn the principles of budgeting and chore sharing first-hand. <u>Since my own family had some chore schedules worked out</u>, I think <u>I'll contribute concrete ideas in this area</u>. However, I worry about all the hidden expenses of independent living <u>that I haven't thought of yet</u>. <u>If I discover that I'm taking on too many responsibilities at once</u>, I might move back in with my folks and brothers for a year. <u>When I look back on it</u>, I'm sure <u>I'll be glad</u> <u>I pursued college work and went on to get my bachelor's degree</u>.

EXERCISE E
Answers will vary. Sample responses are given.

1. There are ten subordinate clauses, some of which have other subordinate clauses inside them.

2. When I am explaining circumstances, reasons for taking certain actions, and contingency plans, I find myself using connecting words such as *since, because, so that, in order to, while,* and so forth. These expressions allow me to add complex information smoothly to my paragraph without tacking it on in choppy short sentences.

Writing Application: Instructions, p. 102
Writing Applications are designed to provide students immediate composition practice in using key concepts taught in each chapter of the *Language and Sentence Skills Practice* booklet. You may wish to evaluate student responses to these assignments as you do any other writing that students produce. To save grading time, however, you may want to use the following scoring rubric.

Scoring Rubric
The instructions teach the task adequately.

   1   2   3   4   5

Most of the sentences are imperatives.

   1   2   3   4   5

The tone is polite but professional.

   1   2   3   4   5

The assignment is relatively free of errors in usage and mechanics.

   1   2   3   4   5

Total Score _____

5 = highest; 1 = lowest

Chapter 5: Agreement, pp. 103–31

Choices: Exploring Agreement, p. 103

Choices activities are designed to extend and enrich students' understanding of grammar, usage, and mechanics and to take learners beyond traditional classroom instruction. To use the Choices worksheet, have each student pick an activity that interests him or her. In some cases, you may wish to assign an activity to a particular student or group of students. You may also want to request that students get your approval for the activities they choose. Establish guidelines for what constitutes successful completion of an activity. Then, help students plan how they will share their work with the rest of the class.

Choices activities can be scored with a pass-fail grade or treated as bonus-point projects. Those activities that require students to research or create a certain number of items might be graded in a traditional manner.

Number, p. 104

EXERCISE A

P **1.** they
S **2.** creature
S **3.** windshield
P **4.** hurricanes
P **5.** brothers-in-law
S **6.** amendment
P **7.** pulleys
S **8.** himself
S **9.** basketball
P **10.** willows
S **11.** inference
P **12.** castles
S **13.** it
S **14.** danger
P **15.** geese
S **16.** crater
S **17.** illness
P **18.** wolves
P **19.** we
P **20.** theorems

EXERCISE B

Answers will vary but should be correct in number.

21. three ripe ___kumquats___
22. many honest ___confessions___
23. a more expensive ___backpack___
24. another bright red ___flag___
25. both successful ___students___
26. every single ___fork___
27. too few ___vacations___
28. either ___door___
29. a traditional ___holiday___
30. at least fifteen ___cups___

Subject-Verb Agreement A, p. 105

EXERCISE A

1. <u>Opinions</u> on the editorial page *(is, <u>are</u>)* often diverse.

2. <u>Ellen Goodman</u>, as well as other writers, *(<u>speaks</u>, speak)* on political issues.

3. A <u>person</u> who reads daily newspapers *(<u>keeps</u>, keep)* up on the issues.

4. One <u>writer</u> of humorous columns *(<u>is</u>, are)* Art Buchwald.

5. Government <u>policy</u>, along with rising taxes, *(<u>receives</u>, receive)* his barbs.

EXERCISE B

6. Her answer to all requests of this kind ~~are~~ is the same.

7. C

8. C

9. The coach of the team, as well as the student co-captains, ~~are~~ *is* going to speak at the banquet.

10. The success of amateur productions ~~depend~~ *depends* largely on the producer.

Subject-Verb Agreement B, p. 106

EXERCISE

1. The <u>color</u> of those daisies (<u>*was*</u>, *were*) bright yellow.

2. Did you know that <u>Principal White</u>, together with the school board, (<u>*has*</u>, *have*) approved the plan for the new gymnasium?

3. Alan said that the <u>dogs</u> in this obedience class (*was*, <u>*were*</u>) rescued from the shelter.

4. The drapery <u>fabric</u> that they finally decided upon (<u>*contains*</u>, *contain*) tiny flecks of yellow and green.

5. <u>Searching</u> for your lost earrings (<u>*is*</u>, *are*) making us late for the party.

6. My twin <u>brother</u>, whom you met yesterday, (<u>*skis*</u>, *ski*) better than I do.

7. <u>To return</u> the tiny robin safely to its nest (<u>*was*</u>, *were*) our goal.

8. In our family, <u>Uncle Jeb</u>, who brings us presents from all over the world, (<u>*is*</u>, *are*) the most popular of the aunts and uncles.

9. The <u>smoke detector</u>, as well as our noses, (<u>*was*</u>, *were*) telling us that something was on fire.

10. The <u>paint</u> for these rooms (<u>*arrives*</u>, *arrive*) tomorrow at the hardware store.

Subject-Verb Agreement: Indefinite Pronouns A, p. 107

EXERCISE A

1. (Anybody) who had his or her parents' permission (*were*, <u>*was*</u>) allowed to go on the field trip.

2. (Several) of our neighbor's puppies (<u>*have*</u>, *has*) found good homes.

3. (Some) of the puzzle pieces (*is*, <u>*are*</u>) missing, but you can still figure out what the picture is.

4. (Everything) you've advised me to do (<u>*has*</u>, *have*) been for the best.

5. (Something) to think about (<u>*is*</u>, *are*) where you expect to be in five years.

EXERCISE B

6. (Some) of the members of the safety patrol ~~is~~ *are* not satisfied with the current regulations.

7. (All) of the marigolds ~~was~~ *were* blooming.

8. (Everyone) with high marks ~~are~~ *is* eligible for the scholarship.

9. Only a (few) of the class members ~~has~~ *have* applied.

10. (None) of the video equipment ~~were~~ *was* salvaged after the devastating flood.

11. (Both) of those answers ~~is~~ *are* correct.

12. (Neither) of the pitchers ~~were~~ *was* able to stop the Hawks from winning the game.

13. C

14. C

15. Of all the blouses on sale, (several) ~~was~~ *were* my size.

Subject-Verb Agreement: Indefinite Pronouns B, p. 108

EXERCISE A

1. (Most) of the ingredients for our supper (<u>*were*</u>, *was*) fresh vegetables from our garden.

2. (None) of the documentary (*have*, <u>*has*</u>) been cut from this videotape.

3. (Several) in the crowd (*is*, <u>*are*</u>) waving banners and hoping to be noticed by the band.

Language and Sentence Skills Practice Answer Key

4. (Everything) on television tonight *(has, have)* [handwritten: s] been on before; I'm tired of re-runs.

5. (All) of us in the forensics society *(is, are)* [handwritten: P] going to the regional competition.

EXERCISE B

6. (Some) of the kittens in this litter ~~is~~ [handwritten: are] gray tabbies like their mother.

7. (All) of the backpacks ~~was~~ [handwritten: were] on sale at Edelmann's Sporting Goods Store.

8. (Anyone) answering all the homework questions correctly ~~are~~ [handwritten: is] excused from taking the quiz.

9. (Several) of the daffodils ~~has~~ [handwritten: have] already sprouted.

10. C

11. (Either) of these tuxedos ~~are~~ [handwritten: is] suitable for the prom, Ernesto.

12. (Both) of the car dealerships ~~is~~ [handwritten: are] offering special deals on financing.

13. C

14. (Neither) of these applicants ~~have~~ [handwritten: has] the necessary experience, Ms. Chao.

15. (Few) of the pages in that old history book ~~has~~ [handwritten: have] pictures.

Agreement with Compound Subjects A, p. 109
EXERCISE

1. Either the <u>dogs</u> or some wild <u>animal</u> *(has, have)* dug a hole under the fence in the backyard.

2. In the past, *(have, has)* <u>juggling</u> and <u>mime</u> been taught at the performing arts summer school?

3. A <u>cup</u> of sugar and three <u>cups</u> of whole wheat flour *(have, has)* been measured and set aside.

4. Either <u>Rick</u> or his <u>brother</u> *(walks, walk)* their dog, Buster, every morning and evening.

5. *(Has, Have)* <u>working</u> at the movie theater and <u>doing</u> your homework been taking up most of your time?

6. *(Is, Are)* <u>Anna</u> or <u>Elise</u> making the costumes for the senior class play?

7. <u>Jonathan</u>, <u>Dana</u>, <u>Leroy</u>, and <u>I</u> *(are, is)* planning a road trip for spring break.

8. <u>Steak</u> and <u>potatoes</u> *(were, was)* my dad's favorite meal until his doctor told him to reduce the amount of cholesterol in his diet.

9. <u>Talking</u> with clients and <u>designing</u> furniture for them *(make, makes)* up most of Dan's day.

10. The large oak <u>tree</u> in the front yard and the smaller <u>one</u> in the back *(are, is)* not in danger of getting oak wilt disease.

Agreement with Compound Subjects B, p. 110
EXERCISE

1. The <u>oboists</u> and the band <u>director</u> ~~is~~ [handwritten: are] scheduled to have the practice room this afternoon.

2. Two <u>physicians</u> or an emergency room <u>nurse</u> ~~have~~ [handwritten: has] agreed to speak to our science class about careers in medicine.

3. Twenty <u>geraniums</u> and an entire <u>flat</u> of petunias ~~is~~ [handwritten: are] what we planted in the window boxes.

4. A good <u>book</u> and a shady <u>hammock</u> ~~is~~ [handwritten: are] going to help me relax this Saturday.

5. Our <u>boss</u>, <u>cheerleader</u>, and <u>role model</u> ~~are~~ [handwritten: is] our store manager, Kris.

6. The student <u>council</u> and their faculty <u>advisor</u> ~~has~~ [handwritten: have] chosen the theme for the prom.

7. During every appointment, the <u>assistants</u> or the <u>veterinarian</u> ~~advise~~ [handwritten: advises] me on tooth care for my basset hound.

8. Cookies or fresh <u>fruit</u> ~~are~~ ^{is} a good dessert to bring to a potluck supper.

9. <u>Macaroni</u> and <u>cheese</u> ~~are~~ ^{is} my little sister's favorite main dish.

10. A <u>dropcloth</u> or even some <u>newspapers</u> ~~helps~~ ^{help} prevent painting accidents.

Special Problems in Subject-Verb Agreement A, p. 111

EXERCISE

1. By the way, ~~where's~~ *where are* the <u>tapes</u> that you borrowed last week?

2. ~~Doesn't~~ *Don't* the <u>fountain</u> and the <u>birdbath</u> freeze in the winter?

3. ~~There's~~ *There are* the exchange <u>students</u> from Germany and Romania.

4. ~~Here's~~ *Here are* the <u>ingredients</u> for the vegetarian lasagna.

5. ~~Is~~ *Are* <u>Jenny</u> and her <u>sister</u> both in the choral ensemble?

6. ~~Where's~~ *Where are* <u>Brent</u> and <u>Joey</u> going over spring break?

7. In addition to your family, ~~was~~ *were* there any <u>friends</u> and <u>neighbors</u> at your grandfather's birthday party?

8. As you know, ~~there's~~ *there are* several <u>items</u> on tonight's PTA agenda that concern us seniors.

9. ~~Don't~~ *Doesn't* this leather-bound <u>journal</u> from the Netherlands belong to you?

10. ~~Here's~~ *Here are* the <u>books</u> about World War II that Ms. Ramos put on reserve for us.

Special Problems in Subject-Verb Agreement B, p. 112

EXERCISE

1. The <u>team</u> (*plan, **plans***) to share their best memories of the coach at his retirement party.

2. At the meeting the <u>staff</u> (*were, **was***) remarking on the new furniture in the conference room.

3. I think the <u>orchestra</u> (*sound, **sounds***) off-key tonight.

4. How often (*have, **has***) our school <u>choir</u> performed at the regional music festival?

5. Principal Smith has asked whether the school safety <u>committee</u> (*want, **wants***) to present their reports.

6. The <u>pride</u> of lions (*were, **was***) resting in the shade of a tree. [or *was*]

7. That <u>litter</u> of puppies (*have, **has***) all different colored coats—brown, black, and white.

8. For this maneuver, the <u>squadron</u> (*fly, **flies***) in a tight formation.

9. The <u>herd</u> (*was, **were***) tagged and vaccinated against common bovine illnesses.

10. The chamber <u>ensemble</u> (*play, **plays***) only music written before 1800.

11. A <u>hive</u> of bees (*work, **works***) hard to feed and protect its queen.

12. The <u>couple</u> that moved in next door (*do, **does***) yard work every Saturday. [or *do*]

13. After a win, the <u>team</u> (*celebrate, **celebrates***) by going out for pizza.

14. The <u>audience</u> usually (***bring**, brings*) their opera glasses with them.

15. Before starting to march, the <u>band</u> (*tune, tunes*) their instruments.

16. After the closing arguments, the <u>jury</u> (*seem, **seems***) to be taking a long time to reach its verdict.

17. The <u>team</u> usually (*donates, **donate***) their old uniforms to a group of disadvantaged youth.

Language and Sentence Skills Practice Answer Key

18. After lunch the <u>staff</u> (*is*, are) going to meet to discuss ways to enhance interdepartmental relationships. [*or* <u>are</u>]

19. The <u>faculty</u> (*is*, <u>are</u>) meeting to decide what to do with the grant money they received.

20. Before the play, the <u>cast</u> (<u>get</u>, *gets*) together to do warm-up vocal exercises.

Special Problems in Subject-Verb Agreement C, p. 113
EXERCISE

1. is
2. Does
3. has
4. is
5. was
6. was
7. have
8. seems
9. participate
10. is

Special Problems in Subject-Verb Agreement D, p. 114
EXERCISE

1. is
2. is
3. Are
4. show
5. has
6. is
7. look
8. explains
9. receive
10. Is

Special Problems in Subject-Verb Agreement E, p. 115
EXERCISE

1. Our greatest <u>concern</u> (*is*, are) the orphaned puppies that were brought in last week.

2. My <u>specialty</u> in the kitchen (<u>is</u>, are) vegetable soups made from fresh produce.

3. Many a <u>student</u> in our calculus class (*have*, <u>has</u>) commented on Mr. Wright's ability to explain complex ideas simply.

4. The <u>acrobats</u> (*was*, <u>were</u>) the best part of the floor show.

5. Every <u>pot</u> and <u>pan</u> in the restaurant (*have*, <u>has</u>) been washed and put away.

6. Many an aspiring <u>actor</u> (*find*, <u>finds</u>) himself or herself waiting tables to pay the bills.

7. (*Is*, <u>Are</u>) sequined evening <u>dresses</u> the most becoming choice for your bridesmaids?

8. One <u>thing</u> I can never have enough of (<u>is</u>, are) colored pencils.

9. Not every high school <u>athlete</u> (*go*, <u>goes</u>) on to play his or her sport in college.

10. These days, many a computer <u>enthusiast</u> (*send*, <u>sends</u>) electronic greeting cards.

11. <u>One</u> of my chores (<u>is</u>, are) washing and drying the dishes after supper.

12. <u>Strawberries</u> and <u>peaches</u> (<u>were</u>, *was*) the dessert.

13. Every <u>employee</u> and <u>volunteer</u> (*look*, <u>looks</u>) forward to the technology fair.

14. <u>Labrador retrievers</u> (*is*, <u>are</u>) my favorite kind of dog.

15. <u>One</u> of the vegetables she has never eaten (<u>is</u>, are) rutabagas.

16. <u>Kites</u> and other flying <u>objects</u> (*was*, <u>were</u>) the main attraction at the fair.

17. Every <u>parent</u> and <u>child</u> (<u>is</u>, are) invited to attend the school picnic.

18. <u>Peaches</u> (*is*, <u>are</u>) my favorite fruit.

19. Many a young <u>child</u> (<u>has</u>, *have*) been thrilled by a sight of a small puppy.

20. <u>One</u> of the things I have to accomplish today (<u>is</u>, are) mowing and trimming the lawn.

Special Problems in Subject-Verb Agreement F, p. 116
EXERCISE

1. The government needs census (workers) who (<u>are</u>, *is*) fluent in Spanish.

2. He suggested two different window (treatments) that (*seem*, *seems*) perfect for the room.

3. Janice has found an art (program) which (*are*, *is*) perfect for her interests and talent.

4. Ravi has used only two of the sick (days) that (*are*, *is*) allowed.

5. Ask the (editor) who (*coordinate*, *coordinates*) the yearbook schedules if it's too late to place an advertisement.

6. Jerome already has several good ideas for the history (project) that (*were*, *was*) assigned today.

7. Do you remember the names of the (astronauts) who (*was*, *were*) the first to land on the moon?

8. Zack found several (Web sites) that (*contain*, *contains*) useful information for our presentation.

9. Uncle Sean is my one (relative) who (*have*, *has*) an Irish first name.

10. This antique lacquer (tray) which (*are*, *is*) very valuable, belonged to my great-great-grandmother.

Agreement of Pronoun and Antecedent A, p. 117
EXERCISE

1. Please get the (keys) off the counter and bring (*it*, *them*) to me.

2. (Tania) has beaten (*her*, *their*) old record in the 200-meter freestyle.

3. If you see (Dwayne,) please tell (*him*, *them*) to pick up his uniform.

4. My (brother) and (sister) and (I) cleaned the house after school so that (*we*, *they*) could surprise Mom when she got home from work.

5. This (bread) is especially moist and delicious because (*it*, *them*) contains two tablespoons of toasted sesame oil.

6. In a few minutes, our (veterinarian) will tell us what (*she*, *they*) learned from Boots's X-ray.

7. (Mara) and (Alana) are accomplished gymnasts; therefore, (*she*, *they*) make even the most difficult flips look easy.

8. Frank is allergic to (cats) so he tries to stay away from (*it*, *them*).

9. Because of extra piano practice, (Ray) has improved (*his*, *its*) performance of that Chopin nocturne.

10. The (robin) pulled bits of moss from the tree in order to make a nest for (*their*, *its*) eggs.

Agreement of Pronoun and Antecedent B, p. 118
EXERCISE

1. One of the players on the boys' team hurt ~~themselves~~ *himself* badly.

2. Mrs. Jackson asked both of the boys to help, and she paid ~~him~~ *them* well.

3. C

4. One of the girls had left ~~their~~ *her* ticket at home and had difficulty getting into the game.

5. C

6. Neither of my sisters has decided where ~~they~~ *she* will work this summer.

7. C

8. C

9. Anyone who works hard should achieve ~~their~~ *his or her* goal.

10. Most of the salad has wilted, so you can throw ~~them~~ *it* away.

Language and Sentence Skills Practice Answer Key

49

Agreement of Pronoun and Antecedent C, p. 119

EXERCISE

1. they
2. it
3. them
4. their
5. her
6. his
7. their
8. her
9. her
10. their

Special Problems in Pronoun-Antecedent Agreement A, p. 120

EXERCISE A

1. During the meeting, the committee reporting on the company's growth were enthusiastic about (*its*, *their*) data.

2. The bed of tulips that we planted was spectacular; (*it*, they) looked like a crimson carpet.

3. Please ask the staff to check (*its*, *their*) e-mail before coming to the meeting.

4. Our marching band complain that (it, *they*) need new white shoes to match the new uniforms.

5. This bushel of plums will last for many months once we make (*it*, them) into jam.

6. Has the pair of swans selected (*its*, their) nesting site yet?

7. The flock of sheep followed (*its*, their) leader into the pen.

8. Uncle Rob claims that the public do not always vote in ways that support (its, *their*) own best interests.

9. The crowd enjoyed the concert and tossed (*its*, their) hats on stage during the encore.

10. A colony of fire ants can protect (*itself*, themselves) quite effectively.

EXERCISE B

11. Surrounding the embassy, the mob shouted angrily and waved ~~its~~ *their* fists in the air.

12. Did you disturb the swarm of bees or get too close to ~~their~~ *its* hive?

13. That cluster of berries is poisonous, so don't eat anything from ~~them~~ *it*.

14. Arriving in port, the crew looked forward to enjoying ~~itself~~ *themselves* on leave.

15. Only a little nervous, the ensemble are tuning ~~its~~ *their* instruments before the recital begins.

Special Problems in Pronoun-Antecedent Agreement B, p. 121

EXERCISE

1. it
2. it
3. their
4. it
5. it
6. it
7. their
8. it
9. their
10. it

Special Problems in Pronoun-Antecedent Agreement C, p. 122

EXERCISE

1. Physics with Mr. Dejani is such a popular class that students must get on a waiting list to take (*it*, them).

2. The binoculars are broken; (it, *they*) may need to be taken to the repair shop.

3. Blossoms is a local florist shop opening soon, and (*it*, they) will specialize in bouquets made from exotic, tropical flowers.

4. Aunt Sara brought us pajamas made of silk from Thailand, and (it, *they*) must be the most comfortable nightclothes I've ever worn.

5. Ted's older brother is studying economics because he says (*it*, they) will help him prepare for a career in politics.

6. My white shorts turned pale pink when I washed (it, *them*) with my red T-shirt.

7. Have you read "Beliefs and Truths"? (It, They) recently appeared in a collection of poems by young writers.

8. Danny watches the news first thing in the morning; he says (it, they) can oftentimes give him a pleasant start on the day.

9. *Dubliners* by James Joyce reflects the grim reality of Irish life; (it, they) can be difficult to read.

10. Mothers Against Drunk Drivers is holding (its, their) annual fund-raiser next Saturday.

Special Problems in Pronoun-Antecedent Agreement D, p. 123

EXERCISE

1. their
2. her
3. its
4. its
5. its
6. their
7. his
8. themselves
9. her
10. their

Review A: Subject-Verb Agreement, p. 124

EXERCISE

1. ~~There's~~ *There are* only three chapters left to finish.

2. C

3. C

4. ~~Is~~ *Are* these trousers washable?

5. C

6. Basic economics ~~show~~ *shows* that a balance of trade is necessary.

7. Every one of the streets ~~need~~ *needs* to be repaired.

8. C

9. Either the school committee members or the principal ~~have~~ *has* the forms.

10. C

11. C

12. The engine of one of the trucks ~~were~~ *was* sputtering.

13. Many a candidate ~~have~~ *has* spoken out eloquently on the issues.

14. Neither Felicia nor her brother ~~were~~ *was* in the band.

15. He ~~don't~~ *doesn't* intend to debate the issues with you.

16. C

17. ~~Don't~~ *Doesn't* your father come from Hungary?

18. C

19. We live on Oaks Avenue, which ~~run~~ *runs* north and south.

20. C

21. Our baseball team ~~are~~ *is* going to Dallas for a tournament this weekend.

22. ~~Here's~~ *Here are* the pictures I had developed last week.

23. Jane thinks that linguistics ~~are~~ *is* a fascinating field of study.

24. She ~~don't~~ *doesn't* know whether she should wash the car first or rake up the leaves in the yard.

25. Either Marguarita or Pilar ~~are~~ *is* auditioning for the lead in the school play.

Review B: Pronoun-Antecedent Agreement, p. 125

EXERCISE A

1. Neither Mr. Syms nor Mr. Karras had worn ~~their~~ *his* glasses.

2. Whether a candidate wins or not, ~~they~~ *he or she* must submit a report about campaign expenditures.

3. C

4. That is a decision that everyone must make for ~~themselves~~ *himself or herself*.

5. C

6. No one on the city council has suggested that ~~they~~ *he or she* will vote for the new ordinance.

7. C

8. C

9. Many of the Rotary Club members
expressed ~~his~~ *their* appreciation to the speaker.

10. C

EXERCISE B

11. their
12. her
13. it
14. it
15. it
16. She
17. his or her
18. he or she
19. his or her
20. her

Review C: Agreement, p. 126

EXERCISE

1. Neither the secretary nor the treasurer ~~have~~ *has* been paid.

2. There ~~was~~ *were* still a few questions that had not been answered.

3. The price of diamonds ~~vary~~ *varies* from year to year.

4. Each of the girls paid for ~~their~~ *her* own dinner.

5. No one will be excused from physical education classes unless ~~they bring~~ *he or she brings* a note signed by a doctor.

6. C

7. ~~When's~~ *When are* the primary and the general elections?

8. Our team ~~are~~ *is* playing the Eagles next Sunday on television.

9. Several of the members of last year's graduating class ~~is~~ *are* enrolled at the University of Wisconsin.

10. One of the canaries had gotten ~~their~~ *its* foot caught in the cage door.

11. Neither Tien nor her sister ~~appear~~ *appears* ready to leave for the concert yet.

12. My English teacher said that ethics might be very interesting for me to study in college. He said that ~~they~~ *it* may be taught in the philosophy department.

13. Nearly one third of the band members carried ~~its~~ *their* instruments in cases to the performance.

14. That bird in the trees ~~don't~~ *doesn't* look like the ones I have seen before.

15. C

16. The class will go on a field trip to the Museum of Science to do research for ~~its~~ *their* projects.

17. Several of the children ate ~~his or her~~ *their* lunches outside because the weather was so beautiful.

18. Almost every book about insects that Sarah reads ~~contribute~~ *contributes* to her ever-increasing knowledge of entomology.

19. Todd explained that the jury would probably take several hours to come to ~~their~~ *its* collective decision.

20. Either her roommates or her sister ~~are~~ *is* throwing a big surprise party for Samantha.

Review D: Agreement, p. 127

EXERCISE

1. her
2. is
3. requires
4. have
5. has
6. he
7. have
8. remembers
9. was
10. his or her
11. its
12. their
13. has
14. Has
15. are
16. is
17. his or her
18. is
19. is
20. are

Proofreading Application: Letter to the Editor, p. 128

Dear Editor:

I fully understand that mathematics, as well as other basic courses, ~~are~~ *is* an essential part of the education one needs to be successful in life. Undoubtedly, many a high school graduate who has not performed well in such courses ~~have~~ *has* had problems later on. If you were to ask any one of them, ~~they~~ *he or she* would probably express regret at not having exerted more effort in science, mathematics, and reading. However, learning the fundamentals ~~are~~ *is* not enough. When the goal of the education system is to produce a well-rounded and complete person, courses not considered basic, such as art or music, ~~is~~ *are* also of extreme importance.

The current rumor going around Lincoln High School is that about two thirds of the art and music courses ~~is~~ *are* going to be eliminated next year. Neither the principal nor the counselors ~~is~~ *are* willing to comment on this.

Students, we must speak out about such a prioritization in how school funds are used! Everyone has to voice ~~his~~ *his or her* protest! Tell parents; I am confident that the number of parents who will side with us ~~are~~ *is* not small. Every one of the fine arts courses—choir, graphic design, jazz band, marching band, etc.—has ~~their~~ *its* own special value. Please join the effort to save them.

Literary Model: Poem, pp. 129–30
EXERCISE A

1. *Each*

2. It determines the number, singular, but does not determine the gender.

3. It determines the gender, masculine.

4. *forefathers*

5. her: __housewife__ __feminine__ __singular__

   their: __children__ __not specific__ __plural__

   his: __sire__ __masculine__ __singular__

EXERCISE B
Each in ___his___ *or* ___her___ *grave*
forever sleeps,

The residents departed of a smaller town.

EXERCISE C
Poems will vary. A sample is given.

His plane went down during World War II.
Barely over thirty himself, he was known as
    "Pops" by the younger troops.
Perhaps it was then he rose to the occasion
And never allowed the pessimism in.

More than half a century later, as full of hope as
    then,
He listened to his grandchildren and smiled on
    their tomorrows.
When his heart gave up, his heart lived on.
This paradox lends comfort to our sorrows.

EXERCISE D
Responses will vary.

(His) plane went down during World War II.
Barely over thirty himself, (he) was known as
    "Pops" by the younger troops.
Perhaps it was then (he) rose to the occasion
And never allowed the pessimism in.

More than half a century later, as full of hope as
    then,
(He) listened to (his) grandchildren and smiled on
    (their) tomorrows.
When (his) heart gave up, (his) heart lived on.
This paradox lends comfort to (our) sorrows.

1. Most pronouns were masculine and singular.

2. Some pronouns might be plural because other people in his life are referred to (specifically, his grandchildren).

Writing Application: College-Admissions Letter, p. 131

Writing Applications are designed to provide students immediate composition practice in using key concepts taught in each chapter of the *Language and Sentence Skills Practice* booklet. You may wish to evaluate student responses to these assignments as you do any other writing that students produce. To save grading time, however, you may want to use the following scoring rubric.

Scoring Rubric

The letter follows the standard format for a business letter.

| 1 | 2 | 3 | 4 | 5 |

The letter is brief, specific, and polite.

| 1 | 2 | 3 | 4 | 5 |

The letter contains no subject-verb or pronoun-antecedent agreement errors.

| 1 | 2 | 3 | 4 | 5 |

The assignment is relatively free of errors in usage and mechanics.

| 1 | 2 | 3 | 4 | 5 |

Total Score _____

5 = highest; 1 = lowest

Chapter 6: Using Pronouns Correctly, pp. 132–54

Choices: Exploring Pronouns, p. 132

Choices activities are designed to extend and enrich students' understanding of grammar, usage, and mechanics and to take learners beyond traditional classroom instruction. To use the Choices worksheet, have each student pick an activity that interests him or her. In some cases, you may wish to assign an activity to a particular student or group of students. You may also want to request that students get your approval for the activities they choose. Establish guidelines for what constitutes successful completion of an activity. Then, help students plan how they will share their work with the rest of the class.

Choices activities can be scored with a pass-fail grade or treated as bonus-point projects. Those activities that require students to research or create a certain number of items might be graded in a traditional manner.

Case Forms of Personal Pronouns, p. 133

EXERCISE A

1. The clerk was very helpful to Ms. Ayala and <u>me</u>. *F—O*
2. Was it <u>he</u> *T—N* who called while <u>I</u> *F—N* was at the recycling center?
3. I didn't know that <u>their</u> *T—P* mother was a published poet.
4. I've decided that <u>I</u> *F—N* thoroughly support <u>your</u> *S—P* point of view.
5. Please provide <u>them</u> *T—O* with your new address and phone number.

EXERCISE B

6. them
7. my
8. We
9. you
10. their

The Nominative Case A, p. 134

EXERCISE A

1. he—S
2. I—S
3. she—PN
4. We—S
5. he—S
6. we—PN
7. they—PN
8. they—PN
9. she—S
10. He—S

EXERCISE B

Sentence-completion answers will vary.

11. S—she
12. PN—he
13. S—they
14. S—I
15. PN—they

The Nominative Case B, p. 135

EXERCISE A

Sentence-completion answers will vary.

1. S—you
2. PN—he
3. S—she
4. S—He
5. S—I
6. PN—we
7. S—she
8. PN—he
9. S—they
10. S—he

EXERCISE B

11. They
12. we
13. you
14. he or she
15. you

The Objective Case A, p. 136

EXERCISE A

1. OP—us
2. OP—her
3. DO—him
4. IO—them
5. DO—them

EXERCISE B

6. him
7. them
8. it
9. them
10. her

The Objective Case B, p. 137

EXERCISE A
Sentence-completion answers will vary.

1. IO—her
2. IO—you
3. IO—me
4. DO—us
5. DO—him, her
6. IO—me
7. IO—them
8. IO—them
9. DO—him
10. IO—them

EXERCISE B
11. me
12. her
13. him
14. me
15. us
16. me
17. her
18. them
19. them
20. us

Nominative and Objective Case Pronouns, p. 138

EXERCISE A
1. IO
2. OP
3. S
4. PN
5. DO

EXERCISE B
Responses will vary. Sample responses are provided.

6. The first ones on the field will be <u>we</u>.
7. Take <u>it</u> to the laboratory.
8. <u>You</u> must be aware of this fact.
9. Come with <u>me</u> please.
10. Will you show <u>her</u> the master document?

The Possessive Case, p. 139

EXERCISE A
Answers may vary, but the case forms of the pronouns chosen should match the case forms of the pronouns below.

1. yours
2. His
3. her
4. our
5. yours

EXERCISE B
6. his—M
7. hers—PN
8. ours—O
9. theirs—O
10. Your—M; mine—S

Case Forms A, p. 140

EXERCISE A
1. we—S
2. she—S
3. me—OP
4. he—PN
5. me—DO
6. they—S
7. Your—M
8. me—OP
9. him—IO
10. we—PN

EXERCISE B
11. me
12. you
13. mine
14. theirs
15. him [*or* her]

Case Forms B, p. 141

EXERCISE
1. Just between you and ~~I~~ *me*, I think he should have studied a bit more.
2. Will Michelle and ~~him~~ *he* post the fliers on campus today?
3. Principal Kostas encouraged the rest of ~~we~~ *us* to volunteer for the project.
4. Mom lent Madeleine and ~~I~~ *me* enough money to buy that book.
5. During the half-time show, ~~them~~ *their* dancing got the most applause.
6. Jamie and ~~her~~ *she* always finish their Spanish assignments.
7. I asked Eva and ~~she~~ *her* to go to the art show with Julie and ~~I~~ *me*.
8. Because Terrence and ~~them~~ *they* have studied Russian, they were asked to translate for the exchange students.

9. Our chemistry teacher strongly objects to ~~us~~ *our*
staging experiments without supervision.

10. While training for the triathlon, make ~~you~~ *your*
exercising a top priority.

11. My grandfather taught ~~we~~ *us* about life in
South Korea after the Korean War.

12. ~~Us~~ *We* should design a mural for the back wall
of the cafeteria.

13. When we were children, Jeff and ~~her~~ *she* could
always run faster than Maya.

14. Josephine and they saw ~~our~~ *us* standing on the
corner, so they honked and waved.

15. ~~He~~ *His* being late has ruined our chance to
compete in the opening match.

16. Do you mind ~~me~~ *my* telling Darla that you are
coming for a visit?

17. We could barely see Alfred and ~~they~~ *them* standing in the back of the theater.

18. His many overseas travels didn't interfere
with ~~him~~ *his* writing.

19. The schedule depended on ~~me~~ *my* performing
all of the research on time.

20. To Ali and ~~she~~ *her*, it was the best graduation
present anyone could give.

Pronouns as Appositives, p. 142
EXERCISE A
1. she
2. me
3. us
4. We
5. we

EXERCISE B
Answers will vary. Sample responses are given.

6. Yes, I got to meet the two star vocalists, him
and Katie.

7. She and I, the biggest fans, were right up
front.

8. The part in the play was reserved just for us
performance artists.

9. The first to help the incoming class were we
seniors.

10. Our class gave the world's best teachers,
him and Mrs. Leopold, a special award.

Pronouns in Elliptical Constructions, p. 143
EXERCISE A
1. I gave him more dessert than *(she, her)*.

   *than I gave her **or** than she gave him*

2. Mr. Moore paid her more money than *(I, me)*.

   *than I paid her **or** than he paid me*

3. No one else I know is as brave as *(she, her)*.

   as she is

4. They see him more often than *(we, us)*.

   *than they see us **or** than we see him*

5. I have written as many pages as *(he, him)*.

   as he has written

EXERCISE B
6. I—N
7. they—N
8. he—N
9. he—N
10. she—N
11. he—N
12. she—N
13. me—O
14. me—O [*or* I—N]
15. she—N

Reflexive and Intensive Pronouns, p. 144

EXERCISE A

1. herself—REF
2. themselves—INT
3. ourselves—REF
4. yourself—REF
5. himself—INT

EXERCISE B

6. My choices for the editors of the paper are Eula and ~~yourself~~ _you_.

7. Thanks to ~~ourselves~~ _us_, the publicity for the drama festival had great results.

8. Lilith introduced herself and ~~myself~~ _me_ to the visiting delegates.

9. *C*

10. Gerald and ~~myself~~ _I_ have set the agenda for the meeting.

Who and *Whom*, p. 145

EXERCISE A

1. *PN*—Did you notice <u>who the goalie was</u>?

2. *S*—The woman <u>who wrote that book</u> is a reporter for *The New York Times*.

3. *OP*—The boy <u>with whom I was sitting</u> is a student from Kenya.

4. *DO*—Coco Chanel was a designer <u>whom many others have imitated</u>.

5. *DO*—We enjoyed our visit with Mr. Cullen, <u>whom we had not seen for months</u>.

EXERCISE B

6. who
7. who
8. Who
9. whom
10. whom
11. whom
12. Who
13. whom
14. Whom
15. who

Special Pronoun Problems, p. 146

EXERCISE A

1. ourselves—I
2. himself—R
3. yourself—R
4. herself—R
5. himself—I

EXERCISE B

6. I
7. who
8. she
9. he
10. he
11. you
12. they
13. Whom
14. whoever
15. her

Review A: Case Forms of Personal Pronouns, p. 147

EXERCISE

1. She
2. her
3. me
4. she
5. her
6. they
7. we
8. me
9. we
10. she
11. me
12. She
13. she
14. them
15. me
16. he
17. her
18. they
19. him
20. her

Review B: Using the Correct Forms of Pronouns, p. 148

EXERCISE

1. Ms. Acosta and ~~myself~~ _I_ do not see eye to eye.

2. Two of the speakers, ~~her~~ _she_ and Senator Haskins, were strongly in favor of the project.

3. *C*

4. *C*

5. We can count on ~~him~~ _his_ cooperating with us.

6. I invited Trulia and ~~she~~ _her_ to the play.

7. We must remember that there are many people in the world who are less fortunate than ~~us~~. *we*

8. They wondered ~~who~~ *whom* she favored as the next editor of the yearbook.

9. Some of ~~we~~ *us* coin collectors wanted to see more commemorative coins.

10. I asked Ms. Savarino, ~~whom~~ *who* has had experience with similar problems.

11. ~~Us~~ *We* citizens have certain rights with which the government cannot interfere.

12. We had high hopes that ~~him~~ *his* running in the track meet would give our team a chance at the title.

13. Jolanda Bradley, ~~who~~ *whom* we had not heard from since last year, finally contacted us.

14. *C*

15. You must keep in mind that your parents are much older than ~~yourselves~~. *you*

16. His cousin from Missouri is younger than ~~him~~. *he*

17. *C*

18. Have you read the article about ~~him~~ *his* signing a contract with the Phillies?

19. Someone on the newspaper's staff, either Margarita or ~~her~~, corrected the typo. *she*

20. *C*

21. *C*

22. Please accept this gift from Ada and ~~myself~~. *me*

23. Neither of the other candidates is as well qualified as ~~her~~. *she*

24. Was Jiro the student ~~whom~~ *who* had entered the mathematics competition?

25. I am grateful for ~~you~~ *your* assisting me with my application.

Review C: Using the Correct Forms of Pronouns, p. 149

EXERCISE A

1. I
2. we
3. whom
4. her
5. she
6. he
7. ourselves
8. who
9. I
10. us

EXERCISE B

11. who—PN
12. whomever—OP
13. who—S
14. who—PN
15. whom—OP

Review D: Using the Correct Forms of Pronouns, p. 150

EXERCISE A

1. his
2. my [or me]
3. me
4. Who
5. they
6. he
7. we
8. me
9. whom
10. whom

EXERCISE B

Some answers will vary, but pronoun case must match the answers shown.

11. your
12. he
13. her
14. her
15. who
16. she
17. whoever
18. him
19. they
20. whom

Proofreading Application: Thank-You Note, p. 151

Dear Mr. Leigh:

We
~~Us~~ Key Club members have frequently remarked on how generous a sponsor Dynamic Software is. However, after cotreasurers Al Muir and *I* me realized the amount of financial support your company is contributing for our upcoming food drive, I took it upon *myself* me to write you a special note of appreciation.

Clearly, the needy people ~~whom~~ _who_ will receive food items during our drive will benefit from your company's generosity. Senior club members such as Ray Gutiérrez and I—people for ~~who~~ _whom_ leadership positions are waiting in their parents' companies—will remember Dynamic Software as a model of community support. ~~You~~ _Your_ contributing to a high school service organization is going to influence Ray and ~~I~~ _me_ to support the efforts of young people when we are running a company.

Sincerely,

Amy Nguyen

Literary Model: Travel Writing, pp. 152–53

EXERCISE A

	CASE	PERSON	NUMBER
1. his	possessive	third	singular
2. it	objective	third	singular
3. Whoever	nominative	third	singular
4. they	nominative	third	plural
5. you	nominative	second	singular or plural
6. who	nominative	third	plural
7. me	objective	first	singular
8. my	possessive	first	singular
9. them	objective	third	plural
10. I	nominative	first	singular

EXERCISE B

Responses will vary. Sample responses are provided.

1. Naturally, the third-person pronouns are used because of all the people the traveler is observing. However, first-person pronouns also figure largely in the account because, after all, the narrative is a first-hand experience and everything happens from the narrator's point of view.

2. By using _you_, Swift seems to be taking a personal tone with the reader, inviting him or her to visualize the narrator's experiences. This personal address creates a sense of immediacy and an informal relationship between reader and writer.

EXERCISE C

Responses will vary. A sample response is provided.

From the perspective of a big-city dweller, the small town at the foot of the Rockies might as well have been on the moon. In the mountain hamlet, people nodded to each other as if they knew each local resident by name, age, and mood swing. I, too, lost my urban reserve and began to use a friendly air to greet people. The absence of gunned car engines made for a lovely, deep silence. The grocer stepped out of his tiny store to swap a bear story with the woman delivering mail. He pointed in the direction of a snow-capped peak, and I was suddenly struck by the majesty of the slope and its surrounding ring of evergreen. You could understand how respect for higher powers had settled long ago into this community.

EXERCISE D

Responses will vary. Sample responses are provided.

1. Three sentences describe the appearance or actions of others.

2. In my paragraph, I used more singular pronouns than plural ones.

3. Slightly fewer sentences express my responses about the new surroundings.

4. A travel journal interests readers most when the account combines narration and emotion. Descriptions of events and scenery provide the objective side of an author's experience. However, the author's emotional responses bring the account to life. Readers need both for a whole understanding.

Writing Application: Writing About Names, p. 154

Writing Applications are designed to provide students immediate composition practice in using key concepts taught in each chapter of the _Language and Sentence Skills Practice_ booklet. You may wish to evaluate student responses to these assignments as you do any other writing that students produce. To save grading time, however, you may want to use the following scoring rubric.

Scoring Rubric

Two appositives and two elliptical constructions are used.

1   2   3   4   5

The meaning of the names is given.

1   2   3   4   5

The report mentions the personal history of the name in some way.

1   2   3   4   5

The assignment is relatively free of errors in usage and mechanics.

1   2   3   4   5

Total Score _____

5 = highest; 1 = lowest

Chapter 7: Clear Reference, pp. 155–69

Choices: Exploring Clear Reference, p. 155

Choices activities are designed to extend and enrich students' understanding of grammar, usage, and mechanics and to take learners beyond traditional classroom instruction. To use the Choices worksheet, have each student pick an activity that interests him or her. In some cases, you may wish to assign an activity to a particular student or group of students. You may also want to request that students get your approval for the activities they choose. Establish guidelines for what constitutes successful completion of an activity. Then, help students plan how they will share their work with the rest of the class.

Choices activities can be scored with a pass-fail grade or treated as bonus-point projects. Those activities that require students to research or create a certain number of items might be graded in a traditional manner.

Pronouns and Their Antecedents, p. 156

EXERCISE A

1. Donna found the keys in the refrigerator, but she cannot explain how they got there.

2. When Elena picks up the posters from the copy shop, ask her to have two more of them made.

3. Before he had read the book, Tyrone had listened to its sequel on tape.

4. Although the directions say this is the right street, it is not on the map.

5. Admirers of the mayor praise him as a reformer who is not afraid to take risks.

6. Do you like that table? David made it himself.

7. Those are the trees the farmers planted to keep the wind from blowing away their crops.

8. Pointing out a small cabin in one of the old photos, Grandma said, "That was my house."

9. The children thought the fountain, which featured a dragon spouting water from each nostril, was the funniest thing they had ever seen.

10. Fiona was delighted when the shopkeeper pointed to a pair of antique bookends and asked, "Are these what you had in mind?"

EXERCISE B

11. Gina could not get back into the house because the door had locked behind her.

12. Gazing up at the stars, both girls were amazed by how immense it was.

13. My brother was exhausted after his first salsa class but is ready for next week's lesson.

14. The park ranger showed the tour group a figure etched into the rock. These are called petroglyphs.

15. Having never tried them, Maurice was eager to order a stuffed eggplant.

Correcting Ambiguous References, p. 157

EXERCISE

Revisions will vary.

1. When he finally met my father, Paolo had plenty to say.

2. Although this mountain bike costs more than that touring bike, the touring bike handles better.

3. As the president and his family passed by, the soldiers saluted them.

4. So that Ariana can complete her volunteer hours, she will help Rachel pick up trash in the park.

5. We should watch the movie after we read the book to see which is better.

6. The main difference between the TV programs aired last week and those from the week before is that the ones last week were mostly reruns.

7. Peter should feel comfortable performing this duet because he has sung with Brent before.

8. Both the Parks and the Morrises drive minivans, but that one is the Parks'.

9. The baby brought the cup down on the edge of the bowl, spilling the cup's contents on the floor.

10. Zora's writing has improved ever since she started working with Bridget.

Correcting General References, p. 158

EXERCISE *Revisions will vary.*

1. My grandfather brought some games and coloring books to Tanya when she was in the hospital. *These gifts* ~~It~~ cheered her up considerably.

2. Trading in the new company's stocks should drop off after a few days, but ~~this~~ *this eventuality* should come as no surprise.

3. The pizza pan should be heated before you put the dough on it. *This technique* ~~That~~ will make your crust crispier.

4. Jacob started exercising regularly, and he felt much better because of ~~it~~ *the exercise*.

5. The tomb was sealed by tons of rock, but *that barrier* ~~that~~ didn't keep thieves away.

6. Seconds before the time ran out, Rosario sank a shot from the three-point line, winning the game for our team. *That spectacular play* ~~That~~ made the crowd go wild.

7. In the past year Marshall has replaced the car's radiator and the coolant hoses, but ~~it~~ *all his efforts have* ~~has~~ not made any difference.

8. The cathedral took almost two hundred years to build, ~~which~~ *and that fact* comes as no surprise when one sees how magnificent ~~it~~ *the cathedral* is.

9. Some people believe the old dam should be breached to allow salmon to swim upstream, but others in the community are opposed to ~~that~~ *such a measure*.

10. More students have been riding the bus to school recently, ~~which~~ *and this increase in passengers* may have been caused by a shortage of parking spaces.

Correcting Ambiguous and General References, p. 159

EXERCISE *Revisions will vary.*

1. The cat was scared when it first met the dog.

2. The clothing drive distributed coats to three thousand families. This drive was a success!

3. Last Saturday, Scott and his father washed Scott's car.

4. When rain ruined our championship soccer game, we were disappointed.

5. Diane told her favorite joke to Ana.

6. The sun came out as soon as we woke up and looked outside our tent. We were relieved to see the sun.

7. Calinda and Ethel wrote a play based on the diary of Calinda's grandmother.

8. The bottle broke into a thousand pieces when it hit the prow of the ship.

9. Before introducing the distinguished speaker, the professor briefly mentioned the speaker's latest book.

10. That global temperatures may be rising is frightening.

Correcting Weak References, p. 160

EXERCISE A *Substitutions may vary slightly.*

1. I was surprised to see Marcus return from the bookstore without buying a single ~~one~~ *book*.

2. Because Lorena grew up on a farm, she was naturally drawn to veterinary medicine, which she saw as a chance to help ~~them~~ *animals*.

3. After the artist visited an Alaskan village to paint an Inupiat ceremony, she was able to

several of her paintings
display ~~several~~ at a museum of American Indian art.

4. Bryce was not able to go ice-skating with us because he hadn't brought ~~his~~. *his ice skates*

5. Since employees commented that departments could communicate with each other more effectively, managers have made ~~it~~ *effective communication* their top priority.

EXERCISE B *Revisions will vary.*

6. Home from the fishing trip, Davida lifted an entire cooler full of fish out of the truck.

7. Lionel has built a potter's wheel in his workroom but so far has not made any pots.

8. Our game has been rained out, and the weather forecast says to expect more rain this week.

9. The review of this strikingly designed computer says that many people buy it because of the design.

10. The museum guide explained the ancient Egyptian practice of mummification and said that these mummies were among the best preserved.

Correcting Indefinite References, p. 161
EXERCISE A

1. At a recent performance in our town, <u>they</u> set Shakespeare's *Othello* in South Africa.

2. Some critics argue that <u>you</u> should set Shakespeare's plays in their original locations.

3. We learned in our British literature class, however, that in Shakespeare's day, the stage was relatively bare and did not have elaborate backdrops or sets on <u>it</u>.

4. Instead of elaborate sets, <u>they</u> depended on spoken descriptions of the scene and elaborate costumes to indicate where and who characters were.

5. Costumes were not always historically accurate; on stage, <u>they</u> basically dressed in the fashions of the day.

EXERCISE B *Revisions will vary.*

6. The bottom of the poster lists a toll-free number that runaways can call for help.

7. The report that aired last night said that fewer asteroids orbit near the earth than had been previously estimated.

8. A sign at the pool warns that swimmers should not bring food into the swimming area.

9. Beside the list of ingredients for this recipe, the article lists metric equivalents for each measurement.

10. To celebrate the store's opening, the company is giving out free groceries to the first fifty customers.

Correcting Weak and Indefinite References, p. 162

EXERCISE *Revisions will vary.*

1. This new atlas shows the recent changes in the countries of Europe and Asia.

2. As the parade passed by, people on several floats threw trinkets to the spectators.

3. Jesse Jackson is an eloquent speaker, and that speech was one of his best.

4. That amusement park has one of the biggest roller coasters in Texas.

5. We found tiny footprints all over the snowdrifts, but didn't actually see the animal that made them.

6. Before 1970, citizens had to be twenty-one to vote.

7. After talking to Mary about the charity event, I decided I wanted to contribute to a charity.

8. We weeded the garden and gave the plants some water.

9. The article said that this year has had the worst hurricane season in recorded history.

10. They wore gorilla masks to the meeting and made everyone laugh.

Review A: Clear Reference, p. 163
Exercise A

1. People write to that columnist because he offers easy solutions for their computer problems.

2. When Ashley peered through the microscope, she was amazed to see the little creatures propel themselves with hundreds of tiny hairs.

3. Entering the subway station, Diane pressed a token into her son's hand and said, "Don't lose this."

4. Amid the docks is a tower that served as a jail before it became an apartment building.

5. Leading Ryan to the display case, Katie said, "These are the watches I described to you earlier."

Exercise B *Revisions will vary.*

6. The officer told Pete that Pete's car had been stolen.

7. This computer-virus warning says to update antivirus software regularly.

8. If only the sun would shine a little, the winter would seem less bleak.

9. After seeing the news report about high-definition television, Grandmother commented that she could remember watching black-and-white television.

10. To ensure the safety of the next flight, the engineers have gone over every inch of wiring in the space shuttle.

Review B: Clear Reference, p. 164
Exercise A *Revisions will vary.*

1. We wanted to buy our movie tickets, but the box office was closed.

2. The receptionist told the patient, "You have laryngitis."

3. Karl's admission that he could not swim came as a surprise.

4. The weather forecaster said on the radio that Monday will be sunny and warm.

5. Having the game canceled because of rain was annoying.

Exercise B *Revisions will vary.*

[6] ~~In this~~ *This* interview, ~~it~~ explains that Ofra Haza was an acclaimed popular singer from Israel. [7] She said that when singing, ~~you feel~~ *a singer feels* as if ~~you are~~ *he or she is* in heaven. [8] ~~Her~~ *Haza's* love for her family, her roots, and her home come across in each ~~one.~~ *song* [9] ~~Its~~ *Her voice is* striking, pure tone gets the message of her words across, even to audiences who do not understand Hebrew and Aramaic. [10] ~~In critical reviews, they~~ *Critics* compare Ms. Haza's voice to those of both America's Whitney Houston and France's legendary cabaret singer, Edith Piaf.

Review C: Clear Reference, p. 165
Exercise *Revisions will vary.*

1. Dad told Juan, "I need to wash the car."

2. This recipe is new. Would you like to try some of the pumpkin bread?

3. In the American League, teams have designated hitters.

4. The pan was still hot when he put it in the water.

5. When I told Mom my essay had won the contest, she said my winning was cause for celebration.

6. Even though drivers, not roads, cause accidents, roads should still be improved.

7. Do the boating regulations allow people to use sailboats on the reservoir?

8. The dictionary says that the word *maverick* was originally someone's name.

9. When the astronaut radioed back, the control room erupted in applause. The noise forced the communications officer to shout in order to be heard.

10. The commercial was very amusing. It showed a man pushing a shopping cart through a maze of grocery store aisles.

Proofreading Application: Pen-Pal Letter, p. 166

Dear Claudia,

In a magazine article I just read, ~~it~~ said that many teens from Ecuador are looking for a pen pal. ~~This~~ *Having a pen pal* interests me a lot. The article named an organization that would help ~~you~~ *teenagers* find a pen pal. So ~~that is what I did,~~ *I wrote to the organization, they sent me your name and address,* and now I am writing to you.

My name is Rose, and I am in the tenth grade. My favorite pastimes are playing the piano and in-line skating. ~~It~~ *In-line skating* is fun to do after working hard at school. I live with my mom and my aunt Eugenia. ~~She~~ *My mom* knows Spanish, but she has not taught it to me yet. I love the language, ~~which is why~~ *so* I hope you will write to me in Spanish. I will respond in English so that you can get practice.

Many students in my class ~~In my class they~~ seem to enjoy writing to pen pals, so I am looking forward to having a pen pal, too. I am anxious to learn more about you and your life, and I will write you another letter soon.

Your new pen pal,

Rose

Literary Model: Narration, pp. 167–68

EXERCISE A

Responses will vary. Sample responses are given.

In excerpt A the antecedent is **building**.

The antecedent is clear because an empty building has a roof and would be able to provide shelter.

In excerpt B the antecedent is **rain**.

The antecedent is clear because only the rain could be beating on the cabbage leaves and beehives and dripping into buckets and pans.

EXERCISE B

Responses will vary. A sample response is given.

This altered version may be somewhat clearer than the original, but it is weaker by far. The elimination of the personal pronouns and the repetition of the words *building* and *traveler* make the altered version much more awkward and less fluid.

EXERCISE C

Responses will vary. Sample responses are given.

1. A blast of frigid air suddenly ripped through nearby trees. The frigid air swept the trees' limbs to one side and the trees seemed to shiver, the trees' backs to the wind. Set loose, the last few autumn leaves swirled wantonly above the ground and then the leaves rushed down the park path as if the leaves were being pursued by a rampaging snowman, closing in on the leaves by the second.

2. A blast of frigid air suddenly ripped through nearby trees. It swept their limbs to one side and they seemed to shiver, their backs to the wind. Set loose, the last few autumn leaves swirled wantonly above the ground and then rushed down the park path as if they were being pursued by a rampaging snowman, closing in on them by the second.

EXERCISE D

Responses will vary. Sample responses are given.

1. The description without pronouns was more challenging to write. Writing without pronouns is awkward, and the writing sounds and feels unnatural. The repetition of *frigid air, the trees,* and *leaves* is cumbersome.

2. The description using pronouns with clear reference is more effective. It's easier to read, it flows better, and it sounds and feels more natural.

HOLT HANDBOOK | Sixth Course

Writing Application: Societal Observation, p. 169

Writing Applications are designed to provide students immediate composition practice in using key concepts taught in each chapter of the *Language and Sentence Skills Practice* booklet. You may wish to evaluate student responses to these assignments as you do any other writing that students produce. To save grading time, however, you may want to use the following scoring rubric.

Scoring Rubric

All the pronouns in the paragraphs have clear and specific antecedents.

   1   2   3   4   5

The paragraphs present a clear thesis in a well-organized manner.

   1   2   3   4   5

Any words quoted from bumper stickers are in quotation marks.

   1   2   3   4   5

The assignment is relatively free of errors in usage and mechanics.

   1   2   3   4   5

Total Score _____

5 = highest; 1 = lowest

Chapter 8: Using Verbs Correctly, pp. 170–99

Choices: Exploring Verbs, p. 170

Choices activities are designed to extend and enrich students' understanding of grammar, usage, and mechanics and to take learners beyond traditional classroom instruction. To use the Choices worksheet, have each student pick an activity that interests him or her. In some cases, you may wish to assign an activity to a particular student or group of students. You may also want to request that students get your approval for the activities they choose. Establish guidelines for what constitutes successful completion of an activity. Then, help students plan how they will share their work with the rest of the class.

Choices activities can be scored with a pass-fail grade or treated as bonus-point projects. Those activities that require students to research or create a certain number of items might be graded in a traditional manner.

The Principal Parts of Verbs, p. 171

EXERCISE

1. talking
2. orbiting
3. hitting
4. saved
5. begun
6. thought
7. catered
8. drawn
9. rising
10. running
11. held
12. stopped
13. wrote
14. saw
15. walked
16. tried
17. sat
18. decided
19. kept
20. sleeping

Regular Verbs, p. 172

EXERCISE A

1. cooked
2. purchased
3. supposed
4. combined
5. pounded
6. poured
7. coated
8. secured
9. arranged
10. used

EXERCISE B

11. stayed
12. imagined
13. fixed
14. supposed
15. matched

Irregular Verbs A, p. 173

EXERCISE

1. worn
2. held
3. made
4. spread
5. forbidden
6. built
7. been
8. read
9. given
10. grown

Irregular Verbs B, p. 174

EXERCISE

1. caught
2. left
3. sent
4. thought
5. arisen
6. driven
7. hidden
8. set
9. spoke
10. woke
11. bound
12. fought
13. lent
14. lost
15. sold
16. spent
17. got
18. chose
19. shrunk
20. crept

Irregular Verbs C, p. 175

EXERCISE

1. cut
2. come
3. eaten
4. felt
5. heard
6. knew
7. paid
8. rang
9. sprung
10. won
11. struck
12. told
13. flung
14. led
15. let
16. began
17. flown
18. fallen
19. done
20. sought

Irregular Verbs D, p. 176

EXERCISE

1. The wind from the storm ~~blowed~~ *blew* all night and howled in the rafters.

2. The cat ~~creeped~~ *crept* into my bed after I turned off the light.

3. My younger sister ~~done~~ *did* that puzzle in less than two minutes.

4. After an all-night bus trip, we ~~fighted~~ *fought* to stay awake during the opening ceremonies.

5. *C*

6. *C*

7. The curator carefully ~~putted~~ *put* the antique toy back into the glass case.

8. The skater ~~spinned~~ *spun* numerous times, making the feat look effortless.

9. Somebody has ~~stealed~~ *stolen* the picture I taped to the outside of my locker!

10. The coach ~~telled~~ *told* us we might see this sort of defense in our next game.

11. If I hadn't bumped into the hive, the bees wouldn't have ~~stinged~~ *stung* me.

12. Cecily grabbed the rope, took a deep breath, and ~~swang~~ *swung* out over the water.

13. Without a map, we couldn't have ~~founded~~ *found* the convention center.

14. After the match, my parents ~~buyed~~ *bought* lunch for the whole team.

15. Marilyn knew that Judith had not yet ~~forgive~~ *forgiven* her for the unkind comment.

16. The window must have ~~broke~~ *broken* when you slammed it shut.

17. *C*

18. I simply could not have ~~bear~~ *borne* one more minute of that awful music!

19. If you had explained the situation, I'm sure he would have ~~understanded.~~ *understood*

20. Before the dinner party, my brother and I ~~shone~~ *shined* the silver candlesticks.

Irregular Verbs E, p. 177

EXERCISE A

1. hurt
2. sold
3. sought [*or* had sought]
4. had
5. lent
6. sung
7. swum
8. written
9. lain
10. ridden

EXERCISE B

11. After I ~~win~~ *won* the race, I must have ~~drank~~ *drunk* a gallon of water.

12. She has already ~~pay~~ *paid* the store for the dishes that she accidentally broke.

13. Mike ~~taked~~ *took* a deep breath, looked down at the water, and dived straight in. [Students should not be penalized if they change *dived* to *dove*.]

14. I'm sorry, but we have already ~~ate~~ *eaten* the whole casserole.

15. LaSandra has ~~chose~~ *chosen* a difficult topic for her final paper.

Lie and *Lay*, p. 178

EXERCISE

1. laying
2. lies
3. lay
4. laying
5. laid
6. laid
7. lying
8. lay
9. laid
10. lie
11. laid
12. lie
13. lay
14. lie
15. laying
16. lain
17. laid
18. laid
19. lying
20. laid

Sit and Set, p. 179

EXERCISE

1. setting
2. sets
3. set
4. sitting
5. sat
6. sitting
7. sits
8. set
9. set
10. sit
11. set
12. Sitting
13. set
14. set
15. sit
16. sat
17. sit
18. set
19. sat
20. set

Rise and Raise, p. 180

EXERCISE A

1. raising
2. rises
3. raised
4. risen
5. raises
6. rising
7. raise
8. risen
9. raised
10. rise

EXERCISE B

11. raised
12. rose
13. rise
14. rising
15. raise

Six Troublesome Verbs, p. 181

EXERCISE A

1. set
2. lying
3. lain
4. rose
5. Lie
6. sat
7. raise
8. rising
9. lay
10. sitting

EXERCISE B

11. The paint set had been ~~laying~~ *lying* in the corner the whole time.

12. C

13. Please do not ~~set~~ *sit* in the chair with the carved legs.

14. The patient was so exhausted she could scarcely ~~rise~~ *raise* her head from the pillow.

15. C

Tense and Form, p. 182

EXERCISE

1. present perfect
2. present, emphatic
3. past, progressive
4. present
5. past perfect
6. past
7. present perfect
8. past, emphatic
9. future perfect
10. future, progressive

Correct Use of Verb Tenses A, p. 183

EXERCISE

1. have put
2. will have finished
3. had left
4. trained
5. played
6. is
7. gave
8. has been collecting
9. was
10. do call

Correct Use of Verb Tenses B, p. 184

EXERCISE

1. Nicole <u>walked</u> *(past)* to school every day last year.

2. Next fall, when she <u>goes</u> *(present)* to college, she <u>will live</u> *(future)* at home for a semester.

3. By then, she <u>will have saved</u> *(future perfect)* enough to buy a small car.

4. She thought she <u>had saved</u> *(past perfect)* enough, but then she <u>remembered</u> *(past)* the additional cost of insurance.

5. Textbooks and other supplies <u>are</u> *(present)* usually very expensive.

6. She <u>has registered</u> *(present perfect)* for classes and <u>will meet</u> *(future)* the professors during orientation week.

7. Some of her friends <u>will be going</u> to the *[future]* same college. [*or future progressive*]

8. Others <u>plan</u> to work in a community volun- *[present]* teer program for a year.

9. Nicole's sister <u>joined</u> the Navy after she *[past]* graduated.

10. Nicole <u>had considered</u> military service but *[past perfect]* <u>decided</u> to go to college first. *[past]*

Sequence of Tenses, p. 185
EXERCISE

1. After blowing her whistle, the official explained that the player's right foot ~~has~~ *[had]* touched the sideline.

2. She ~~delivered~~ the mail when the regular let- *[delivers]* ter carrier is sick. [*or She delivered the mail when the regular letter carrier* ~~is~~ sick.] *[was]*

3. My cousin and I ~~quarreled~~ earlier, but we *[had quarreled]* were friends again by the end of the day.

4. We would have eaten outdoors if the rain ~~would have~~ stopped. *[had]*

5. C

6. By next summer, my family will ~~be~~ living in *[have been]* this house for five decades.

7. I wish that you hadn't ~~been telling~~ her that *[told]* secret.

8. C

9. I have just learned that Jimmy Carter will ~~have spoken~~ at our commencement *[speak]* ceremony.

10. By the time you returned, we ~~will have~~ *[had]* been waiting for half an hour.

Infinitives and Participles, p. 186
EXERCISE
Answers may vary slightly.

1. ~~Leaving~~ my book at home, I ~~had borrowed~~ *[Having left]* *[borrowed]* another copy from the teacher.

2. My ten-year-old brother hopes to ~~have become~~ an architect. *[become]*

3. Ten minutes ago, Ms. Shane said, "You should choose a classmate to ~~have worked~~ *[work]* with on this project."

4. The little girl stood on the curb, ~~having looked~~ both ways for cars before *[looking]* ~~she crossed~~ the street. *[crossing]*

5. Excited to ~~be~~ elected class president, *[have been]* Carlotta outlined her ideas for the year.

6. Cole would ~~like~~ to take physics with us this *[have liked]* semester, but he had to take another math class instead.

7. ~~Having waited~~ for the light to change, I *[Waiting]* gazed out the windshield.

8. Not wanting to ~~have waked~~ the sleeping *[wake]* baby, Emma tapped on the window.

9. I hope to ~~have read~~ all of Shakespeare's *[read]* tragedies this summer.

10. ~~Have shaken~~ his head and ~~muttered~~ to *[Shaking]* *[muttering]* himself, the team captain walked off the field.

Active and Passive Voice, p. 187
EXERCISE A
1. PV 　　3. PV 　　5. AV
2. PV 　　4. AV

EXERCISE B

6. PV—none

7. AV—By discussing and debating the prob-lem openly, the <u>group</u> reached a consensus.

8. PV—More data will be gathered by the research <u>team</u> during the expedition.

9. AV—The local <u>newspaper</u> publishes letters and articles by student reporters.

10. PV—Two award-winning features were written by <u>students</u> from our school.

Language and Sentence Skills Practice Answer Key

Uses of the Passive Voice, p. 188

EXERCISE

Sentences may vary.

1. The owners of the antique store have collected items from all over the country.

2. Correct

3. Correct [*or* My grandfather, who built many pieces of furniture for the family, encouraged my mother's interest in woodworking.]

4. She collected woodworking books, in addition to the tools themselves.

5. We found cans and bottles of all sizes, colors, and shapes along the highway.

Mood, p. 189

EXERCISE A

1. SUB	5. SUB	8. IND
2. IND	6. SUB	9. IMP
3. SUB	7. IND	10. SUB
4. IMP		

EXERCISE B

11. If I ~~was~~ *were* the coach, I would make a different play call.

12. C

13. The room would seem larger if that wall ~~was~~ *were* a lighter color.

14. I wish that my television set ~~wasn't~~ *weren't* broken so that I could watch the game.

15. The veterinarian has recommended that Tucker ~~is~~ *be* vaccinated.

Modals A, p. 190

EXERCISE

1. could [*or* might]
2. can
3. may
4. must
5. May
6. could [*or* might *or* may]
7. must [*or* might *or* may]
8. must
9. Can [*or* Could]
10. might [*or* may]
11. must
12. might [*or* may *or* must *or* could]
13. could [*or* can]
14. can
15. must [*or* might *or* could]
16. can [*or* could *or* must]
17. must
18. could; can [*or* could]
19. Must
20. might [*or* may]

Modals B, p. 191

EXERCISE

1. ought
2. would [*or* should *or* will]
3. should [*or* would *or* will]
4. Would
5. would [*or* shall *or* will]
6. Should
7. would
8. should
9. would
10. should
11. should
12. would [*or* should]
13. ought
14. will [*or* should]
15. Should
16. will [*or* shall *or* should]
17. will [*or* shall *or* should]
18. ought
19. would
20. would [*or* should]

Review A: Principal Parts of Verbs, p. 192

EXERCISE A

1. I had ~~did~~ *done* most of my packing the previous evening.

2. My two best friends had ~~drove~~ *driven* across town to attend the party.

3. Each of us had already ~~chose~~ *chosen* a college to attend, and we spent much of the evening debating the merits of our respective schools.

4. *C*

5. I guess old Molly had ~~hear~~ *heard* it all before.

6. When silence at last ~~come~~ *came*, she woke up suddenly.

7. Then the doorbell ~~rung~~ *rang*, and Molly started barking furiously.

8. At the door were my friends Fritz and Melanie, whom Molly had ~~meet~~ *met* several times before.

9. Fritz and Melanie joined in the party, and before long we had ~~putted~~ *put* aside our debate and had ~~began~~ *begun* a game of charades.

10. *C*

EXERCISE B

11. seen

12. taking

13. rang

14. spoken

15. singing

Review B: Tense, Voice, Mood, and Modals, p. 193

EXERCISE A

Answers may vary.

1. ~~Having been~~ *Being* a poet in an age of prose often makes life difficult for a sensitive person.

2. *C*

3. *C*

4. Whoever expects to find great poetry among Pope's childhood writings undoubtedly will ~~have been~~ *be* disappointed.

5. On the other hand, Mozart ~~is writing~~ *wrote* brilliant works when he was fifteen.

6. Subsequent generations have been delighted to ~~have listened~~ *listen* to these compositions.

7. If he ~~would have~~ *had* written nothing in his youth, would he have become a composer later?

8. Mozart's father began to teach his son composition when Mozart ~~is~~ *was* only five years old.

9. By the time he was ten, Mozart ~~composed~~ *had composed* dozens of lovely works.

10. *C*

EXERCISE B

11. Soledad reviewed all the notes she ~~took~~ *had taken* the week before.

12. If she ~~would have~~ *had* taken more notes, she would have been better prepared.

13. She had hoped to ~~have written~~ *write* a good report on U.S. presidents.

14. If I ~~was~~ *were* a harder worker, she thought, I'd get higher grades.

15. In her notes, she had written that the first six presidents ~~come~~ *came* from Virginia and Massachusetts. [*or* ~~had written~~ *wrote* . . . ~~come~~ *came*]

16. Then Andrew Jackson ~~is~~ *was* elected in 1828.

17. If Jackson ~~came~~ *had come* from Virginia, he would have carried on the tradition.

18. *C*

19. If Soledad's report ~~would have~~ *had* been nothing more than a chronology, it would have lacked interest.

20. She managed to ~~have included~~ *include* all kinds of interesting facts, though.

Review C: Six Troublesome Verbs, p. 194

EXERCISE

1. The letter from my older sister, who is in college, ~~laid~~ *lay* on my computer desk.

2. He has never once ~~risen~~ *raised* his voice in anger.

3. My dog was ~~laying~~ *lying* peacefully by the front window, when suddenly a squirrel ran across the lawn.

4. *C*

5. The pen has ~~laid~~ *lain* on the floor all day.

6. We ~~lain~~ *laid* the folded clothes on top of the dresser.

7. Where was Julia ~~setting~~ *sitting* when you saw her last?

8. *C*

9. The temperature ~~raised~~ *rose* another twenty degrees before the rain started.

10. As soon as he ~~laid~~ *lay* down, the telephone rang.

11. The cost of gasoline has ~~rose~~ *risen* sharply because of cuts in production.

12. *C*

13. Frank ~~rose~~ *raised* the lid off the terrarium and added a little water.

14. Melting icebergs rumbled and cracked as the temperature ~~raised~~ *rose*.

15. My bicycle was ~~laying~~ *lying* on the garage floor in pieces.

16. How many people do you know who have ~~rose~~ *raised* their grade-point average so much?

17. Heavy rains have ~~rose~~ *raised* the water level of the lake more than a foot.

18. Please ~~sit~~ *set* the groceries on the kitchen counter.

19. The crane lifted the steel girder and ~~sat~~ *set* it on top of the structure.

20. Strong winds ~~raised~~ *rose* from the valley and whistled through the trees.

Review D: Correct Use of Verb Forms, p. 195

EXERCISE A

1. "Anybody can fix a leaky faucet," I ~~says~~ *said* to him.

2. Dad ~~brang~~ *brought* me the tools from the basement, and I ~~creeped~~ *crept* under the sink to turn off the water.

3. I ~~knowed~~ *knew* how to begin, and soon I was hard at work.

4. Tools and faucet parts ~~laid~~ *lay* strewn about.

5. I ~~seen~~ *saw* right away that a new washer would do the job, and I ~~swang~~ *swung* into action with complete self-assurance.

6. My father ~~come~~ *came* into the room just as I was finishing.

7. With the water back on, I ~~raised~~ *rose* in triumph, ~~flinged~~ *flung* the wrench aside, and turned on the faucet.

8. *C*

9. *C*

10. "I've never ~~swam~~ *swum* in the kitchen before," Dad said softly.

EXERCISE B

Students' corrections may vary, but the revised paragraph should make sense as a whole.

[11] In the current job market, your abilities ~~have been~~ *will be* examined on a questionnaire as well as during one or more face-to-face interviews. [12] Some interviewers will ~~have asked~~ *ask* you questions about your qualities as a leader. [13] Other interviewers ~~may be requesting~~ *might request* information about your skill as a team player. [14] Knowing your own strengths and weaknesses ~~would~~ *could* prevent your being taken by surprise. [15] Keep these hints in mind the next time you ~~set~~ *sit* down for an interview.

Proofreading Application: Personal Narrative, p. 196

    Some people believe that dreams are ~~suppose~~ *supposed* to be predictions of the future. If this ~~was~~ *were* true, I soon would be living in a fairly marvelous situation. In various dreams I have ~~saw~~ *seen* myself living in a fifteen-room villa overlooking the Caribbean Sea, sailing on a yacht, and snorkeling among rainbow-colored fish. The life ~~lived~~ *I live* ~~by me~~ in these dreams is lacking only one thing: challenges. In these dreams I ~~set~~ *sit* on the terrace of the villa, never having to lift a finger for its maintenance. When I ~~lay~~ *lie* on the deck of the yacht, the sun never burns my skin. The sea ~~presented~~ *presents* as many dangers as a tabletop aquarium would.

    Frankly, I am happy that these dreams have not ~~came~~ *come* true—the reason being that I ~~thrived~~ *thrive* on challenges. I ~~will have gone~~ *go* cross-country skiing in subzero weather, and I am a card-carrying member of the Polar Bear Club.

    If my *conscious* dreams are realized, by the time I am sixty, I will ~~be~~ *have been* responding to challenges for forty-two years.

Literary Model: Verbs in Poetry, pp. 197–98

EXERCISE A

1. groaned, stirred, moved, steered, moved, raised
2. Any form of *rose* is from the verb *rise*, which never takes a direct object. A form of *raise* must be used in the last sentence to take the direct object *limbs*.
3. began to work
4. spake, wont
5. Part A: one ("It had been . . .")
   Part B: one ("We were . . .")

EXERCISE B

Responses will vary. A sample response is given.

The duties of the sailors are varied, the challenges of navigating are critical and changing, and the movement of the water is never-ending. The steady stream of action verbs helps sustain seafaring suspense.

EXERCISE C

Responses will vary. A sample response is given.

The Roller Coaster

The bar across my lap locked shut,
Someone cranked a lever, gears engaged;
Inch by inch the caravan of cars lurched
upward on its narrow tracks
To the scaffolded crest, then paused, where
escape escaped us all,
And teased us to remorse—

But fell at once this wild string of chairs, or
faster flew than any gravity could pull
Toward certain oblivion,
Or so it seemed,
And yet with breath and voice regained,
I located myself among the living, on a still
steeper incline;
And grimacing toward its vertical peak,
I braced myself
To scream asunder another sure demise!

EXERCISE D

Responses will vary. A sample response is given.

Using action verbs whenever possible should help enliven writing of any purpose. A linking verb or the passive voice rarely makes as powerful a statement as an action verb.

Writing Application: Directions, p. 199

Writing Applications are designed to provide students immediate composition practice in using key concepts taught in each chapter of the *Language and Sentence Skills Practice* booklet. You may wish to evaluate student responses to these assignments as you do any other writing that students produce. To save grading time, however, you may want to use the following scoring rubric.

Language and Sentence Skills Practice Answer Key

Scoring Rubric

Most of the sentences are in active voice; passive voice is used when appropriate.

   1   2   3   4   5

The steps of the recipe are chronologically ordered.

   1   2   3   4   5

The recipe includes sensory details appropriate to the cooking process.

   1   2   3   4   5

The assignment is relatively free of errors in grammar, usage, mechanics, and spelling.

   1   2   3   4   5

Total Score _____

5 = highest; 1 = lowest

Chapter 9: Using Modifiers Correctly, pp. 200–224

Choices: Investigating the Correct Use of Modifiers, p. 200

Choices activities are designed to extend and enrich students' understanding of grammar, usage, and mechanics and to take learners beyond traditional classroom instruction. To use the Choices worksheet, have each student pick an activity that interests him or her. In some cases, you may wish to assign an activity to a particular student or group of students. You may also want to request that students get your approval for the activities they choose. Establish guidelines for what constitutes successful completion of an activity. Then, help students plan how they will share their work with the rest of the class.

Choices activities can be scored with a pass-fail grade or treated as bonus-point projects. Those activities that require students to research or create a certain number of items might be graded in a traditional manner.

Adjective or Adverb? p. 201

EXERCISE

1. All a shadow puppet show requires is a translucent screen, a light source, and some opaque, two-dimensional *ADJ* figures to cast the shadows.

2. Traditionally, shadow *ADJ* puppets have been made of leather.

3. The puppeteer skillfully *ADV* manipulates the puppet using thin rods.

4. The audience usually sits on the other *ADJ* side of the screen to watch the shadows.

5. Shadow puppetry is an extremely *ADV* ancient art.

6. Experts believe that in India shadow puppets performed onstage *ADV* long before human actors.

7. Pretending to be someone else was strictly *ADV* forbidden in ancient Indian culture.

8. However, puppets were not *ADV* bound by such restrictions.

9. A Chinese *ADJ* legend dates shadow puppetry in China to 120 B.C.

10. The legend says that a man named Chiao-meng cleverly *ADV* devised a plan to trick the emperor.

11. The empress had recently *ADV* died, and the emperor mourned for her.

12. Chiao-meng placed an elaborate silhouette of the empress between a light and a cotton *ADJ* screen.

13. The emperor apparently thought the shadow was his deceased *ADJ* wife.

14. He listened attentively *ADV* to "her" advice on state matters.

15. Chiao-meng's great *ADJ* influence ended, as did his life, when the emperor discovered the trick.

16. However, Chiao-meng is duly *ADV* remembered as the original shadow puppeteer of China.

17. In Bali today, *ADV* shadow puppetry survives in an ancient form.

18. There, the puppeteer plays a spiritual *ADJ* and ceremonial role.

19. In fact, a priest must ordain the puppeteer and write a mystic *ADJ* symbol on his tongue before he may perform.

20. An important part of traditional events such as weddings, the puppet play, or *wayang*, often *ADV* lasts all night.

Phrases Used as Modifiers, p. 202

EXERCISE

1. The man with the intelligent dog *ADJ* won the contest.

2. **ADV** | After class, Penelope and Cary Ann (shared) a granola bar.

3. **ADV** | Because of the mud stains, Tom (took) his suit to the dry cleaner.

4. **ADV** | To me, summer (seemed) a long, long time away.

5. The (boat) **ADJ** in the harbor was searched for illegal goods.

6. **ADV** | With all of his belongings on his back, he (crossed) the river.

7. **ADV** | Because of the new job, my life (has) improved.

8. My (friend) **ADJ** in the band plays both the saxophone and the clarinet.

9. (Come) **ADV** inside the building to avoid the heavy rain.

10. The (seal) **ADJ** with the insignia belongs to the governor of the state.

11. (Walk) **ADV** to the store and take your little brother with you.

12. Hanging inside the coliseum, **ADJ** there is a (photograph) of all of the players on the team.

13. The speaker (talked) **ADV** about crime prevention.

14. Of all the (singers) **ADJ** in the world, I like Neil Young best.

15. The (box) **ADJ** inside the trunk rattled the whole way to Cleveland.

16. She took a picture of the (bird) **ADJ** sitting on the fence.

17. (Articles) **ADJ** about his astounding discovery were in all the papers.

18. **ADJ** | Finishing the text first, (Jim) appeared happy with himself.

19. **ADV** | In case of fire, (move) quickly and calmly to the nearest exit.

20. (Light) **ADJ** from the bedroom window indicated someone was awake.

Clauses Used as Modifiers, p. 203
EXERCISE

1. **ADV** | Because my sister was in the shower, I had to wait fifteen minutes to get into the bathroom.

2. I was a bit late for breakfast, **ADJ** which was cereal and low-fat milk.

3. I had to run all the way to the bus stop **ADV** since I was behind schedule.

4. The bus, **ADJ** which was early, had left without me.

5. I had to walk to school, **ADJ** which is only a few blocks from my house.

6. I arrived at school just **ADV** as the bell was ringing.

7. I was happy about that **ADV** until I found out that we were having a pop quiz in my first class.

8. Fortunately, I was well prepared for the quiz **ADV** because I had studied the night before.

9. In biology class my lab partner, **ADJ** who is great at dissections, was absent.

10. The lab project **ADJ** that we did today didn't involve dissections.

11. **ADV** | After I finished the project, I was ready for a nice quiet hour in study hall.

12. However, the workers **ADJ** who were repairing the roof created a lot of noise.

13. At 3:30 P.M., I went to the gym **ADJ** that is in my school to get some exercise.

14. When I walked in the door, *ADV* I saw my two best friends, Lisa and Peter.

15. Although we are not great players, *ADV* we still decided to play a few games of basketball.

16. This afternoon I had a piano lesson with Ms. Lufler, who has won many competitions as a pianist. *ADJ*

17. For dinner Mom, who is an excellent cook, *ADJ* prepared grilled chicken and mashed potatoes.

18. After we ate, *ADV* my sister and I offered to wash the dishes.

19. Mom was very happy that we were helping out because she needed to do some other chores around the house. *ADV*

20. Before I went to bed, *ADV* I read several chapters in my history book.

Uses of Modifiers, p. 204
EXERCISE

1. The brain processes information very rapidly. *ADV*

2. Think of all the numbers, names, and other information you remember easily. *ADV*

3. The memory-enhancing system called mnemonics is fascinating. *ADJ*

4. Let me explain it quickly. *ADV*

5. The system is simple: *ADJ* Imagine you meet someone named Art Baker.

6. What if you forget the person's name immediately? *ADV*

7. Making a mental image to help you remember the name is important. *ADJ*

8. Try simply *ADV* imagining a painting.

9. It could be a painting of a man who is skillfully *ADV* baking pastries.

10. Now, associate that image consistently *ADV* with the person you met named Art Baker.

11. See how easy *ADJ* it can be?

12. The process just described may seem silly, *ADJ* but you will be surprised at how well it works.

13. For names that are less visual than "Art Baker," you have to think more creatively. *ADV*

14. Forming mental pictures moves information more reliably *ADV* from short-term to long-term memory.

15. In order to succeed, you must think associatively. *ADV*

16. Of course, memory becomes crucial *ADJ* when taking tests.

17. Stress can sometimes interfere substantially *ADV* with memory.

18. The results can be terrible *ADJ* (a bad grade, for example).

19. Memory is complex *ADJ* and occasionally frustrating.

20. Don't forget to make mental pictures regularly *ADV* if you want to improve your ability to recall.

Bad and Badly; Good and Well, p. 205
EXERCISE

1. well	11. well
2. good	12. bad
3. badly	13. badly
4. well	14. good
5. good	15. badly
6. well	16. good
7. badly	17. badly
8. bad	18. well
9. good	19. bad
10. well	20. well

Real and Really; Slow and Slowly, p. 206
EXERCISE

1. slowly
2. slow
3. really
4. real
5. really
6. slowly
7. really
8. slow
9. really
10. really
11. slowly
12. really
13. really
14. slowly
15. really
16. really
17. slowly
18. slowly
19. real
20. slowly

Eight Troublesome Modifiers, p. 207
EXERCISE

1. well
2. slowly
3. really
4. well
5. badly
6. really
7. slowly
8. badly
9. really
10. slowly
11. well
12. slowly
13. really
14. badly
15. slow
16. well
17. badly
18. slowly
19. well
20. well

Regular Comparison, p. 208
EXERCISE

1. *long*; *longer*; longest
2. silly; *sillier*; *silliest*
3. *comical*; *more comical*; most comical
4. *absorbent*; *more absorbent*; most absorbent
5. *pretty*; prettier; *prettiest*
6. *boring*; less boring; *least boring*
7. wild; *wilder*; *wildest*
8. *troublesome*; *less troublesome*; least troublesome
9. *unsettling*; more unsettling; *most unsettling*
10. *flimsy*; flimsier; *flimsiest*
11. *carefully*; *more carefully*; most carefully
12. *interesting*; more interesting; *most interesting*
13. *curious*; *more curious*; most curious

14. *heavy*; heavier; *heaviest*
15. *young*; younger; *youngest*
16. *funny*; *funnier*; funniest
17. *honest*; less honest; *least honest*
18. *ridiculous*; *more ridiculous*; most ridiculous
19. large; *larger*; largest
20. *grown-up*; more grown-up; *most grown-up*

Irregular Comparison, p. 209
EXERCISE

1. more
2. best
3. better
4. further
5. best
6. worse
7. better
8. worse
9. more
10. much
11. more
12. more
13. best
14. little
15. worst
16. better
17. more
18. better
19. worse
20. better

Regular and Irregular Comparison, p. 210
EXERCISE A

1. better; best
2. more; most
3. thicker; thickest
4. softer; softest
5. more; most
6. more smoothly; most smoothly
7. more useful; most useful
8. littler; littlest
9. less; least
10. more selective; most selective

EXERCISE B

11. less angry; least angry
12. less ill; least ill
13. less difficult; least difficult
14. less clear; least clear
15. less tolerant; least tolerant

Uses of Comparative and Superlative Forms A, p. 211

EXERCISE

1. hottest
2. smarter
3. brighter
4. most infuriating
5. warmer
6. tallest
7. less effective
8. more dangerous
9. tastiest
10. colder
11. more difficult
12. trickier
13. more comfortable
14. less rapidly
15. worst
16. less frequently
17. most
18. more skilled
19. better
20. funniest

Uses of Comparative and Superlative Forms B, p. 212

EXERCISE

1. Dorrie is happier than anyone _else_ I know.
2. C
3. This is the ~~most~~ juiciest orange!
4. Our team won more games than any _other_ team in the league.
5. You received more votes than anyone _else_ who was running.
6. C
7. My sister is better at skiing than any _other_ member of my family.
8. Which is the ~~most~~ hardest material in the world?

9. That egg is smaller than any _other_ egg in its nest.
10. The train is less ~~likelier~~ _likely_ to be on time than the plane is.
11. I am ~~more~~ better at grammar now than I was last year.
12. He was less ~~friendlier~~ _friendly_ to me than he was to her.
13. I'm sure Susan can outrun any _other_ girl on her track team.
14. That coffee pot is ~~more~~ fuller than this one.
15. C
16. C
17. Our puppy was the ~~most~~ cutest one in the litter.
18. You are just as important as every _other_ member of your team.
19. Gloria sold more boxes of cookies than anyone _else_ in the troop.
20. You are ~~more~~ luckier than I am.

Uses of Comparative and Superlative Forms C, p. 213

EXERCISE

1. This semester I joined the ~~better~~ _best_ group in the whole school—the drama team.
2. I wanted to join it more than any _other_ team.
3. I was the ~~happier~~ _happiest_ kid around when I found out that I had been selected.
4. I was even ~~most~~ _more_ excited than that when I heard we were doing a play soon.
5. The play was *Macbeth*, by Shakespeare, who may be the ~~more~~ _most_ revered British writer.
6. The choice of play was great because I like *Macbeth* better than any _other_ Shakespeare play.
7. C

8. However, I got to do the ~~more~~ *most* fun thing of all—I was the understudy for everyone ^*else*.

9. I got to play more roles in rehearsal than anyone ^*else* in the group.

10. Fortunately, I have a greater knack for memorizing lines than anyone ^*else*.

11. It was the ~~more~~ *most* challenging thing ever to play a different part at each rehearsal.

12. The director had the ~~most~~ silliest superstitions about the play, though.

13. C

14. Even ~~more~~ weirder than that, we had to call the play "The Scottish Play."

15. I think our director is more superstitious than any ^*other* team sponsor at school.

16. However, the rehearsals did seem ~~most~~ *more* exciting after he told us about the "curse."

17. He thought that if anyone said "Macbeth," the show would be the ~~worse~~ *worst* performance ever.

18. C

19. We were having a lot of fun, and our enjoyment seemed to make the time go by ~~fastest~~ *faster* ^.

20. Soon it was opening night, and I think we put on the ~~better~~ *best* show ever, if I do say so myself!

Clear Comparisons and Absolute Adjectives A, p. 214

Exercise

Students' revisions may vary, but comparisons should be clear and sensible.

1. Howard told me more about ice fishing than you ^*told me*.

2. I have heard more about the new class than Dr. Taylor ^*has*.

3. It seems as if my uncle's collection of books is larger than the ~~library~~ *library's*.

4. This book is as long ^*as* if not longer than, *A Tale of Two Cities.*

5. Our coaching staff has ~~the most~~ unique training techniques.

6. Dad gave me a longer speech than ^*he gave* you.

7. Copernicus thought it was ~~more~~ true that the earth orbited the sun ^*rather* than the other way around.

8. This essay is as good ^*as* if not better than, any I have written thus far.

9. My hero, Stephen Hawking, has used mathematics to try to develop a ~~more~~ complete model of how the universe works.

10. Do hawks eat more small animals than eagles ^*do*?

Clear Comparisons and Absolute Adjectives B, p. 215

Exercise

Students' revisions may vary, but comparisons should be clear and sensible.

1. The panelists decided that Dan's research proposal was more interesting than ~~Phil~~ *Phil's*, so they gave Dan the grant.

2. Of all the ice skaters, Joan was the ~~most perfect~~ *best* because of her style and grace.

3. Betsy talks to her plants more often than Patricia ^*does*.

4. Those injured birds need as much care ^*as* if not more care than, the healthy ones.

5. Theo and Susan enjoy Renaissance writers more than Catherine ^*does*.

6. Rafael speaks as many different languages ^*as* if not more than, Beverly.

7. The ~~very~~ unique properties of this element have intrigued scientists.

8. Exaggerating somewhat, Jane said that the coming weekend offered ~~a more~~ _{an} infinite number of possibilities.

9. Temika likes to challenge her sister to a game of chess more often than _she challenges_ Bill.

10. Kim reads as much Russian literature, _as_ if not more than, her roommate Sandra does.

Comparisons Review, p. 216

EXERCISE

Students' revisions may vary, but comparisons should be clear and sensible.

1. I am much _better_ ~~gooder~~ at doing jigsaw puzzles now than I used to be.

2. When I was ~~more~~ younger, I used to feel frustrated when I worked on puzzles.

3. Finally, though, I realized that it was less _difficult_ ~~impossible~~ than I had thought.

4. I watched my neighbor Sarah, who was ~~more~~ better at puzzles than I was.

5. I noticed that I was not as patient with puzzles as Sarah _is_.

6. Once I learned to go slowly and be patient, I was better at doing jigsaw puzzles than anyone _else_ on our block.

7. I like jigsaw puzzles more than my dad _does_, but he helps me put them together sometimes.

8. Last year, my dad and I put together a puzzle that was more challenging than any _other_ one we have ever done.

9. The picture on the box was ~~more~~ harder to model than any other I had seen.

10. _C_

11. After we solved that puzzle, which was more difficult than any _other_ puzzle you could buy, I became interested in making my own puzzles.

12. I like making jigsaw puzzles as much, _as_ if not more than, putting them together.

13. First I draw a design on thick cardboard— the ~~more~~ thicker the better.

14. Then I carefully cut out the pieces with my dad's jigsaw, which is the ~~most~~ perfect tool for the job.

15. With the jigsaw, I can make the pieces _more_ ~~most~~ easily than I could by using scissors or a knife.

16. Now that I know how to make my own puzzles, I can make my friends the _best_ ~~better~~ gifts ever.

17. Sometimes I have photographs enlarged, and I make puzzles out of them that are ~~very~~ unique.

18. I think I like making puzzles for my friends even better than _I like making them for_ myself.

19. Recently, I made ~~the most~~ _a_ unique one—a picture of us doing a jigsaw puzzle.

20. Isn't that the ~~most~~ coolest thing?

Review A: Forms of Modifiers, p. 217

EXERCISE

1. Socrates, Plato, and Aristotle share the honor of molding the Western <u>philosophical</u> [ADJ] tradition.

2. Socrates gained a reputation <u>for wisdom</u> [ADJ] early in his life.

3. In fact, he was declared the wisest of men by the <u>revered</u> [ADJ] oracle at Delphi.

4. Socrates lived very <u>humbly</u> [ADV] and focused his energies on other people and on Athens.

5. During the Peloponnesian War, he was a
ADV
foot soldier and reportedly a good fighter.

6. Socrates' extreme patriotism even con-
ADJ
tributed to his death.

7. After he was convicted on charges that he
ADV
considered false, Socrates would not let his
friends help him escape.

8. He said that the verdict, even though
unfair, must be obeyed because the court
ADJ
was a legitimate institution.

9. Socrates' execution in 399 B.C. had a large
ADJ
impact on Plato's life.

10. Plato had probably met Socrates
when Plato was a boy.
ADV

11. Plato's family, which was one of the most
ADJ
distinguished families in ancient Athens,
was well acquainted with Socrates.

12. After Socrates was forced to drink hemlock,
ADV
a poison, Plato and several other friends
and followers of Socrates left Athens for
some time.

13. Plato made Socrates the subject of many of
his greatest written works.
ADJ

14. That he did so is fortunate as Socrates
ADJ
himself did not write anything.

15. Plato eventually returned to Athens and
ADV
founded his Academy there.

16. Although it was not the only such center
ADV
for learning, Plato's Academy is sometimes
considered to have been the first university.

17. Plato's Academy also played an important
role in the life of Aristotle.
ADJ

18. Aristotle went to the Academy as a youth
and studied there for twenty years.
ADV

19. He later founded his own school called the
Lyceum, and he is also well-known for
tutoring the young Alexander the Great.
ADJ

20. Aristotle's influence dominated Western
thought until the end of the seventeenth
ADV
century.

Review B: Eight Troublesome Modifiers, p. 218

EXERCISE

1. well	11. really
2. badly	12. good
3. good	13. well
4. slowly	14. real
5. badly	15. really
6. really	16. bad
7. well	17. slowly
8. slowly	18. slowly
9. bad	19. well
10. well	20. really

Review C: Comparison, p. 219

EXERCISE

Some revisions may vary, but comparisons should be clear and correct.

1. This is the ~~worse~~ *worst* casserole I have ever tasted.

2. I am as tall, *as* if not taller than, John.

3. That was the ~~most~~ perfect double play!

4. This spider is ~~more~~ bigger than that one.

5. That was the ~~less~~ *least* useful suggestion of all.

6. I think the African gray parrot is a better talker than any *other* bird.

7. He is getting ~~more~~ stronger every day.

8. I like your plan better than ~~Lisa.~~ *Lisa's*

9. The water is as cold, *as* if not colder than, the air above it.

10. I built my bicycle myself, so it is ~~more~~ unique.

11. Until you joined, I was the ~~stronger~~ *strongest* swim-
mer in our club.

12. This is the ~~most~~ fastest car on the market.

13. I think Aunt Colleen chose the ~~most~~ *more* elegant
of the two gowns.

14. C

15. Cousin Nora sent me more postcards than
she sent you.

16. The pizza crust is ~~least~~ *less* crispy than it usually
is.

17. Darren prefers his mom's cooking to *that of* any
professional chef.

18. Their dog is ~~more~~ better at fetching than
our dog.

19. I am as upset, *as* if not more upset than, you
are.

20. Our treasurer is more responsible than anyone *else* in the club.

Review D: All Types of Problems, p. 220
EXERCISE A

1. Elephants reputedly have better *ADJ* memories
than other animals have.

2. My old *ADJ* shoes are very comfortable.

3. We will definitely *ADV* consult more experts the
next time.

4. I think your first *ADJ* answer was correct.

5. Watch closely, everyone, because *ADV* we are
now entering the lions' habitat.

6. That smoking *ADJ* volcano is the most active
one on the island.

7. When we go *ADV* swimming, I usually get hungry around eleven in the morning.

8. In a can of mixed *ADJ* nuts, which kind of nut
do you prefer?

9. Edgar and I wished fervently *ADV* for snow, so
we could ride our sleds.

10. I don't think I have ever been more sleepy
than I was after we stayed up all night. *ADV*

EXERCISE B *Some revisions may vary, but compar-
isons should be clear and correct.*

11. Training to run a full marathon can seem
~~slowly~~ *slow*.

12. Of the three violinists who performed, Ms.
Buchanan played ~~better~~ *best*.

13. I was the ~~worse~~ *worst* player on our rugby team,
but I had a wonderful time.

14. I have always thought that our dog Samson
is braver than any *other* animal.

15. The narrow pass through the ravine is ~~most~~ *more*
treacherous than the longer road around
the mountains.

16. I think we will have ~~a more~~ *an* equal amount
of work if you handle the most recent
account.

17. The meeting will probably run as late, *as* if not
later than, four o'clock.

18. I believe Joe's account of events more than
~~Ana~~ *Ana's*.

19. Sonja doesn't feel ~~good~~ *well*; she has a high
fever.

20. Our new dog is no longer acting ~~bad~~ *badly*.

Proofreading Application: Formal Letter, p. 221
Some revisions may vary.

TO: jchen@houserep.la.gov

SUBJECT: Visit to Williamson High School

As student council secretary at Williamson
High School, I have been asked to invite you to
address our student body. We would sincerely
like you, more than any *other* state legislator, to
speak to us about the positive aspects of a

democratic form of government. Your life expe-

riences are ~~most~~ *more* interesting than *those of* ˄ many

representatives. After all, none of your other

colleagues grew up in possibly the ~~less~~ *least* demo-
˄
cratic country in the world. Among all the rep-

resentatives, you alone moved to the United

States in your teens and worked ~~hardly~~ *hard* to
˄
make your life ~~more~~ better. More recently, you

have spoken so *enthusiastically* ~~enthusiastic~~ about the positive
˄
role that young people have to play in govern-

ment.

We students realize that you are a *really* ~~real~~ busy
˄
man. However, we also know that you are

a
˄ ~~the most~~ unique person in state government

today. You are certain to receive the *strongest* ~~most~~
˄
~~strong~~ welcome you have ever been given in

your career.

Literary Model: Narrative, pp. 222–23

Exercise A

1. *Any ten of the following:* dull, dark, soundless, oppressively, low, alone, singularly,
   dreary, melancholy, not, first, insufferable

2. *Any ten of the following:* During the whole; of
   a dull, dark, and soundless day; in the
   autumn; of the year; in the heavens; on
   horseback; through a singularly dreary
   tract; of country; at length; of the evening;
   within view; of the melancholy House of
   Usher; of Usher; with the first glimpse; of
   the building; of insufferable gloom

Exercise B

Responses will vary. Sample responses are given.

1. I had been passing through a tract, and
   found myself at the House of Usher. When
   I glimpsed the building, gloom pervaded
   my spirit.

2. The modifiers set the tone and mood, helping the reader feel the narrator's sense of
   gloom.

Exercise C

Responses will vary. A sample response is given.

With my heart in my throat, I stepped off the
plane into Heathrow Airport in London, the
bustling capital of jolly old England. It was my
first solo vacation, the only trip I'd ever taken
outside the States. I couldn't wait to experience
the historic city: to see the famed British
Museum, filled with treasures from all over the
world; to watch the celebrated changing of the
guard at Buckingham Palace; to see a
Shakespearean play performed by struggling
young artists in one of the city's many theaters;
and to eat fish-and-chips from a grease-soaked
newspaper cone.

Exercise D

Responses will vary. A sample response is given.

1. I stepped off the plane into Heathrow
   Airport. It was my vacation. I couldn't wait
   to experience the city: to see the British
   Museum; to watch the changing of the
   guard at Buckingham Palace; to see a play;
   and to eat fish-and-chips.

2. Modifiers in my story opener give details
   that help the reader feel my excitement and
   expectation.

3. It would be very hard to set the mood, tone,
   and setting of the story without using modifiers. Modifiers help a reader see and feel
   what the narrator is seeing and feeling;
   without them, a story is boiled down to the
   essentials and has little spice.

Writing Application: Essay, p. 224

Writing Applications are designed to provide
students immediate composition practice in
using key concepts taught in each chapter of
the *Language and Sentence Skills Practice* booklet.
You may wish to evaluate student responses to
these assignments as you do any other writing
that students produce. To save grading time,
however, you may want to use the following
scoring rubric.

Scoring Rubric

A single chore—how it was done in the past and how it is done at present—is discussed adequately.

   1   2   3   4   5

A clear organizational plan includes points of comparison and points of contrast.

   1   2   3   4   5

The paragraphs use sensory details to bring the past to life.

   1   2   3   4   5

The assignment is relatively free of errors in grammar, usage, mechanics, and spelling.

   1   2   3   4   5

Total Score _____

5 = highest; 1 = lowest

Chapter 10: Placement of Modifiers, pp. 225–38

Choices: Exploring Modifier Placement, p. 225

Choices activities are designed to extend and enrich students' understanding of grammar, usage, and mechanics and to take learners beyond traditional classroom instruction. To use the Choices worksheet, have each student pick an activity that interests him or her. In some cases, you may wish to assign an activity to a particular student or group of students. You may also want to request that students get your approval for the activities they choose. Establish guidelines for what constitutes successful completion of an activity. Then, help students plan how they will share their work with the rest of the class.

Choices activities can be scored with a pass-fail grade or treated as bonus-point projects. Those activities that require students to research or create a certain number of items might be graded in a traditional manner.

Misplaced Modifiers A, p. 226

EXERCISE A

1. A woman showed us how to bead necklaces <u>near the judges' stand</u>.

2. The woman giving the demonstration <u>in her hair</u> wore beaded jewelry.

3. A Blackfoot artist <u>on one dress</u> had sewn numerous shells.

4. *C*

5. The contestant earned a cash prize <u>whose costume was chosen</u>.

EXERCISE B

Revisions may vary. Sample revisions are given.

6. Ever since she was young, Michelle had wanted to attend the college where her mother taught.

7. Using fancy lures, the man and woman caught several fish.

8. A single Canada goose was all the birdwatchers spotted after sitting in the cold for hours.

9. When you pick Joshua up at school, could you ask him what he plans to sing for everyone?

10. The slamming door sent the kitten, startled by the noise, dashing headlong from the room.

Misplaced Modifiers B, p. 227

EXERCISE

Revisions may vary. Sample revisions are given.

1. After the election results were announced, the losing candidate gave a gracious speech in which he thanked all voters for taking part in the democratic process.

2. Tricia proudly displayed on her desk a picture of her three children.

3. The climber's family were glad that their son, stranded on the mountain, had learned survival skills.

4. The new community centers that are being built downtown will be paid for with city funding and corporate contributions.

5. At the end of her presentation, the astronomer explained how a telltale wobble could indicate that one or more planets are in orbit around a star.

6. Safety Guide listed in its newsletter children's toys that could cause injury.

7. Next season, we will see the ballet that caused such a stir when it was first performed.

8. Fortunately, thanks to the firefighters' efforts, the house missed being burned by the brush fire.

9. When you have the time, please sing me the song Nana taught you.

10. Visiting an American supermarket for the first time, Ty was overwhelmed by the size of the store.

Squinting Modifiers A, p. 228

EXERCISE A

1. S
2. S
3. S
4. S
5. C

EXERCISE B

Revisions may vary. Sample revisions are given.

6. The scientists explained the oil slick should continue to break up throughout the week.

7. Dad promised I could use the car after he ran some errands.

8. During their stay in Istanbul, many visitors to the historic mosque say they have never seen a building of such beauty.

9. Ms. Singh requested we read quietly when we were finished with the test.

10. Before the plane took off, the pilot told the passengers they should turn off any personal electronic devices.

Squinting Modifiers B, p. 229

EXERCISE A

1. Having weathered the drought, the farmers hoped <u>in the fall</u> more rain would come.

2. Four of the doctors were convinced <u>because of the positive test results</u> their patients would want to undergo the treatment.

3. C

4. The company's spokesperson said <u>during a press conference</u> investors were getting nervous about the company's future.

5. Paul assured us <u>after an hour of hiking</u> the trail would become less rugged.

EXERCISE B

Revisions may vary. Sample revisions are given.

6. The committee agreed <u>over the holidays</u> we should sponsor some kind of service project.

7. Daniel had suggested <u>throughout the semester</u> we encourage more students to volunteer regularly.

8. Jeanette argued <u>on one occasion</u> we could get more students to work at smaller projects, thus helping more people.

9. Jeanette explained <u>afterwards</u> some volunteers would be inspired to volunteer more regularly.

10. Kahlil said <u>by the end of the meeting</u> we should generate a list of agencies for which students could volunteer.

Dangling Modifiers A, p. 230

EXERCISE A

1. D
2. D
3. D
4. C
5. D

EXERCISE B

Revisions may vary. Sample revisions are given.

6. After I spent all day Saturday reading, my eyes ached.

7. To give ourselves enough time, we had the taxi pick us up an hour and a half before our train left.

8. While Sora was working in New York, her family lived in California.

9. Peering at my map, I realized that the streets looked completely unfamiliar.

10. Although he is not usually shy, public speaking upset his stomach.

Dangling Modifiers B, p. 231

EXERCISE A

1. D
2. D
3. D
4. D
5. C

EXERCISE B

Revisions may vary. Sample revisions are given.

6. For returning the videotape early, you will receive the next rental free.

7. While Jordan was on her backpacking trip, the compass proved essential.

8. To set the clock, you must first press the "mode" button.

9. Not one to give up easily, she knew that the second attempt to climb the mountain would be a success.

10. As the acrobats were cartwheeling head over foot, the spectators gasped at the spectacle.

Review A: Placement of Modifiers, p. 232

EXERCISE A

1. D
2. D
3. S
4. M
5. D

EXERCISE B

Revisions may vary. Sample revisions are given.

6. The museum seemed huge to the preschoolers holding hands to keep from being separated.

7. Carla assured me she would stop more often to take pictures once we had entered the national park.

8. Stunned by the news of the earthquake, people from everywhere donated food and money.

9. Tina showed her parents the goldfish, which had grown since she put it in a larger bowl.

10. Having won first place in the obedience contest, Mr. Sawyer's schnauzer, Wolfy, won a year's supply of dog food.

Review B: Placement of Modifiers, p. 233

EXERCISE

Revisions may vary. Sample responses are given.

1. She stared with open amazement at the poster Elias was tacking up.

2. The teacher sent the students arriving in class without any books to the office.

3. Remind Dr. Scoffield her appointment at three o'clock has been canceled.

4. In this medieval book, the artist used a brush with only a few hairs to paint this tiny angel.

5. Sung Li has determined we can, with considerable effort, finish the job.

6. While I was crossing the street, the red light caught me halfway across.

7. No one whose driver's license has been revoked is allowed to drive a car.

8. Maya had thought her friends would meet her by the ticket counter before the movie.

9. Having learned to cook in home economics, I surprised Dad with my culinary skills.

10. To find out how the contraption works, you should not push buttons at random.

Review C: Placement of Modifiers, p. 234

EXERCISE

Revisions may vary. Sample revisions are given.

1. Through the binoculars Luke saw a bird with a long bill.

2. When this song is over, tell the dance instructor I need to review the steps.

3. To recognize a talented player, you must understand the game.

4. We're sponsoring a dance in the gym to raise money for famine victims.

5. My parents congratulated me for having finally made the honor roll.

6. On his little finger the man wore a ring with a large red ruby.

7. Riding on the school bus this morning, Bruno saw a deer.

8. A mysterious woman warned the king he would regret his rash decision before he had reigned a year.

9. Leaving the store, I slipped on the icy sidewalk.

10. After Jodi found the diary, her first inclination was to read it.

Proofreading Application: Script, p. 235

Revisions may vary. Sample revisions are given.

Marty: It's true that most students at Powell High School stay busy. They know that to succeed in life ~~a great deal of studying is required~~ they must study a great deal.

Leah: Don't you think that teenagers need to do more than study (tr) ⌢trying to achieve success⌣?

Marty: Yes, Leah—and after hearing what you and I are about to say, *these students obviously will see* a way to make their lives more multidimensional ~~will be obvious~~.

Leah: That's right. The key word is *multidimensional*. We want to talk about a pleasant way to

(tr) take a break from studying (with all of you Powell juniors and seniors).

(tr) Marty: We're here (at Powell High) to encourage you to join the Dimensions Club. Recognizing how high school students can benefit from helping others, *Mr. Guthrie formed* this community service organization ~~was formed by Mr. Guthrie~~ three years ago. Growing each month, the *club is* ~~members are~~ planning several big service events to be held throughout the year. We also provide an ongoing tutoring service at two elementary schools.

Literary Model: Epic Poem, pp. 236–37

EXERCISE A

Responses will vary. Students should underline at least ten modifiers in all and should include one-word modifiers, phrase modifiers, and clause modifiers among their answers.

Of living strong men he was the strongest,

Fearless and gallant and great of heart.

He gave command for a goodly vessel

Fitted and furnished; he fain would sail

Over the swan-road to seek the king

Who suffered so sorely for need of men.

And his bold retainers found little to blame

In his daring venture, dear though he was;

They viewed the omens, and urged him on.

Brave was the band he had gathered about him,

Fourteen stalwarts seasoned and bold,

Seeking the shore where the ship lay waiting,

A sea-skilled mariner sighting the landmarks.

From *Beowulf: The Oldest English Epic,* translated by Charles W. Kennedy. Copyright 1940 by **Oxford University Press, Inc.**; copyright renewed © 1968 by Charles W. Kennedy. Reprinted by permission of the publisher.

EXERCISE B

Responses may vary. Sample responses are given.

1. Beowulf contains so many modifiers so that the audience listening to the story can picture it in their minds. Descriptive language is used to create a vivid verbal picture, to stir the listeners' imaginations, and to sustain the listeners' interest.

2. The modifiers must be placed correctly so that listeners can clearly picture the characters, places, and actions without becoming confused.

EXERCISE C

Responses will vary. Sample response is given.

A long time ago on an island faraway,

The citizens of a kingdom ruled by a warrior-king

Dwelled in terror that they could not overcome.

The source of their fears, which grew gradually more intense,

Was a huge, fiendish creature named Mologar,

Who fiercely roamed the countryside at night,

Every moonlit night, to satiate his appetite,

His obviously unsatiable appetite,

For more human flesh and blood.

The brighter the moon, the hungrier Mologar became.

Too powerful and fearless and cunning

For the king's warriors, who grew more cowardly each night,

Molagar soon faced little resistance from his delectable prey.

EXERCISE D

Responses will vary. Sample responses are given.

1. I used several modifiers to describe Mologar and his appetite and to describe the fear of the citizens and the king's warriors.

2. I think the audience will picture a monstrous predator who, under the cover of night, devours the helpless citizens while the warriors hide in fear.

Language and Sentence Skills Practice Answer Key

Writing Application: Valentines, p. 238

Writing Applications are designed to provide students immediate composition practice in using key concepts taught in each chapter of the *Language and Sentence Skills Practice* booklet. You may wish to evaluate student responses to these assignments as you do any other writing that students produce. To save grading time, however, you may want to use the following scoring rubric.

Scoring Rubric

The assignment includes two messages for women, two for men, and two for friends.

  1   2   3   4   5

The modifiers used are appropriate and correctly placed.

  1   2   3   4   5

The sentiment of the messages is appropriate and could apply to most flower recipients.

  1   2   3   4   5

The assignment is relatively free of errors in usage and mechanics.

  1   2   3   4   5

Total Score _____

5 = highest; 1 = lowest

Chapter 11: A Glossary of Usage, pp. 239–53

Choices: Exploring Usage, p. 239

Choices activities are designed to extend and enrich students' understanding of grammar, usage, and mechanics and to take learners beyond traditional classroom instruction. To use the Choices worksheet, have each student pick an activity that interests him or her. In some cases, you may wish to assign an activity to a particular student or group of students. You may also want to request that students get your approval for the activities they choose. Establish guidelines for what constitutes successful completion of an activity. Then, help students plan how they will share their work with the rest of the class.

Choices activities can be scored with a pass-fail grade or treated as bonus-point projects. Those activities that require students to research or create a certain number of items might be graded in a traditional manner.

Glossary of Usage A, p. 240

EXERCISE

1. a
2. a lot
3. number
4. etc.
5. all right
6. accepted
7. alumnae
8. a while
9. have it
10. anywhere
11. as far as
12. all right
13. isn't
14. effect
15. amount
16. adapting
17. illusion
18. adopt
19. a
20. ensured

Glossary of Usage B, p. 241

EXERCISE

1. My teacher invented a popular math trivia game; now he's ~~notorious~~! *famous*

2. C

3. ~~Being as~~ my father received a promotion, our family moved to Chicago. *Because*

4. ~~Less~~ teenagers were able to find jobs this summer. *Fewer*

5. Owen and Chad split the meal ~~among~~ themselves. *between*

6. C

7. Odessa ~~don't~~ know where the microscope should go. *doesn't*

8. How did you ~~bust~~ your arm? *break*

9. After lunch, Hisako and I ~~done~~ the dishes while the others picked berries. *did*

10. The reason I was late for class is ~~because~~ my dad's car wouldn't start. *that*

11. Who ~~discovered~~ the electron microscope? *invented*

12. How many people had to ~~immigrate~~ from Ireland during the potato famine? *emigrate*

13. The data ~~was~~ carefully reviewed by our panel of experts. *were*

14. Their efforts to prevent the fire from spreading were ~~credible~~. *creditable*

15. Sure, I would be happy to ~~borrow~~ you my lawnmower. *lend*

16. C

17. Did the police ~~bust~~ anyone for trespassing? *arrest*

18. When you leave tonight, ~~bring~~ this umbrella with you. *take*

19. He's so ~~creditable~~; he believed that the moon was really made of green cheese. *credulous*

20. We ~~doesn't~~ care how far it is—we're going! *don't*

Glossary of Usage C, p. 242

EXERCISE

1. If you have never heard of cyclo-cross racing, I ~~had~~ ought to tell you about it.

2. The race, which takes place in open country, ~~it~~ is usually about ten to fifteen miles long.

3. The obstacles, of which there are plenty, ~~they~~ can include ditches or even flights of stairs.

4. The bikers often have to pick up their bikes *themselves* ~~theirselves~~ and carry them over obstacles.

5. *C*

6. From the large crowd at the last race I attended, I can *infer* ~~imply~~ that the sport has some real fans.

7. My brother, the great athlete, ~~he~~ took me to my first cyclo-cross race.

8. *This sort* ~~These sort~~ of event was not my usual Saturday afternoon fare.

9. I went, though, because my brother had helped set up the event *himself* ~~hisself~~.

10. When we got there, we walked right *into* ~~in~~ the registration tent.

11. My brother had not told me that I would actually be helping with the race, but I guess he had *implied* ~~inferred~~ it.

12. It was *somewhat [or rather]* ~~kind of~~ exciting to be a part of the event staff.

13. We even got to wear *this type* ~~these type~~ of badge that looked really snappy.

14. But what would I have to do—what kind of job had I gotten myself *into* ~~in~~?

15. *I hoped [or I hoped that]* ~~Hopefully,~~ it wouldn't be anything too boring.

16. I *ought not* ~~hadn't ought~~ to have worried about that.

17. A girl named Jen, who had worked at several races, ~~she~~ explained what I had to do.

18. During a race, each helper ~~had~~ ought to stand on the course with a spare bike.

19. This was in case any rider's bike, which can get damaged or bogged down with mud, ~~it~~ was unfit to finish the race.

20. Being that close to the action was *somewhat [or rather]* ~~sort of~~ intimidating, but it was fun!

Glossary of Usage D, p. 243
EXERCISE

1. I saw a design for a *kind of* ~~kind of a~~ clock that wakes you by dropping corks on your face.

2. I won't see that film, because I am *liable* ~~likely~~ to have nightmares.

3. I know that Layla and *I* ~~myself~~ can paint the backdrop this afternoon.

4. My uncle is the man who *taught* ~~learned~~ me how to play the guitar.

5. Do you think Dad will *let* ~~leave~~ me go to the concert?

6. Jerold will call for Evelyn and *us* ~~ourselves~~ at eight o'clock.

7. *C*

8. I feel *as if* ~~like~~ I will never finish my homework.

9. The day is not going *as* ~~like~~ I had planned.

10. Betsy has promised to *teach* ~~learn~~ me about my new computer this weekend.

11. This is a *kind of* ~~kind of a~~ problem we don't encounter very often.

12. If we don't leave soon, we are *likely* ~~liable~~ to arrive late.

13. Do you mean he *literally* ~~figuratively~~ spilled the beans—he dumped a bag of dry beans onto the table?

14. *C*

15. I'm sorry, but I cannot *let* ~~leave~~ you have the car this weekend.

16. *C*

17. Karen and *I* ~~myself~~ are going out for ice cream tonight.

18. Unfortunately, this is not the right *sort of* ~~sort of a~~ wrench for the job.

94

HOLT HANDBOOK | Sixth Course

19. C

20. Bill is ~~liable~~ *likely* to show up any time now.

Glossary of Usage E, p. 244

EXERCISE

1. That particular ~~phenomena~~ *phenomenon* has never been explained.

2. C

3. My aunt is a lawyer—she ~~persecutes~~ *prosecutes.* people.

4. You ~~ought to of~~ *ought to have* seen how deep the snow was in my backyard.

5. I will neither resign ~~or~~ *nor* apologize.

6. We ~~should of~~ *should have* made reservations for dinner.

7. Does the old regime have a history of ~~prosecuting~~ *persecuting* minorities?

8. I got this Sammy Sosa rookie card ~~off~~ *from* my cousin.

9. Either you have the item, ~~nor~~ *or* you don't.

10. The number of people who signed up ~~were~~ *was* surprising.

11. I need to sit down; I'm feeling ~~nauseous~~ *nauseated*.

12. Did you get any good debate tips ~~off of~~ *from* that guy?

13. I ~~could of~~ *could have* brought an extra plate if I had known we needed one.

14. This store ~~persecutes~~ *prosecutes* all shoplifters.

15. I have neither approved ~~or~~ *nor* disapproved her proposal.

16. C

17. A number of applications ~~was~~ *were* waiting for me on my desk.

18. Someone ~~must of~~ *must have* told them about the secret meeting.

19. I can't believe they didn't win either first ~~nor~~ *or* second place.

20. A number of strange ~~phenomenon~~ *phenomena* have been reported in this area recently.

Glossary of Usage F, p. 245

EXERCISE *Revisions of item 6 may vary.*

1. The Reverend ~~Allan~~ *Mr. Allan* spoke to our class on Monday.

2. C

3. Mr. Allan ~~use~~ *used* to be a family counselor.

4. He looked at us seriously and ~~says~~ *said* that communication was always a big issue.

5. He said that family members ~~which~~ *who [or that]* communicate well have happier home lives.

6. Good communication is ~~where~~ *interaction in which* each person talks and listens in a caring and constructive way.

7. C

8. We were each ~~suppose~~ *supposed* to choose a partner.

9. He gave each pair of us a hypothetical situation, and ~~than~~ *then* we had to act it out.

10. First, we acted out ~~that there~~ *that* situation in an angry way.

11. ~~Than~~ *Then*, we talked about the words most of us had used to express ourselves.

12. We had been saying "you always do this" and that ~~type~~ *type of* thing.

13. When we used ~~them~~ *those* accusing words, our partners felt defensive.

14. We realized ~~where~~ *that* we had not been focused on solving the problem.

15. Next, we tried the same discussion, except it was ~~some~~ *somewhat* different.

16. This time we had to ~~try and~~ *try to* keep the other person's feelings in mind.

17. Immediately after deciding on this new approach, we began to feel as if tensions had eased ~~some~~ *somewhat*.

Language and Sentence Skills Practice Answer Key

18. Before we even started the discussion, my partner turned to me and ~~says~~ _said_ that our friendship is more important than our problems.

19. After ~~that there~~ _that_ statement, I felt much more inclined to listen and compromise.

20. Mr. Allan said we had come a long ~~ways~~ _way_ toward having better relationships.

The Double Negative and Nonsexist Language, p. 246

EXERCISE

Replacements for gender-specific terms may vary.

1. Last week a number of ~~businessmen~~ _businesspeople_ came to the city convention center.

2. They were looking for more ~~manpower~~ _workers_ for their businesses.

3. I ~~hadn't never~~ _hadn't ever (or had never)_ been to a career fair before, so I decided to attend.

4. The recruiters seemed like ~~salemen~~ _salespeople_ trying to sell their companies.

5. At first, I didn't think they had ~~nothing~~ _anything_ that would interest me.

6. C

7. I ~~couldn't hardly~~ _could hardly_ find any booths there that weren't for computer companies.

8. There ~~weren't but~~ _were but (or were only)_ a few tables for more old-fashioned professions.

9. One company was looking for ~~seamstresses~~ _needleworkers_ to do complicated alterations.

10. I ~~wasn't nowhere~~ _wasn't anywhere (or was nowhere)_ close to being qualified for that job, but it sounded interesting.

11. I think the most interesting booth was the one the ~~firemen~~ _firefighters_ had set up—it had real fire-fighting equipment and uniforms.

12. I bet I ~~wouldn't hardly~~ _would hardly (or wouldn't)_ look bad in one of those outfits.

13. C

14. I ~~can't never~~ _can't ever (or can never)_ imagine myself carrying a gun, though.

15. I have a cousin who is a ~~stewardess~~ _flight attendant_, so I looked at the airlines' booths.

16. I wouldn't be good at that, because I already know I'm a lousy ~~waiter~~ _server_.

17. I did well as a ~~deliveryman~~ _delivery person_ for a pizza chain last summer, though.

18. I noticed that there ~~weren't no~~ _weren't any (or were no)_ booths for some of the jobs I respect most.

19. My mother is a ~~housewife~~ _homemaker_, and I think that's a very worthwhile profession.

20. I'm sure that once I find the right career, there ~~won't be nobody~~ _won't be anybody (or will be nobody)_ else better at it than I am!

Review A: Glossary of Usage, p. 247

EXERCISE

Replacements for gender-specific terms may vary.

1. Nan and Jo were the two ~~policemen~~ _police officers_ ~~which~~ _who_ were in charge of patrolling the carnival.

2. I read in the paper ~~where~~ _that_ the team lost again yesterday.

3. Her remarks ~~inferred~~ _implied_ that she was not happy in her new school.

4. C

5. Some illnesses may ~~effect~~ _affect_ the brain.

6. C

7. She borrowed five dollars ~~off~~ _from_ her sister.

8. According to the ~~chairman~~ _chairperson_, the plan was ~~kind of~~ _somewhat (or rather)_ complicated.

9. The children built the treehouse ~~theirselves~~ _themselves_, without any help from their parents.

10. There were ~~less~~ _fewer_ people in the audience than there were on the stage.

11. The ~~mailman~~ *mail carrier* said that the package required a large ~~amount~~ *number* of postage stamps.

12. We noticed that there ~~weren't hardly~~ *were hardly* enough test booklets for everyone in the class.

13. C

14. Shall we ~~except~~ *accept* the Smiths' invitation to dinner?

15. I read ~~where~~ *that* Bethune-Cookman College in Florida is named after Mary McLeod Bethune.

16. Gwendolyn Brooks was a poet ~~which~~ *who (or that)* won a Pulitzer Prize in 1950.

17. ~~Being as~~ *Because* the lake was frozen, we decided to ice-skate.

18. C

19. They found ~~less~~ *fewer* wild strawberries than they had expected.

20. The students had to explain the differences ~~among~~ *between* nouns, verbs, and adjectives.

Review B: Glossary of Usage, p. 248

EXERCISE

1. the Reverend Edward Jackson
2. into
3. emigrated
4. Because
5. liable
6. way
7. as if
8. fewer
9. This kind of
10. assured
11. those kinds of
12. take
13. affected
14. could have
15. implied
16. number
17. creditable
18. as if
19. from
20. feeling

Review C: Glossary of Usage, p. 249

EXERCISE

Replacements for gender-specific terms may vary.

1. In 1612, Shah Jahan of India married a woman ~~which~~ *who (or that)* would become the love of his life.

2. They were ~~literally~~ inseparable—she went almost everywhere with him, even to war.

3. Shah Jahan, who loved his wife very much, ~~he~~ gave her a special name: "Mumtaz Mahal."

4. ~~That there~~ *That* name means "Chosen One of the Palace."

5. Queen Mumtaz was ~~notorious~~ *famous* in India for her kindness.

6. She inspired Shah Jahan to commit many ~~credible~~ *creditable* acts of charity.

7. They also had a large ~~amount~~ *number* of children together.

8. It ~~must of~~ *must have* been a terrible shock, then, when she died suddenly.

9. ~~Being as~~ *Because* Shah Jahan was so grief-stricken, he mourned for eight days in a locked room.

10. I read ~~where~~ *that* his black hair had turned almost completely white by the time he came out of the room.

11. He decided to build the world's finest mausoleum to ~~assure~~ *ensure* that Mumtaz's memory would be preserved.

12. ~~No one isn't~~ *No one is* certain about the origin of the name "Taj Mahal" for the mausoleum, but it is thought to be an abbreviation of Mumtaz Mahal's name.

Language and Sentence Skills Practice Answer Key

13. Twenty thousand ~~workmen~~ *workers* were used in the colossal building effort.

14. No ~~less~~ *fewer* than 1,000 elephants hauled the building materials from all over the Far East.

15. Artisans decorated the inside of the building with gold, turquoise, precious gems, ~~and~~ etc.

16. C

17. Legend says that Shah Jahan intended to build a second mausoleum for himself, but his son, who seized the throne and imprisoned his father, would not ~~leave~~ *let* him do it.

18. I think that the Taj Mahal has the most beautiful architecture of any building ~~anywheres~~ *anywhere*.

19. According to the original design, the interior ~~had~~ ought to be perfectly symmetrical.

20. The reason it is not is ~~because~~ *that*, after Shah Jahan's death, his cenotaph was placed beside that of his beloved wife, upsetting the perfect balance of the room.

Proofreading Application: Letter, p. 250

Dear Ms. Delahoussaye:

~~Being as~~ *Because [or Since]* your company, Griffin Press, is in need of a production assistant for the summer, I am sending you my résumé. The reason I am interested in working at Griffin is ~~because~~ *that* I intend to study communications in college. In addition, I read ~~where~~ *that* Griffin is ~~notorious~~ *famous* for publishing science-related books. As you will probably infer from my résumé, ~~between~~ *among* all my school subjects, biology and chemistry are my favorites. I ~~ought to of~~ *ought to have* decided to major in a science, but my love for the printed word is too great. I think it is wonderful that one of your company's goals is to ~~try and~~ *try to* help more people understand science.

I am sure that the ~~amount~~ *number* of résumés you receive will be ~~kind of~~ *somewhat [or rather]* large. ~~Hopefully,~~ *I hope [or I hope that]* you will find my résumé creditable enough to consider me for the job.

Sincerely,

Caroline Sato

Literary Model: Dialogue, pp. 251–52
EXERCISE A

'Look'ee here, Pip. I'm your second father. . . . When I was a hired-out shepherd in a solitary hut, <u>not seeing no</u> faces but faces of sheep till I half forgot wot men's and women's faces wos like, I see yourn. . . . I see you there a many times, as plain as ever I see you on <u>them</u> misty marshes. "Lord strike me dead!" I <u>says</u> each time—and I goes out in the air to say it under the open heavens—"but wot, if I gets liberty and money, I'll make that boy a gentleman!" And I <u>done</u> it. Why, look at you, dear boy! Look at <u>these here</u> lodgings o' yourn, fit for a lord! . . . Don't you mind talking, Pip. . . . You <u>ain't</u> looked slowly forward to this as I have; you wosn't prepared for this, as I wos. But <u>didn't you never</u> think it might be me?"

EXERCISE B
Answers will vary. Sample responses are given.

1. The irony of this situation is that the very person that made Pip a gentleman would not be considered a gentleman himself. Pip is shocked to learn that this man, with his language, crude manner, and background, is his benefactor.

2. Yes, Dickens skillfully depicts the character of Magwitch through his speech. Pip becomes a gentleman who uses correct English due to the efforts and money of an untutored man.

EXERCISE C
Answers will vary. Sample responses are given.

"Betsy, answer the telephone, please."

"Ms. Delacroix, right away."

"And when you are finished, I desire lunch."

Betsy hung up the telephone. "You won't never believe what just happened, ma'am. My mother she bought a lottery ticket last week and said she aimed to split the winnin's with me, if she were lucky enough to win. She just called. I won twenty million dollars!"

"Why, Betsy, that's fabulous. I'll let you have the afternoon off, after you prepare the lobster bisque for lunch, of course."

"Ms. Delacroix, I ain't gonna be fixin' lunch no more. From now on, I hadn't ought to work anymore."

EXERCISE D
Answers will vary. Sample responses are given.

The effect I planned to achieve is the relationship between Betsy, the servant, and Ms. Delacroix, the wealthy woman. Ms. Delacroix is a bit snobbish and bossy toward Betsy. While Betsy may not have the education that Ms. Delacroix has, by winning the lottery, Betsy is now her equal monetarily and won't be bossed around by her anymore. Ms. Delacroix expects Betsy to keep working even after winning the money: "Why, Betsy, that's fabulous. I'll let you have the afternoon off, after you prepare the lobster bisque for lunch, of course."

Writing Application: Thank-You Note, p. 253

Writing Applications are designed to provide students immediate composition practice in using key concepts taught in each chapter of the *Language and Sentence Skills Practice* booklet. You may wish to evaluate student responses to these assignments as you do any other writing that students produce. To save grading time, however, you may want to use the following scoring rubric.

Scoring Rubric

The letter thanks the teacher for a specific incident.

| 1 | 2 | 3 | 4 | 5 |

The letter's tone and diction are appropriate.

| 1 | 2 | 3 | 4 | 5 |

The letter mentions specific details of the incident.

| 1 | 2 | 3 | 4 | 5 |

The assignment is relatively free of errors in usage and mechanics.

| 1 | 2 | 3 | 4 | 5 |

Total Score _____

5 = highest; 1 = lowest

Chapter 12: Capitalization, pp. 254–75

Choices: Investigating Capitalization, p. 254

Choices activities are designed to extend and enrich students' understanding of grammar, usage, and mechanics and to take learners beyond traditional classroom instruction. To use the Choices worksheet, have each student pick an activity that interests him or her. In some cases, you may wish to assign an activity to a particular student or group of students. You may also want to request that students get your approval for the activities they choose. Establish guidelines for what constitutes successful completion of an activity. Then, help students plan how they will share their work with the rest of the class.

Choices activities can be scored with a pass-fail grade or treated as bonus-point projects. Those activities that require students to research or create a certain number of items might be graded in a traditional manner.

First Words, *O*, and the Pronoun *I*, p. 255

EXERCISE

1. When asked his favorite sport, Lloyd said, "basketball to watch and tennis to play."

2. The resolution began with "Resolved: that support for day care be increased by 15 percent."

3. for breakfast, i had two bowls of cereal and two bananas because, Oh, was I hungry.

4. Claire, I have one thing to say: college admission requirements are more stringent than you think.

5. Measure my humble self against your vastness, o majestic sky.

6. Butler wrote, "an expert is one who knows more and more about less and less."

7. I believe that Dr. Kimura's point is, exercise is essential for good health.

8. The epitaph that my grandfather Tomás wrote for himself is an enigma: "he always strove to look beyond harmony."

9. Luisa closed her letter to her aunt with "yours truly."

10. My question to you is, do you think it is worth your time to finish this project?

Proper Nouns A, p. 256

EXERCISE

1. adela rogers st. johns was a famous journalist.

2. I've had my parakeet tweety for two years.

3. Have you heard of George s. Patton, an important military figure in World War II?

4. Sabrina's uncle, dr. Ray Hinojosa, jr., is a well-known surgeon in Boston.

5. Did your parents use to watch the television program about lassie, the dog?

6. Our guest speaker is heidi v. martenson, president of the Chamber of Commerce.

7. My cousin ambrosio is named for st. ambrose, patron saint of Milan, Italy.

8. C

9. The First Baptist Church minister, the rev. Carlton H. Colson, has announced his retirement.

10. It gives me great pleasure to introduce Lt. taneesha wilson of the United States Army.

11. C

12. My sister just became engaged to a man named john doe.

13. C

14. "Auntie Louise" is mrs. Burnside's nickname.

15. Roy Higginbotham, ~~sr.~~ —not his son ~~mor~~-
    gan—wants to buy our farm.
    [S above sr., M above mor]

16. The course in twentieth-century philosophy
    will be taught by ~~dr.~~ Jean Marchand.
    [D above dr.]

17. C

18. Do you think I should send the letter today,
    ~~mr.~~ Goldblatt?
    [M above mr.]

19. The Broadway musical *Cats* is based on
    ~~t. s.~~ Eliot's humorous poems about cats.
    [T S above t. s.]

20. Peter the ~~great~~ made great efforts to mod-
    ernize Russia in the late 1600s and early
    1700s.
    [G above great]

Proper Nouns B, p. 257
EXERCISE A

1. the largest ~~Ocean~~, the Pacific [o above Ocean]

2. floating down the Blanco ~~river~~ [R above river]

3. C

4. on Thirty-Eighth ~~street~~ [e above Eighth, S above street]

5. on the other side of the ~~Lake~~ [l above Lake]

6. in Madison ~~township~~ [T above township]

7. sailing on ~~lake~~ Buchanan [L above lake]

8. a view of ~~mount~~ McKinley [M above mount]

9. Niagara ~~falls~~ in ~~Western~~ New York [F above falls, W above Western]

10. a trip to ~~new~~ Zealand [N above new]

EXERCISE B

11. Turn ~~East~~ on Route 56, and follow it until
    you reach the ~~Town~~ of Oak Grove.
    [e above East, t above Town]

12. Which United States ~~Rivers~~ flow into the
    Gulf ~~Of~~ Mexico?
    [r above Rivers, o above Of]

13. Do you agree that the railroads were a sig-
    nificant factor in the settlement of the ~~west~~?
    [W above west]

14. The Canary ~~islands~~ were so named because
    wild dogs (called *canes* in Latin) roamed
    them.
    [I above islands]

15. You can hunt for diamonds at a place just
    ~~North~~ of the town where I grew up.
    [n above North]

16. My grandfather lived in ~~egypt~~ twenty years
    ago.
    [E above egypt]

17. Miami is located in Dade ~~county~~, near the
    southernmost tip of Florida.
    [C above county]

18. Many of Georgia O'Keeffe's paintings
    depict the American ~~southwest~~.
    [S above southwest]

19. Abby's family is planning to go to Zion
    ~~national park~~ in July.
    [N P above national park]

20. The town of Grand ~~gulf~~ is a few miles
    south of Vicksburg on the Mississippi ~~river~~.
    [G above gulf, R above river]

Proper Nouns C, p. 258
EXERCISE

1. the Biltmore Hotel
2. on Saturdays and Sundays
3. chief of the Central Intelligence Agency
4. a celebration on the Fourth of July
5. at James Bowie High School
6. C
7. the Battle of Gettysburg
8. C
9. in M. D. Anderson Hospital
10. the War of Independence
11. Cedar Valley Community College
12. the last Sunday in December
13. the Underground Railroad
14. the Cleveland Browns
15. C
16. Cannes Film Festival
17. C
18. the Hundred Years' War
19. members of the United Nations
20. the Age of Enlightenment

Proper Nouns D, p. 259
EXERCISE A

1. a sixteenth-century ~~arabic~~ philosopher [A above arabic]
2. a group of ~~haitian~~ immigrants [H above haitian]

3. on ~~e~~aster Sunday *[E]*

4. the ~~h~~opi language *[H]*

5. ~~s~~hinto priests in Japan *[S]*

6. Shiva, the ~~h~~indu goddess *[H]*

7. South ~~a~~fricans from Johannesburg *[A]*

8. the ~~o~~ld ~~t~~estament of the Bible *[O] [T]*

9. from ~~m~~ercury, the Roman messenger of the ~~G~~ods *[M] [g]*

10. C

EXERCISE B

11. The ~~s~~panish conquistadors applied the name *Inca* to a ~~n~~ative ~~a~~merican people in present-day South America. *[S] [N] [A]*

12. The new ~~m~~ethodist minister is ~~a~~ustralian. *[M] [A]*

13. In ~~h~~induism, the god ~~v~~ishnu is regarded as the preserver of the universe. *[H] [V]*

14. On what day of the week does ~~c~~hristmas fall this year? *[C]*

15. One of the ~~m~~ormons' sacred scriptures is called the ~~b~~ook of ~~m~~ormon. *[M] [B] [M]*

Proper Nouns E, p. 260

EXERCISE

1. In 1928, two Australian and two American fliers flew an airplane called the ~~s~~outhern ~~c~~ross 11,910 kilometers from Oakland, California, to Sydney, Australia. *[S] [C]*

2. Has Anna Maria decided to buy a ~~c~~ompaq or a Dell ~~C~~omputer? *[C] [c]*

3. Charles Darwin was employed as a naturalist aboard the sailing vessel the ~~b~~eagle. *[B]*

4. Arnulfo is going to test drive a new Dodge ~~T~~ruck. *[t]*

5. The first manned spacecraft to land on the moon was the lunar module ~~e~~agle. *[E]*

6. Did you know that the origins of ~~r~~eebok ~~i~~nternational ~~l~~td., the athletic shoe company, go back to 1890? *[R] [I] [L]*

7. C

8. The first Harley-Davidson ~~M~~otorcycle, built in 1903, was basically a motor-equipped bicycle—the rider had to pedal uphill. *[m]*

9. Ahmed's uncle Ibrahim has applied for a job at Amoco ~~c~~orporation. *[C]*

10. In December 1986, an ultralight experimental aircraft called ~~v~~oyager completed the first nonstop flight around the world without refueling. *[V]*

Proper Nouns F, p. 261

EXERCISE

1. Who won the ~~a~~cademy ~~a~~ward for ~~b~~est ~~d~~irector in 1998? *[A] [A] [B] [D]*

2. Green Bay Packer Paul Vernon Hornung had won the Heisman ~~t~~rophy in 1956 when he was on the University of Notre Dame team. *[T]*

3. Is a visit to the ~~w~~hite ~~h~~ouse included in your tour of Washington, D.C.? *[W] [H]*

4. In New Jersey can be found several ~~M~~onuments that commemorate the American Revolution. *[m]*

5. The Aswan ~~d~~am is located in southern Egypt. *[D]*

6. Is Mr. Ling going to the ~~k~~ennedy ~~c~~enter to see the Alvin Ailey Dance Theater? *[K] [C]*

7. You're sure to see the works of some well-known twentieth-century artists at the Hirshhorn ~~m~~useum. *[M]*

8. Gregory Hines received a ~~t~~ony ~~a~~ward in 1992 for his work in the Broadway production of *Jelly's Last Jam*. *[T] [A]*

9. We're planning to visit the alamo [A] while in San Antonio; it's a former Franciscan mission and now a state monument.

10. You shouldn't leave New York City before going to the Empire state [S] building [B].

Proper Nouns G, p. 262

EXERCISE

1. The first-magnitude giant star beta [B] orionis [O] is also called rigel [R].

2. Patricia is going to sign up for Calculus [C] if the Algebra II class is full.

3. The cluster of stars that we know as the pleiades [P] was named by the ancient Greeks after the "Seven Sisters" of mythology.

4. C

5. In his art [A] 301 class, Mr. Holtzman tends to concentrate on the Renaissance era.

6. Which is greater, the distance between Venus and earth [E] or between earth [E] and Mars?

7. The star algol [A] in the constellation Perseus is an eclipsing variable star.

8. C

9. A requirement for that german [G] course is Ms. Torres's class called Foundations of Language I.

10. Does it amaze you, as it does me, that people living thousands of years ago gazed at the same Moon [m] that we do?

Proper Nouns Review, p. 263

EXERCISE

1. Frances Perkins, the first female member of the cabinet

2. C

3. going to eastern California

4. the National Science Foundation

5. actors Edward James Olmos and Sidney Poitier

6. Japanese paper folding

7. Bill Yellowtail, Jr.

8. paddling a canoe down the Suwannee River

9. Dr. Jemison, an astronaut

10. famous Asian American cellist Yo-Yo Ma

11. two miles west of Denver

12. the headquarters of the Chrysler Corporation

13. the third Friday in March

14. the constellations Aries and Virgo

15. the prestigious Student of the Year Award

16. C

17. a bowl of Breyer's ice cream

18. an Islamic holy man

19. the War Between the States

20. Mount Vernon, home of George Washington

Personal Titles and Titles Showing Family Relationships, p. 264

EXERCISE

1. Did you know that senator [S] Phil Gramm is the son of an army Sergeant [S]?

2. The last person to leave the party was my seventy-year-old Grandmother [g].

3. We saw Ex-president [e][P] Jimmy Carter at a baseball game last night.

4. Lucy's Uncle Percy is writing his autobiography.

5. C

6. The defense wishes to call lieutenant [L] Michael O'Reilly to the stand.

7. The committee is headed by Former [f] Justice Billig.

8. Thank you, professor [P] Eaton, for presenting your views on the topic.

9. I fully expect ~~aunt~~ [A] Josie to join in the protest.

10. The ~~Captain~~ [c] of the ship has called the entire crew on deck.

11. Every ~~Judge~~ [j] has an office at the courthouse.

12. The ~~Secretary-Treasurer~~ [s][t] of the Ecology Club can give you a check.

13. C

14. At last count, ~~cousin~~ [c] Edna had fourteen cats and three dogs.

15. Ask your ~~Father~~ [f] if you can borrow his car this afternoon.

16. The archbishop and ~~father~~ [F] Banks have known each other for twenty years.

17. The press release said that ~~mayor~~ [m] Watkins will be at the ground-breaking ceremony.

18. The Community Services Division is sending ~~sergeant~~ [s] Raymond to talk to the students.

19. Nominations for ~~Club President~~ [c][P] and ~~Vice President~~ [v][P] are still open.

20. Will she be a ~~Doctor~~ [d] when she graduates from medical school?

Titles and Subtitles, p. 265

EXERCISE

1. The PBS series *Sister Wendy's Story ~~Of~~* [o] *Painting* included a discussion of Millet's ~~the gleaners~~ [T][G].

2. Have you heard a CD called *Reggae: ~~past~~* [P], *~~present~~* [P], *and ~~future~~* [F]?

3. For tomorrow's class, read the chapter titled "~~the~~ [T] Consequences of ~~urbanization~~ [U]."

4. My little brother's favorite poem is Shel Silverstein's "~~sarah cynthia sylvia stout~~ [S][C][S][S] ~~would not take the garbage out~~ [W][N][T][G][O]."

5. Ray Bradbury's "All Summer ~~In A~~ [i][a] Day" is about a family who lives on Venus.

6. In addition to writing the book *What ~~To~~* [t] *Listen ~~For In~~* [F][i] *Music*, the American composer Aaron Copland wrote the music for the film *~~of mice and men~~* [O][M][M].

7. Child actress Judy Garland played Dorothy in *The ~~wizard of oz~~* [W][O].

8. George Bernard Shaw wrote the play *Arms and ~~The~~ Man* and the political essay *The Intelligent Woman's ~~guide~~ [G] to ~~socialism~~ [S] and ~~capitalism~~ [C]*.

9. American colonists were vehemently opposed to the ~~stamp act~~ [S][A], which required them to buy revenue stamps to put on all official documents.

10. Leonard Bernstein, winner of the 1985 Grammy Lifetime Achievement Award, wrote the musical *~~west side story~~* [W][S][S] in 1957.

Abbreviations A, p. 266

EXERCISE

1. my vet, Roberto Guzmán, D.V.M.

2. C

3. the TV in the living room

4. American novelist E. L. Doctorow

5. the Rev. Martin Luther King, Jr.

6. my neighbor, *Mr.* Garofolo

7. a policy of the ACLU

8. the speaker, Dr. Jeanne Li [*or* the speaker, Jeanne Li, Ph.D.]

9. C

10. C

Abbreviations B, p. 267

EXERCISE

1. Julio needs to leave for school by ~~eight~~ [8:00] A.M. today.

2. The recipe calls for ~~2 tsp~~ [two teaspoons] of olive oil.

3. C

4. In the ~~A.D. first century~~ [first century A.D.], when Romans occupied Britain, London was already an important town.

5. When Mr. and Ms. Appelbaum lived in the ~~U.S.~~ *United States*, they visited eight national parks.

6. In 51 ~~b.c.~~ *B.C.*, when Cleopatra was about seventeen years old, she succeeded to the throne of Egypt with her brother Ptolemy XIII.

7. The Juárez family lived at 260 Mesquite ~~Ave.~~ *Avenue* in Phoenix, ~~Ariz.~~ *Arizona*, for ten years.

8. The experiment requires ~~3~~ *three* milliliters of boric acid.

9. Only two of the five states you mentioned are west of the Mississippi River: ~~ND~~ *North Dakota* and ~~NV~~ *Nevada*.

10. *C* [or *New York*]

Titles and Abbreviations Review, p. 268

EXERCISE

1. E. B. White, author of *Charlotte's Web*

2. my great-uncle Norbert

3. the MTV channel

4. our good friend, Mr. Lepage

5. *C*

6. the house at 601 East Republic Street

7. found in the unit titled "A World at War"

8. Barbara Eastman, Ph.D.

9. lacking five cups of sugar

10. the recently released CD, *Love in Winter*

11. *C*

12. an appointment with Dr. Kelly Thomas [or Kelly Thomas, M.D.]

13. by 3:00 P.M.

14. an interview with Senator Hutchinson

15. *C*

16. the former Speaker of the House Sam Rayburn

17. the daily newspaper *USA Today*

18. the Shakespearean play *As You Like It*

19. jobs at the IRS

20. *C*

Review A: Capitalization, p. 269

EXERCISE

1. B	**11.** N
2. N	**12.** B
3. A	**13.** B
4. A	**14.** B
5. A	**15.** N
6. N	**16.** B
7. N	**17.** B
8. B	**18.** A
9. A	**19.** B
10. A	**20.** A

Review B: Capitalization, p. 270

EXERCISE

1. Last ~~S~~summer Ricardo became ~~C~~captain of the school's basketball team, the Reagan ~~R~~rockets.

2. In 1900, the Standard Oil ~~c~~company held virtually a monopoly position in the petroleum-refining industry of the ~~U.S.~~ *United States*.

3. According to family tradition, my mother, an English ~~S~~scientist, calls our dog *Dig*: ~~t~~The dog likes to "~~D~~dig for gold" in our yard.

4. One of the oldest known handbooks on ~~M~~mathematics is an Egyptian papyrus scroll dating from about 1700 B.C.

5. *C*

6. The Greek ~~G~~gods supposedly dwelt on the peaks of Olympus, a mountain range in the ~~C~~central part of Greece.

7. Today's assignment in ~~h~~History IV is to read Chapter 11, "The Beginning ~~Of The~~ *of the* Industrial Revolution," in *History ~~I~~in Perspective*.

8. Candace, ~~Prof.~~ *Professor* Donatello told us that the correct answer was "2 tsp." [or two teaspoons]

9. Please send this ~~v.c.r.~~ *VCR* to 88 Forty-~~Fifth~~ *Street* ~~St.~~ in Terre Haute, ~~IN~~ *Indiana*.

10. The point is, the ~~k~~*K*oran has been sacred to Muslims for many centuries.

11. You can take ~~l~~*L*atin or one of three ~~M~~*m*odern ~~L~~*l*anguages at our ~~H~~*h*igh ~~S~~*s*chool.

12. Turn left, or ~~E~~*e*ast, on Central ~~ave.~~ *Avenue*.

13. Should the closing be "~~s~~*S*incerely" or "~~v~~*V*ery truly yours"?

14. Please get some tape when you go to ~~e~~*E*dam's ~~c~~*C*orner ~~s~~*S*tore.

15. Which planet, Jupiter or Saturn, has more ~~M~~*m*oons?

16. The important question is, ~~w~~*W*hat do we do now?

17. Right this minute, ~~i~~*I*'d like to be on an island somewhere in the Caribbean ~~s~~*S*ea.

18. When my ~~M~~*m*om and ~~D~~*d*ad were young, school didn't start until after Labor ~~d~~*D*ay.

19. We'll stop at ~~Nasa~~*NASA*'s Johnson Space ~~Ctr.~~ *Center* on our way to the ~~g~~*G*ulf ~~c~~*C*oast.

20. Gina heard him say he was "~~D~~*d*eathly afraid of roller coasters."

Review C: Capitalization, p. 271

EXERCISE A

[1] ~~d~~*D*ear ~~m~~*M*auricio,

[2] Here I am, back on dry land, sorely missing the Pacific ~~o~~*O*cean and wishing I were still about 3,000 ~~mi~~ *miles* ~~W~~*w*est of Reno. [3] Now ~~i~~*I* understand why you told me you would give the ~~M~~*m*oon and stars to be able to move back to the ~~I~~*i*sland of Kauai—its beauty is the stuff of dreams.

[4] We landed at Hanamaulu at 2:00 P.M. on a ~~Thurs.~~ *Thursday*, and the fun didn't stop until we left ten days later. [5] ~~w~~*W*e hiked across lava flows, visited the Waikiki ~~a~~*A*quarium in Honolulu, and saw waterfalls in Puaa Kaa ~~state park~~ *State Park* on Maui. [6] We also spent time at the ~~polynesian cultural center~~ *Polynesian Cultural Center* on Oahu. [7] We went to a *luau*—it's a ~~h~~*H*awaiian feast—where I watched people dancing the *hula*. [8] (Did you know that the *hula* used to be performed not only for entertainment, but also as a ~~R~~*r*eligious exercise to honor the goddess ~~l~~*L*aka?) [9] We spent our final day on Oahu so that my ~~D~~*d*ad could take us to the USS *Arizona* ~~m~~*M*emorial at Pearl Harbor.

[10] The question I leave you with is, ~~h~~*H*ow are you and I going to save enough money so that we can go to Hawaii together the day after we graduate from ~~H~~*h*igh ~~S~~*s*chool?

EXERCISE B

11. tour the ~~H~~*h*eadquarters of the ~~Fbi~~ *FBI*

12. well-known ~~n~~*N*orse myths

13. New Year's ~~d~~*D*ay holiday

14. ~~t~~*T*he company name is Neville & ~~assoc.~~ *Associates*

15. Theodore Roethke's poem "The ~~f~~*F*ar ~~f~~*F*ield"

16. at the intersection of Broad ~~ave.~~ *Avenue* and Fifty-Sixth ~~St.~~ *Street*

17. to meet us in, ~~O~~*o*h, ten ~~min.~~ *minutes*

18. near the ~~L~~*l*ake on the ~~W~~*w*est side of town

19. ~~d~~*D*ear ~~prof.~~ *Professor* Barrientos:

20. one of my favorite Mexican ~~R~~*r*estaurants

Proofreading Application: Announcement, p. 272

To all students of Three Rivers ~~high school~~ *High School*:

If you have ever said, "~~history~~ *History* is boring!" you're going to love the field trip that the

History teachers have planned for the weekend of april 27–28. You'll return on sunday with a very different perspective of the civil rights movement of the 1960's.

Our destination is the 54-mile Selma to Montgomery National Historic Trail, created in 1996 by the national park service to commemorate a historic march. On March 21, 1965, more than 3,000 people, the reverend Martin Luther King, jr., nobel peace prize winner Ralph Bunche, and rabbi Abraham Heschel set out from Brown Chapel African Methodist Episcopal church in Selma. They wanted to bring attention to their efforts to end segregation and to secure their voting rights in the south. The following Summer, congress passed the Voting Rights Act, which guaranteed all americans over 21—including african americans—the right to register and vote.

Buses will leave the Nola b. Walker community center at 8:00 A.M. and arrive in Selma around 10:00. we'll stop along highway 80 at points of interest, spend Saturday night in Montgomery, and return about 4:00 on Sunday.

This fascinating field trip is guaranteed to make history come alive for you!

Literary Model: Capitalization in Poetry, pp. 273–74

EXERCISE A

1. Capitalize the first and last words and all important words in titles and subtitles. For example, in the title of Gray's poem, the words *Elegy*, *Written*, *Country*, and *Churchyard* are capitalized. *In* and *a* are not capitalized because they are not important words.

2. Capitalize the first word in a line of poetry. Examples in Gray's poem include *Here*, *A*, *Fair*, and *And*.

3. Capitalize the pronoun *I*. Wordsworth capitalizes *I* in the first, fourth, fifth, and eighth lines of his poem.

4. Capitalize a word referring to a personified entity. Examples in Gray's poem are *Earth*, *Fortune*, *Fame*, *Science*, and *Melancholy*.

EXERCISE B
Responses may vary. A sample response is given.

1. The personified entities perform human actions. For example, Melancholy "marked" the subject of the epitaph "for her own."

2. He causes readers to see *Child* as representing all children or the concept of *child*. Similarly, *Man* represents adult humans in general.

3. The reader might wonder, What child and what man is he talking about? The meaning could be confusing since no child or man was introduced.

EXERCISE C
Responses will vary. A sample response is given.

Pledge to My Future

To my friends I will be Loyal;
To my ideals I will be True.
I'll welcome Dreams as blessings
And Future as my friend,
And Music will surge through my veins.

EXERCISE D
Responses will vary. Sample responses are given.

1. My writing included fewer references to nature—none, in fact. When I thought of the important pledges I could make, nature did not occur to me. Instead, friends, the future, and my goals and dreams came to mind.

2. Poets may see the end of youth as the end of an important era; therefore, they try to capture the beauty and purity of childhood in a poem, and they use personification to show the importance of certain ideals and concepts. Poems on other topics may tell a story or present a conversation in which personification would only be confusing. Regular punctuation would be needed for the story or dialogue.

Writing Application: Travel Itinerary, p. 275

Writing Applications are designed to provide students immediate composition practice in using key concepts taught in each chapter of the *Language and Sentence Skills Practice* booklet. You may wish to evaluate student responses to these assignments as you do any other writing that students produce. To save grading time, however, you may want to use the following scoring rubric.

Scoring Rubric

Specific travel information is included in the itinerary.

   1   2   3   4   5

Proper nouns and adjectives are capitalized.

   1   2   3   4   5

Format is clear; information is easy to locate.

   1   2   3   4   5

The assignment is relatively free of errors in spelling and punctuation.

   1   2   3   4   5

Total Score _____

5 = highest; 1 = lowest

Chapter 13: Punctuation, pp. 276–97

Choices: Exploring Punctuation, p. 276

Choices activities are designed to extend and enrich students' understanding of grammar, usage, and mechanics and to take learners beyond traditional classroom instruction. To use the Choices worksheet, have each student pick an activity that interests him or her. In some cases, you may wish to assign an activity to a particular student or group of students. You may also want to request that students get your approval for the activities they choose. Establish guidelines for what constitutes successful completion of an activity. Then, help students plan how they will share their work with the rest of the class.

Choices activities can be scored with a pass-fail grade or treated as bonus-point projects. Those activities that require students to research or create a certain number of items might be graded in a traditional manner.

Using End Marks, p. 277

EXERCISE A

1. *Q*—Have you ever read Robert Frost's poem "Fire and Ice"**?**

2. *S*—Unable to open the door, Sofia called loudly for help**.**

3. *C*—Watch out, Tony**!**

4. *R*—Please read JoBeth Hall's column**.**

5. *E*—What an incredible catch he made**!**

EXERCISE B   *Some answers may vary.*

"I've been working on this comic strip for hours**!**" she exclaimed**.** She glanced at the clock**.** Yikes**!** How could it already be 4:30**?** The strip was due to the paper by 5:00**.** Becca knew that all she needed was a good punchline**.** How could she come up with a good idea**?** "I know," she thought. "I'll just have the dog slip on a banana peel**!**" She giggled**.**

Abbreviations A, p. 278

EXERCISE A

1. Was W**.** E**.** B**.** Du Bois an early civil rights leader?

2. Now that I've graduated, I sign my name "Jayson Byars, M**.** Ed."

3. Address your letter of thanks to Mr**.** and Mrs**.** Tsao.

4. The students rose and applauded when Sen**.** Brenda Gomez was introduced.

5. Have you read any of D**.** H**.** Lawrence's works?

EXERCISE B

6. Dr. Shawna Brown [*or* Shawna Brown, M.D.]

7. Pres. Les Simont

8. T. Mays, Jr.

9. Sra. Carlotta Sanchez

10. Prof. Jon Katz

Abbreviations B, p. 279

EXERCISE

Answers will vary. Sample responses are given.

1. 1572 Madison Ave.
   Atlanta, GA 44229

2. River Valley High School
   929 Academic Ln.
   Cincinnati, OH 77477

3. North Methodist Hospital
   247 Emergency St.
   Memphis, TN 38114

4. Hit Records Store
   1295 Compact Disc Dr.
   Lexington, KY 40502

5. MADD
   1456 Anderson Rd.
   Chicago, IL 57592

Abbreviations C, p. 280

EXERCISE A

1. 16 ft by 12 ft

2. Mon., Oct. 12

3. Fri. at 8:30 A.M.

4. 100 lbs

5. 2 doz

6. 5:00 P.M.

7. 3 ft, 5 in. wide by 4 ft, 2 in. long

8. tsp

9. 19th century A.D.

10. 15 mph

Some answers may vary.

11. The ingredients for a grilled cheese sandwich are two slices of bread, one slice of cheese, one teaspoon of butter, and one tablespoon of mayonnaise.

12. Spread one tablespoon of mayonnaise on the inside of a slice of bread, and top with cheese.

13. Heat the griddle with one teaspoon of butter.

14. Grill the sandwich at 250 degrees centigrade for two minutes on each side.

15. Serve the sandwich with eight ounces of cold milk.

Abbreviations D, p. 281

EXERCISE A

1. 2 ft, 3 in.
2. 2:00 P.M. on Mon., Nov. 2
3. Mr. Joseph Chen
4. A.D. 2003
5. Sen. Kata Rodriguez
6. 10:00 A.M., Sun., Apr. 1
7. Prof. Kyle Mannon
8. 8 sq km
9. Dr. Martin Luther King, Jr.
10. Oak St. and Maple Ave.

EXERCISE B

11. Dr. Angela Mehran
12. 2:00 P.M.
13. Robert E. Lee Middle School [Accept other reasonable answers.]
14. SPCA
15. 15 mph

End Marks and Abbreviations, p. 282

EXERCISE

1. When my little sister turned four, I agreed to help plan her birthday party. ___C___

2. After all, what could be so difficult about having three little friends over for cake and ice cream? ___C___

3. Two wks before the party, we bought all the supplies at the grocery store on Main St. ___weeks, Street___

4. The day before the party, which was scheduled for Sat, we picked up the brightly iced cake that read, "Happy Birthday to Our Big Girl." ___Saturday___

5. My little sister was thrilled when her three friends arrived with presents. ___C___

6. They came at 9:00 A.M., and that's when the trouble started. ___C___

7. We had bought cartoon trading cards for party favors, even though we knew that Rafe Miller, M.D., our pediatrician, thinks they are not good toys for little kids. ___C___

8. We found out why when one kid began to cry because his card pack was missing his favorite character, Squirrely Squirrel, Junior. ___Jr.___

9. Sounds of crying and yelling could probably be heard all the way to the state of WA. ___Washington___

10. Just then, my sister surprised me by saying, "Here, KC, you can have my Squirrely." ___K. C.___

Commas A, p. 283

EXERCISE A

Optional commas are underlined.

1. In early spring, daffodils, irises, tulips, and crocuses bloom.

2. Did Bob, Rafael, or Bart start as quarterback after the half?

3. C

4. I like Renee because she is such a dependable, sensitive person.

5. Vermont has green, rolling valleys and lofty, pine-crested mountains.

6. I have visited Mississippi, Louisiana, and New Mexico.

7. He cooked me chicken fajitas with jalapeño peppers, nopales, and avocado.

8. Prague was a graceful, pastel city.

9. Ahmed, Sheryl, Fred, and Suzi went to the library; but Harriet, Kate, and Jim ran.

10. My dog, Daisy, is brown, black, and white.

EXERCISE B
Optional commas are underlined.

[11] Lillie Patterson has worked as a teacher, librarian, and children's author. [12] As a child, Patterson lived with her grandmother in South Carolina. [13] Her grandmother was an interesting, well-read person, who instilled in Patterson her early love for books. [14] Patterson has written biographies, poems, and non-fiction articles for children. [15] The subjects of her biographies have included Frederick Douglass, Booker T. Washington, and Dr. Martin Luther King, Jr.

Commas B, p. 284
EXERCISE A
1. Fire-breathing dragons never really existed, but most ancient peoples believed in them.

2. Dragons appeared in legends, and they were often portrayed as fire-breathing monsters.

3. C

4. Beowulf killed the monster Grendel, yet Beowulf was later killed by a dragon.

5. Chinese legends differ from Western ones, for in Asian cultures the dragon is revered as sacred.

EXERCISE B
Some answers may vary.
6. We planned a picnic, but it rained.

7. Shawndra practiced her speech, and she felt confident.

8. I may go to Tulane or Ohio State next year.

9. We'll wait for you at the theater, so don't be late.

10. I thought we would make it to the game on time, but the traffic was terrible.

Commas C, p. 285
EXERCISE
1. Only dogs that are on leashes are allowed in the park.

2. Theseus, who was a figure in Greek myths, battled the Minotaur.

3. All people found guilty will be fined or sent to jail.

4. The playwright whom I admire the most is August Wilson.

5. All trains using Track 4 will be slightly delayed.

6. Dr. Kyoshi is the only man I know who likes opera as much as I do.

7. He cuts his lawn, which is full of dandelions, only once a month.

8. I recently spoke to a woman who had lived for two years in Taiwan.

9. The bread that we brought to the dinner party was fresh and hot.

10. Fifteen flags, rippling in the breeze, could be seen from the hilltop.

11. Samantha, whom I've known since we were both two, is my best friend.

12. I've always liked people who are considered eccentric.

13. The island that was covered with poppies was called Delos.

14. My dog is the one splashing in the mud puddle.

15. South Indian food, which is sometimes served on a banana leaf, is delicious. *(N over "which is sometimes")*

16. The man wearing the hat gave up his seat on the bus for the elderly woman. *(E over "wearing")*

17. My little sister, crowing like a rooster, woke the guests. *(N over "crowing like a rooster")*

18. The girl wearing the fedora wandered along the sidewalk. *(E over "wearing")*

19. My father, who was Hungarian, taught me to cook. *(N over "who was Hungarian")*

20. The performance that I enjoyed the most involved break dancing. *(E over "that I enjoyed the most")*

Commas D, p. 286
EXERCISE A
1. Walking as fast as possible, we reached the store just before it closed.
2. In the scene at the end of *Casablanca*, Rick says goodbye to Ilsa.
3. C
4. C
5. Often mistaken for Mel Gibson, my uncle Pierre is really handsome.
6. Whenever I see an old Fred Astaire film, I regain my interest in dancing.
7. Why, let's take dancing lessons together.
8. No, I really have neither the time nor the talent.
9. At the corner of Fourteenth Street and Broad Street, you'll see a beautiful fountain.
10. When Principal Carson retired, my uncle took over the job.

EXERCISE B
Sentences will vary. Sample responses are given.
11. Well, I don't think the test is tomorrow.
12. Because I enjoy adventure movies, we went to see the latest Jackie Chan film.
13. At the top of the hill behind the school, we set up the decorations for the school fair.
14. While sitting in the restaurant, we decided that we would spend the afternoon in the park.

15. In June, I will be a bridesmaid in my sister's wedding.

Commas E, p. 287
EXERCISE A
1. Michael Jordan will be remembered, I am sure, as a great basketball player.
2. Joseph, right now I don't have time to play catch.
3. C
4. Edmund Spenser, an Elizabethan poet, wrote *The Faerie Queene*.
5. C
6. The character's name was Indiana Jones, not Oklahoma Jones!
7. Tawny's cousin, a freshman, just joined a fraternity at Arizona State.
8. Nikki, have you got any ideas that you'd like to share with us?
9. Alfred Nobel, the man who established the Nobel Prize, was a scientist.
10. Nobel, by the way, was the person who invented dynamite.

EXERCISE B
Sentences will vary. Sample responses are given.
11. I didn't want to attend the science fair; nevertheless, I did.
12. I studied very hard for the math test; however, it wasn't difficult.
13. Jamie wanted, as if it mattered, to go to the concert.
14. I thought John was the winner of the talent contest; in fact, it was Samantha.
15. James had the highest grade in the class, naturally.

Commas F, p. 288
EXERCISE
1. advisor,
2. table,
3. smiled,
4. Yes,
5. thirteenth,
6. summers,
7. class,
8. cool,
9. said,
10. bland,

Commas G, p. 289

EXERCISE A

1. Rafael's address is 13 Henry Avenue, Akron, OH 44301.
2. On August 9, 1934, my grandfather was born in San Juan, Puerto Rico.
3. Marissa Valdez, Ph.D., will be our guest on the fifth of October.
4. Harold P. Levinson, Jr., opened a law office at 5 Dale Street in Ames, Iowa.
5. *C*

EXERCISE B

Dear Mr. Roosevelt:

On August 24, 2003, I will be leaving to attend Ohio State University. Therefore, I will be terminating my employment at Bob's Diner as of August 22. I look forward to working for you again during my winter vacation, which begins on December 15. Meanwhile, please send my final paycheck to Box 1415, Ohio State University, Columbus, OH 43212.

Sincerely,

Eugene Goldstein, Jr.

Commas H, p. 290

EXERCISE

1. Jim and Pedro sat enthralled during the long, exciting basketball game.
2. I drove to the lake with my sister, and several of her friends soon joined us there.
3. Mr. Haynes, who was once a professional baseball player, gave us some tips about hitting and fielding.
4. On April 6, 1917, the United States entered World War I.
5. By the way, did you know that the Robertsons have moved to Palo Alto, California?
6. Sacagawea, the famous interpreter and explorer, was a Shoshone.

7. The reporters, many of whom had covered the trial from the very first day, said that the defense lawyers had handled the case extremely well.
8. As soon as Alaqua arrived in Seattle, she called her parents, who had been waiting anxiously to hear from her.
9. *C*
10. Ambassador Williams, returning from her successful mission, was met at the airport by a crowd of reporters and press photographers.

Review A: End Marks and Abbreviations, p. 291

EXERCISE *Some answers may vary.*

1. *Q*—Are you satisfied with your hiking boots?
2. *C*—Stay in your seats.
3. *R*—Please order me a sandwich when our server comes.
4. *S*—I decided to take tae kwon do next year at our YMCA.
5. *S*—All papers must have bibliographies.
6. *S*—All the world's a stage.
7. *Q*—Have you ever read T. S. Eliot's poem "The Hollow Men"?
8. *E*—Your car is rolling into the river!
9. *Q*—What time is it?
10. *R*—As soon as you have a chance, read Anna Quindlen's column in *Newsweek* called "The Last Word."
11. *C*—Stop that dog fight!
12. *Q*—May I answer that question?
13. *C*—Drive carefully.
14. *S*—I'd like to invite Uncle Rafael to my graduation.

Language and Sentence Skills Practice Answer Key

15. Q—Didn't Carolyn Kizer write the poem "The Ungrateful Garden"?

16. Q—What did Elsa have in mind when she said that?

17. R—Please walk down to the corner store for a loaf of bread.

18. S—The British poet Alfred Tennyson wrote "The Kraken."

19. Q—Do you want to walk to the concert with me?

20. E—What a fantastic singer Leontyne Price is!

Review B: Commas, p. 292

1. Writing letters to the editor is one of my favorite activities.

2. Yes, if you are sure you want to enroll in the program, Bernie, by all means do so.

3. C

4. Emma Lazarus, who wrote the sonnet engraved on the pedestal of the Statue of Liberty, was born in New York City.

5. The miners carried picks, shovels, and pans along the banks of the creek where gold had been discovered, Lost Creek.

6. C

7. No one in the band, it seemed to me, had ever played better than on that gray, cold day.

8. Listening to the news on the radio, I failed to notice that my cousin had left the house.

9. C

10. Viewers who enjoy sitcoms will like the series that features a Martian running a diner.

11. When the cold, lonely winter evenings came, we would huddle near the fireplace.

12. The surgeon's face showed no emotion, but she felt anxious as she performed the operation.

13. "How would you like to go to the game with me tomorrow?" she asked, taking me by surprise.

14. C

15. On the contrary, the first attempts to improve farming techniques yielded few positive results.

Review C: End Marks and Commas, p. 293

Optional commas are underlined.

1. All school buses needing repairs will be out of service next week.

2. That song was sung by either Nancy Wilson or Natalie Cole.

3. No, I never heard Billie Holiday sing; was she good, Clive?

4. Sitting on that rickety chair, I felt very nervous.

5. I like films starring Humphrey Bogart, so I know I'd enjoy *The African Queen*.

6. Isn't George P. Steiner, Sr., the comptroller of Baldwin Corp.?

7. Is Emilio R. Gustavo, Jr., still a corporate attorney with Ames, Johnson, & Co.?

8. Before he could say another word, the doorbell rang.

9. I went swimming in the ocean, visited Hal, and played soccer.

10. The Dixtro Co. opened an office at 4 Rikes Blvd., Chicago, IL 60606.

11. We walked on the beach, collected some shells, and had a long, pleasant talk.

12. Dave Barry, once a staffer for a local news-paper, became a syndicated columnist.

13. "Is writing a newspaper column challeng-ing?" wondered Pat.

14. On Saturday, June 6, 1992, my sister moved to Chester County in Pennsylvania.

15. Are you sure that a flowered, bright-red scarf will go with this dress?

16. Well, look at the picture and try to find me.

17. People who don't bother to vote shouldn't complain about the outcome of the election.

18. Working hard should help you achieve the goals that you have set for yourself.

19. "After you're finished with your chores, do you want to go to a movie, Bill?"

20. Neither the coach nor the players are happy.

Proofreading Application: Business Letter, p. 294

Dr. Rodrigo Espinosa

University of the Americas

1200 Sedona Parkway

Phoenix, AZ 85082

Dear Dr. Espinosa:

Last spring I spent three exciting, fabulous days exploring the ruins of Chichén Itzá, in Mexico's Yucatán Peninsula. Inspired by this experience, I have chosen the Mayas as the topic for my research project in world history. Since you are a renowned expert on the Mayas, Ms. Garza, my history teacher, suggested that I write to you to reques information about the history of this indigenous people. In particular, do you have any material concerning the theories of why Chichén Itzá, the most important city of the Mayas, was abandoned around A.D. 670?

Dr. Espinosa, thank you in advance for your time and attention to this matter.

Sincerely,

Guadalupe Martinez

Literary Model: End Punctuation in a History, pp. 295–96

EXERCISE A *Some answers may vary.*

The passage contains declarative, interroga-tive, and exclamatory sentences.

sentence 1: declarative

sentence 2: interrogative

sentence 3: exclamatory

sentence 4: declarative

sentence 5: interrogative

sentence 6: exclamatory

EXERCISE B

Answers will vary. A sample response is given.

The use of different sentence types conveys emotion and tone. Exclamatory and interroga-tive sentences re-create the thoughts of the peo-ple who were actually involved in the revolu-tion. Using only declarative sentences would make the passage dull.

EXERCISE C

Answers will vary. A sample response is given.

It was the last ten seconds of the state cham-pionship game. The score was 42 to 42, and our team, the Bradford Bears, was at the free-throw line. Would we win the game? We waited breathlessly as James took the shot. "Go, James, go!" the crowd cheered. "Please, make the shot," I said to myself. The ball rattled into the basket. He scored! The Bradford Bears were the new champs!

EXERCISE D

Answers will vary. A sample response is given.

The paragraph would not have conveyed the anticipation and excitement of actually being at the event. Using only declarative sentences would sound more like reporting than being present at the event.

Writing Application: Letter, p. 297

Writing Applications are designed to provide students immediate composition practice in using key concepts taught in each chapter of the *Language and Sentence Skills Practice* booklet. You may wish to evaluate student responses to these assignments as you do any other writing that students produce. To save grading time, however, you may want to use the following scoring rubric.

Scoring Rubric

The letter's tone and word choice are appropriate for the audience.

   1   2   3   4   5

The letter adequately defends the choice of motto.

   1   2   3   4   5

The letter makes effective use of exclamation points.

   1   2   3   4   5

The assignment is relatively free of errors in usage and mechanics.

   1   2   3   4   5

Total Score _____

5 = highest; 1 = lowest

Chapter 14: Punctuation, pp. 298–335

Choices: Exploring Punctuation, p. 298

Choices activities are designed to extend and enrich students' understanding of grammar, usage, and mechanics and to take learners beyond traditional classroom instruction. To use the Choices worksheet, have each student pick an activity that interests him or her. In some cases, you may wish to assign an activity to a particular student or group of students. You may also want to request that students get your approval for the activities they choose. Establish guidelines for what constitutes successful completion of an activity. Then, help students plan how they will share their work with the rest of the class.

Choices activities can be scored with a pass-fail grade or treated as bonus-point projects. Those activities that require students to research or create a certain number of items might be graded in a traditional manner.

Semicolons A, p. 299

EXERCISE A

1. The wind is fierce; it sounds like a locomotive.
2. The workers were dissatisfied; therefore, they considered a strike.
3. We are eager to go on vacation; the past few weeks have been strenuous.
4. Tony has accomplished quite a lot; on the other hand, Janis hasn't.
5. Begonias thrive in the shade; marigolds need more sun.

EXERCISE B

6. We were late for the game; as a result, we missed the kickoff.
7. Jules is the yearbook editor; he also works on the school newspaper.
8. C
9. C
10. Many events have been scheduled; for example, there are two concerts coming up.

Semicolons B, p. 300

EXERCISE

1. Among the people who contributed to the book are Dr. Newman, who did the research; Ms. Lewis, who provided the photographs; and Mr. Jung, who wrote the introduction.
2. Her best friends' birth dates are December 31, 1984; February 10, 1985; and March 21, 1985.
3. He was busy raking the yard, cleaning the gutters, and pulling out items for his garage sale, which he intended to have the next Saturday; but he longed to submerge himself in a novel.
4. The members of the committee who helped the most are Sharon, who handled the publicity; Betty, who led the finance subcommittee; and Bart, who built all the booths.
5. We did not, for the most part, want to be identified with that organization, its leaders, or its cause; nor did we want to sign the petition.
6. Stan realized that spilling juice on his keyboard is, of course, what damaged his computer; that he should never, ever leave a drink sitting close to it again; and that he was lucky to find a replacement keyboard so quickly.
7. The finalists were from Grand View, Idaho; Big Horn, Wyoming; and Sunburst, Montana.
8. On her day off, she had plans to take a cooking course, visit a friend, and tutor a third-grade student; and after all that, she might take in a movie.
9. In 1992, the candidates vying for president were George Herbert Walker Bush, who was the current president; William Jefferson Clinton, who was the governor of Arkansas; and Ross Perot, who had never held public office.
10. We hope to visit Lexington, Charlottesville, and Harrisonburg, Virginia; and if we have any time remaining, we would like to drive on to Gettysburg, Pennsylvania.

Semicolons Review, p. 301

EXERCISE

1. Her grandparents had their first date on September 5, 1945; became engaged on February 14, 1947; and were married on June 28, 1952.

2. Some people can play musical instruments by ear without formal training; others need years of lessons and practice to play an instrument well.

3. He started first grade in Waycross, Georgia; attended junior high in Thomasville, Georgia; finished high school in Macon, Georgia; and ended up in Memphis, Tennessee, for college.

4. Sandy excelled in Latin; that is, she won numerous honors.

5. He stayed up until 4 A.M.; consequently, he slept through his 7 A.M. alarm.

6. Irving Berlin composed hundreds of songs, including "God Bless America," "Easter Parade," and "Always"; but "White Christmas" may be his best-known song.

7. I must answer his letter straightaway; otherwise, I'm afraid that I will forget.

8. Forty years ago, Jane broke her arm by falling off a horse; this time she lost her balance on some steps.

9. Bonnie designs most of her clothes; for example, she sewed the lovely coat and dress that she wore Sunday.

10. *C*

Colons A, p. 302

EXERCISE

1. Hikers need the following: sturdy boots, light clothing, and waterproof jackets.

2. The actor gave me this advice: Learn your lines, be on time, and don't get emotional.

3. *C*

4. The protests had a positive effect: They grabbed the governor's attention.

5. President Franklin D. Roosevelt issued his famous statement about fear in his first inaugural address: "So, first of all, let me assert my firm belief that the only thing we have to fear is fear itself. . . ."

6. The ballet troupe will perform in the following cities: New York, Chicago, and London.

7. These words are from Eleanor Roosevelt's first autobiography: "No one can make you feel inferior without your consent."

8. There is one thing I am sure about now: At that point in my life, I should not have let my friends influence me so much.

9. Stella has two annoying habits: entering my room without knocking and borrowing my things without asking.

10. We have no school on these holidays: New Year's Day, Martin Luther King Day, Presidents' Day, and Memorial Day.

Colons B, p. 303

EXERCISE

1. Both Matthew 6:28 and Luke 12:27 refer to the lilies of the field.

2. The letter began, "Dear Sir or Madam: I am writing on behalf of my son."

3. She intends to be ready by 8:30 in the morning.

4. He would like to depart by 7:15 tomorrow evening.

5. My paper was titled "The Rain Forest: Harvest of Shame."

6. Their flight left on time at 7:12 A.M.

7. Her father often quoted Micah 6:8.

8. In theory, I should be at my desk by 8:15.

9. You should take the 3:32 train to Columbus, where you will catch the 5:07 to Dayton.

10. The imagery in Isaiah 11:6 always intrigued her.

11. He decided to name his paper "Satchmo: Musical Shaper of the Twentieth Century."

12. Jamie's letter began, "Dear Mr. Clark: Please find enclosed two copies of my résumé."

13. Worship began with a congregational reading of Psalms 96:1–6.

14. I arrived at 7:37, about five minutes after the movie began.

15. I enjoyed the article "Cats: Can They Be Trained?"

16. Her friends asked her to read I Corinthians 13:1–13 at their wedding.

17. The invitation says that the brunch is to begin at 10:30.

18. The lyrics of that song are taken from Ecclesiastes 3:1–8.

19. One of the albums she received for her birthday was Wynton Marsalis' *Standard Time, Vol. 5: The Midnight Blues*.

20. I promised that I would be prompt for our 12:45 lunch date.

Semicolons and Colons, p. 304

EXERCISE A

1. Sharon's alarm is set for 6:30 A.M.

2. Most tickets for the event are sold out; however, there is a waiting list for remaining seats.

3. Eight pounds, three ounces; seven pounds, four ounces; and eleven pounds, four ounces are the current weights of my cats.

4. The following items are required at this course: spikeless golf shoes, collared shirts, and one set of clubs per player.

5. The living room carpet has been vacuumed; the kitchen floor is being scrubbed right now.

EXERCISE B

Dear Mr. Livingston:

We have checked into connecting flights for you through the following cities: Birmingham, Alabama; Jackson, Mississippi; New Orleans, Louisiana; and Houston, Texas. The flight that seems to suit your schedule best is the one that departs Houston at 9:05 A.M. and arrives in Dallas at 9:55 A.M. (You would need to be at the airport no later than 8:15.)

We would like to know if this is agreeable with you; otherwise, we will examine the remaining flight options. One thing is certain: We need to make your reservation soon in order to secure a low fare.

Very truly yours,

Tim Horne

Italics (Underlining) A, p. 305

EXERCISE

1. South Pacific; Carousel

2. 60 Minutes

3. Evening Bulletin

4. American Gothic

5. Peanuts

6. The New Yorker; Talk

7. Aida

8. All Things Considered

9. Frequency

10. Friends

11. A Lesson Before Dying

12. Twelfth Night

13. Myst; Riven

14. Good Housekeeping

15. Gone with the Wind

16. The Birthday

17. John Brown's Body

18. La Bamba

19. The Bridge of San Luis Rey

20. George

Italics (Underlining) B, p. 306
EXERCISE

1. <u>California Zephyr</u>
2. <u>shlemil</u>
3. <u>affect</u>; <u>effect</u>
4. <u>Titanic</u>
5. <u>v</u>; <u>f</u>; <u>w</u>; <u>v</u>
6. <u>et cetera</u>; <u>etc.</u>
7. <u>Flyer</u>
8. <u>Semper fidelis</u>
9. <u>Veni</u>; <u>vidi</u>; <u>vici</u>
10. <u>Rapido</u>

Italics (Underlining) Review, p. 307
EXERCISE

1. <u>SS</u>; <u>HMS</u>
2. <u>The Washington Post</u>
3. <u>Challenger</u>
4. <u>ex animo</u>
5. <u>vacuum</u>; <u>c</u> ; <u>u</u>
6. <u>Sense and Sensibility</u>
7. <u>People</u>
8. <u>Hurricane, Bahamas</u>
9. <u>Doonesbury</u>
10. <u>The Women</u>

Quotation Marks A, p. 308
EXERCISE

1. I describe my aunt Luna by saying, "Her words are candy, but her actions are cod liver oil."
2. Teresa hollered across the yard, "Have you seen my car keys?"
3. He ran down the street yelling, "Wait for me!"
4. "The first step in cooking ratatouille," my teacher said, "is to clean and salt the eggplant."
5. Who said, "Beauty seen is never lost"?

6. Clare warned, "If you keep eating, you'll ruin your supper"; she sounded like my mother.
7. Colleen stopped me to inquire, "When have you heard from Ken?"
8. "If you ask me," Ned asserted, "that board is too thick to use for your shelves."
9. The poem begins, "Who has seen the wind?"
10. He shouted his admonition: "Don't put your fingers near the fan!"

Quotation Marks B, p. 309
EXERCISE A

[1] The Greek philosopher Diogenes the Cynic lived in a huge barrel. [2] One day, Alexander the Great peered in to see the great philosopher. [3] "Is there anything that I can do for you?" Alexander asked. [4] ¶ "Yes," answered Diogenes. [5] "I'd like you to stop blocking my light."

EXERCISE B

[6] The call came into Woodhaven Fire Station at 9:07. Firefighters reacted immediately and were at the McAllister residence within four minutes. [7] "That's an unusually quick response time considering there are still some patches of ice on the streets, but when you hear someone say, 'There's smoke pouring out of my attic,' it's an incentive," stated Chief Grant Hughes. [8] ¶ "I have nothing but praise for the local firefighters," offered Ed McAllister. [9] "Not only did they save my house, they rescued our family's dog." [10] ¶ Chief Hughes smiled modestly and shrugged.

Quotation Marks C, p. 310
EXERCISE

1. Thurber's short story "The Night the Bed Fell" is very funny.
2. Is Chapter 3 of *Winter Tales* called "Up the Creek"?

3. The title of my essay is "What Is the Point of Arguing?"

4. The Sanskrit word *ahimsa* means "reverence for life; a principle of nonviolence."

5. He told me of a BBC Radio 2 program on a jazz composer; specifically, he mentioned the episode "The Romance and the Reality."

6. Your assignment is to read the excerpt from Emerson's essay titled "Nature."

7. For years, people incorrectly coined the word *prioritize*, but it is now in the dictionary, meaning "to arrange (items) in order of priority."

8. He compared the grimness of his relatives' house to the House of Usher, referring, of course, to Poe's short story "The Fall of the House of Usher."

9. Rebecca's pet peeve is the conversion of nouns to verbs; for example, she really dislikes hearing anyone say "partnering."

10. Stephen decided to memorize "The Road Not Taken," a poem by Robert Frost.

Quotation Marks Review, p. 311

Exercise

1. Sherry inquired, "Have you read the story 'The Open Window'?"

2. Emily Dickinson's "Success is counted sweetest" is one of Ellen's favorite poems.

3. "*Arizona* means 'little springs,'" she explained.

4. The only tough part of the interview occurred when he asked, "What do you see yourself doing in fifteen or twenty years?"

5. Halle said, "I'm sure I have some royal blue thread"; then, she proceeded to dig for it in the drawer.

6. "Please finish your paper," he pleaded, "so you can go to the movie with me."

7. He quoted from Nelson Mandela's 1994 inaugural speech: "Our deepest fear is not that we are inadequate. Our deepest fear is that we are powerful beyond measure. It is our light, not our darkness, that frightens us."

8. "Mom said, 'Not tonight,'" he reminded me with a frown.

9. "That a man can influence a woman with jewels I find 'opalling,'" he teased.

10. The last thing I remember is someone shouting, "Look out!"

Italics (Underlining) and Quotation Marks, p. 312

Exercise A

1. Yeats's poem "When You Are Old"

2. his weekly column in <u>The Washington Post</u>

3. the ship <u>Titanic</u>

4. the Gershwin tune "I've Got Rhythm"

5. Carson McCullers's play <u>The Member of the Wedding</u>

Exercise B

6. O. Henry's story "The Ransom of Red Chief" is included in the movie <u>O. Henry's Full House</u>.

7. Mr. Darcy's proposal to Elizabeth Bennet comes in Volume Two, Chapter XI of <u>Pride and Prejudice</u>; in consecutively numbered editions, however, it is in Chapter XXXIV.

8. A portion of James Baldwin's book <u>The Fire Next Time</u> first appeared in <u>The New Yorker</u> in November 1962.

9. "The Latin term <u>res ipsa loquitur</u> means 'the thing speaks for itself,'" the instructor reminded us.

10. The poem "Lucinda Matlock" is found in Edgar Lee Masters' <u>Spoon River Anthology</u>.

Ellipsis Points, p. 313

Exercise

1. "I'd like to learn to dance! . . ." she said.

2. "Open your eyes to the opportunities around you. . . . [N]ever say 'I can't.'"

3. "Donnie came over. . . . He left a note on the door."

4. "Wishes . . . can come true."

5. "Well, . . . I'm almost speechless," Ashley replied.

Apostrophes A, p. 314

EXERCISE

1. a two weeks' vacation
2. the wolves' den
3. her children's teacher
4. my niece's cat
5. Bess's home
6. the constituents' complaints
7. the amateurs' trophies
8. Jesse's agility
9. the decade's sale
10. the mice's nest
11. the sheep's coat
12. the Joneses' backyard
13. the audio's clarity
14. Achilles' heel
15. Paris's lights
16. the sun's rays
17. Keats's poems
18. the women's identities
19. her sons' gift
20. the stars' brilliance

Apostrophes B, p. 315

EXERCISE A

1. Your
2. their
3. hers
4. its
5. whose

EXERCISE B

6. Nobody else's; C
7. everyone's
8. C
9. No one's; C

10. somebody else's
11. everybody's
12. Somebody's
13. somebody else's; C
14. anybody's; whose
15. yours

Apostrophes C, p. 316

EXERCISE

1. NATO's members
2. her mother-in-law's input
3. Yvonne's, Daphne's, and my efforts
4. a week's plans
5. National Public Radio's schedule
6. Randy's and Kevin's uniforms
7. the attorney general's conference
8. three dollars' worth
9. the Boy Scout Council's fund-raiser
10. Clinton and Gore's administration

Apostrophes D, p. 317

EXERCISE A

1. lady's; ladies'
2. brother-in-law's; brothers-in-law's
3. dime's; dimes'
4. committee's; committees'
5. gentleman's; gentlemen's

EXERCISE B

6. sisters-in-law's
7. nobody else's
8. C
9. somebody's
10. C; C; C
11. week's; doctor's
12. anybody's
13. Beverly and Bob's
14. Brad's and Terry's
15. council's

Apostrophes E, p. 318

EXERCISE

1. We've
2. You're
3. there's
4. hasn't
5. can't
6. could've
7. It's
8. they're
9. He'll
10. Wasn't
11. can't
12. Who's
13. I've
14. She'd
15. haven't
16. We'll
17. That's
18. Wouldn't
19. couldn't
20. isn't

Apostrophes F, p. 319

EXERCISE

1. He's crashed two CPUs by spilling water in them.—CPU's [*or* ⊂]
2. She has lost all her photo IDs.—ID's [*or* ⊂]
3. Johnny could count by 2s but not by 3s.— 2's [*or* ⊂]; 3's [*or* ⊂]
4. They've made all As the past two years.— A's
5. The police department had issued only a few APBs.—APB's [*or* ⊂]
6. Carter knew his ABCs but got his ks and ls out of order.—ABC's [*or* ⊂]; k's; l's
7. All the members were either J.D.s or M.D.s.—J.D.'s; M.D.'s
8. They've bought two VCRs this year alone.—VCR's [*or* ⊂]
9. I have too many IOUs.—IOU's [*or* ⊂]
10. Few people like to hear *I told you so*s.—*I told you so*'s
11. How many @s appear in an e-mail address?—@'s [*or* ⊂]
12. How many TVs do you have in your house?—TV's [*or* ⊂]

13. He had used too many *therefores* in his essay.—*therefore*'s
14. Both of my cousins have B.A.s from the same university.—B.A.'s
15. Sheila revised her paper to reduce the number of *ands* and *buts*.—*and*'s; *but*'s
16. The Gs stand for "good," and the Es stand for "excellent."—G's [*or* ⊂]; E's [*or* ⊂]
17. Her extended family includes five R.N.s.— R.N.'s
18. Henry's handwritten 8s sometimes look like 0s.—8's [*or* ⊂]; 0's [*or* ⊂]
19. Spell out the word *and*; don't use &s.—&'s [*or* ⊂]
20. Don't forget to dot your *is* and cross your *ts*.—*i*'s; *t*'s

Apostrophes G, p. 320

EXERCISE

1. can't; *e*'s; *i*'s
2. We're; A's; B's
3. J.D.'s; '87
4. *no*'s; *yes*'s
5. *t*'s; *l*'s
6. '57; isn't
7. I'm; CD's [*or* ⊂]
8. She'd; M.A.'s
9. *hello*'s
10. *uh*'s

Apostrophes Review, p. 321

EXERCISE A

1. woman's; women's
2. father-in-law's; fathers-in-law's
3. dollar's; dollars'
4. association's; associations'
5. major general's; major generals'
6. Hughes's; Hugheses'
7. his; theirs
8. minute's; minutes'
9. kiss's; kisses'
10. cowboy's; cowboys'

11. Who's
12. D.D.S.'s
13. everybody's
14. 7's
15. two o'clock

16. Z's
17. won't
18. they've
19. 1990's [*or* '90s]
20. *p*'s and *q*'s

Hyphens A, p. 322

EXERCISE

Some dictionaries may show other hyphenations.

1. eighty-nine
2. mid-dle
3. hand-bag
4. no hyphen
5. no hyphen
6. ski-ing
7. no hyphen
8. teeny-bopper
9. no hyphen
10. sta-tion

11. con-scious
12. sci-en-tif-ic
13. no hyphen
14. feud-ing
15. twenty-five
16. set-tle-ment
17. all-purpose
18. no hyphen
19. ham-mer-ing
20. fi-nan-cial-ly

Hyphens B, p. 323

EXERCISE

1. a wooded island in the mid-Pacific
2. a four-fifths majority
3. a self-fulfilling prophecy
4. *C*
5. twenty senators-elect
6. a noise-free atmosphere
7. one-fourth cup of molasses
8. their great-grandmother
9. a much-admired teenager
10. an anti-European attitude
11. her ex-husband
12. all-school picnic
13. an all-American basketball player
14. *C*
15. a full-moon night
16. a half-baked idea
17. a dramatic re-creation of the event
18. a sugar-free snack

19. a well-attended banquet
20. a frost-free refrigerator

Hyphens Review, p. 324

EXERCISE A

1. pre-fix
2. suf-fix
3. T-shirt
4. go-between
5. proof-read

6. no hyphen
7. trim-ming
8. president-elect
9. no hyphen
10. re-bate

EXERCISE B

11. a two-thirds approval
12. an ex-football player
13. an anti-Irish vote
14. a self-starting approach
15. our great-grandparents
16. an anti-inflammatory medication
17. twenty-two travelers
18. a well-liked relative
19. *C*
20. a smoke-free lobby

Dashes, p. 325

EXERCISE

1. That movie—perhaps you've already seen it—is excellent.
2. Have you read his recent book—the one in paperback?
3. We should pack rain gear—tarpaulins, boots, and ponchos.
4. Please hand me the hammer and a—oh, never mind.
5. Lucille Ball had three television series—*I Love Lucy, The Lucy Show,* and *Here's Lucy.*
6. His answer—the logic of which I couldn't follow—seemed to satisfy the judges.
7. You should have no problem getting into the show—there are plenty of free tickets.
8. The point is—and you should listen closely—to make sure everyone follows instructions.

9. Some of the earliest New Orleans jazz musicians—King Oliver, Louis Armstrong, and Sidney Bechet, for instance—found fame first outside that city.

10. The author of the play—I can't recall her name—won a Pulitzer Prize.

Parentheses, p. 326
EXERCISE

1. Marilyn Bennett (do you know her?) is my lawyer.

2. Rep. Patrick Kennedy (D–Rhode Island) was head of the committee.

3. We should plan to have dinner Monday night. (Do you think your plane will arrive on time?)

4. Your win (way to go!) was extraordinary.

5. Of all the nominees (four total) I like him the best.

6. The Nile River (see map on page 620) is the longest in the world.

7. The Luces (Harry was in third grade with you) are moving next door.

8. His letter (how thrilled I was to receive it!) enclosed recent photos.

9. The photography exhibit (January 28 through May 24) contains several of his pictures.

10. Lisa Richter is in your graduating class. (It is her sister that I knew from junior high.)

Brackets, 327
EXERCISE

1. I		**6.** C	
2. C		**7.** C	
3. I		**8.**	
4. I		**9.** I	
5. I		**10.** C	

Dashes, Parentheses, and Brackets, p. 328
EXERCISE A

1. P	**4.** D [*or* P]
2. D [*or* P]	**5.** B
3. B	

EXERCISE B

6. Thomas Paine (1737–1809) wrote the pamphlet *Common Sense*.

7. Chadds Ford (in southeastern Pennsylvania) is the home of Andrew Wyeth. [*or* Chadds Ford, in Southeastern Pennsylvania, is the home of Andrew Wyeth.]

8. C

9. The speaker quoted from the poem "The Hollow Men" (T. S. Eliot [1888–1965]).

10. The Dudleys—do you know their son Jim?—plan to be there. [*or* The Dudleys (do you know their son Jim?) plan to be there.]

Review A: Using Punctuation Correctly, p. 329
EXERCISE A

1. terms:

2. Saturday;

3. scholarships: University; Stanford;

4. plans;

5. C

EXERCISE B

6. Who wrote the poem "Elegy in a Country Churchyard"?

7. "If I'd known that you were going to the party," Norris said, "I'd have offered you a ride."

8. Aldous Huxley's essay "Music at Night" appears in the anthology Adventures in English Literature.

9. Salvador announced proudly, "I've learned to play 'The Star-Spangled Banner' on the piano."

10. Daphne told me that she had seen a movie version of the play Hamlet on television.

Review B: Using Punctuation Correctly, p. 330

EXERCISE A

1. pliers;
2. hand;
3. cities;
4. test:
5. action:

EXERCISE B

6. Ralph Ellison's essay "Hidden Name and Complex Fate" is included in his book <u>Shadow and Act</u>.

7. "Is it true," she asked, "that only the anthem 'O Canada' would be sung in a World Series between Toronto and Montreal?"

8. Celeste asked whether the word <u>scissors</u> is considered singular or plural.

9. "I hope," she said, "that you read the editorial in the <u>Daily Record</u>."

10. Do you know who wrote the line "Where are the snows of yesteryear?"

Review C: Using Punctuation Correctly, p. 331

EXERCISE A

1. It was a . . . cedar tree.
2. True sympathy is . . . never condescending.
3. Tony's . . . waiting on the porch.
4. April showers . . . Bring May flowers.
5. Do you want to come hiking with us? . . . I expect that we will be back long before dark.

EXERCISE B

6. (c) a magnificently drawn picture
7. (b) Ohio River (p. 331 [Figure 1])
8. (b) He doesn't think we know.
9. (c) His remarks were pro-Italian
10. (c) a notebook that is yours

Proofreading Application: Excerpt, p. 332

Answers may vary.

What do a totem pole, the nursery rhyme "Jack and Jill," the Uncle Remus stories, the traditions of Kwanzaa (a festival observed by African Americans at the end of December), and the belief that cats have nine lives all have in common? Most of you have probably thrown up your hands and said, "I give up. What's the common element?" They are all considered folklore. Folklore materials can be categorized as follows: folk arts, folk sayings, narratives, traditions, and folk beliefs.

The word <u>folklore</u> was first suggested by an English antiquary (someone who collects and studies old objects such as relics and ancient works of art). His name was William John Thomas (1803–1885). The antiquary's suggestion eventually resulted in the new word's replacing the phrase "popular antiquities," which had been used until then.

Literary Model: Dialogue, pp. 333–34

EXERCISE A

Answers may vary.

1. Cecilia Jupe."
2. number twenty," said Mr. Gradgrind.
3. Who is that girl?"
4. as calls me Sissy, Sir
5. mustn't
6. blushing, standing up, and curtseying.
7. Mr. Gradgrind
8. Mr. Gradgrind, squarely pointing

EXERCISE B

Answers may vary.

Contractions are common in informal speech, but narratives are usually more formal.

HOLT HANDBOOK | Sixth Course

EXERCISE C

Answers will vary. A sample dialogue follows.

"What do you call that?" the man asked Lucy.

"That's the chef salad, Sir," she said, setting down the dressing server.

"And I suppose you're going to say this is romaine lettuce and not iceberg," he challenged her.

"I'm not sure what all Chef puts in there," Lucy admitted. "Was there something else you wanted, Sir?"

"Yeah, right," he sneered, "how about anything that looks remotely like the photo on the menu."

"The photo?"

"You know—a camera? Detail? Accuracy?" He began to wad up his napkin. "Accuracy? Is that a concept you understand, little lady?"

"I've heard about ladies," Lucy spoke up, "and gentlemen, too, but some days they're as hard to find in this restaurant as romaine lettuce."

EXERCISE D

Answers will vary. A sample revision follows.

Customer: "Accuracy? Is that a concept you understand, little lady?"

Lucy: "I'm not sure, Sir," Lucy stammered. "I mean, I don't know. I mean, yes, Sir."

Writing Application: Presentation, p. 335

Writing Applications are designed to provide students immediate composition practice in using key concepts taught in each chapter of the *Language and Sentence Skills Practice* booklet. You may wish to evaluate student responses to these assignments as you do any other writing that students produce. To save grading time, however, you may want to use the following scoring rubric.

Scoring Rubric

The song's title and any quoted lyrics are in quotation marks.

1   2   3   4   5

Three reasons for choosing the song are given.

1   2   3   4   5

The presentation's tone is appropriate to the writing context.

1   2   3   4   5

The assignment is relatively free of errors in usage and mechanics.

1   2   3   4   5

Total Score _____

5 = highest; 1 = lowest

Chapter 15: Spelling, pp. 336–67

Choices: Investigating Spelling, p. 336

Choices activities are designed to extend and enrich students' understanding of grammar, usage, and mechanics and to take learners beyond traditional classroom instruction. To use the Choices worksheet, have each student pick an activity that interests him or her. In some cases, you may wish to assign an activity to a particular student or group of students. You may also want to request that students get your approval for the activities they choose. Establish guidelines for what constitutes successful completion of an activity. Then, help students plan how they will share their work with the rest of the class.

Choices activities can be scored with a pass-fail grade or treated as bonus-point projects. Those activities that require students to research or create a certain number of items might be graded in a traditional manner.

Good Spelling Habits, p. 337

EXERCISE

1. The ~~acter~~ *actor* Boris Karloff was born in England in 1887.

2. In a career that spanned more than fifty years, Karloff became famous in films that repeatedly cast him as a ~~villian~~ *villain*.

3. In one of my ~~favorits~~ *favorites*, *His Majesty, the American* (1919), Karloff played the evil leader of a gang of spies.

4. In one of his final films, *The Incredible Invasion* (1968), he played a scientist ~~who's~~ *whose* body was taken over by an alien from outer space.

5. Other ~~frightning~~ *frightening* films in which Karloff appeared include *The Ghoul, The Mummy, The Raven, The Black Cat*, and *The Terror*.

6. ~~Probly~~ *Probably* the most famous of all of Karloff's screen roles was in *Frankenstein*.

7. This film, based on a ~~novell~~ *novel* by Mary Shelley, was first released in 1931.

8. Movie versions of Frankenstein have since been made many times, but Karloff was the first person to bring the role of the ~~monstor~~ *monster* to the ~~screan~~ *screen*.

9. *C*

10. Karloff also starred in some ~~humerous~~ *humorous* films that made fun of ~~tipical~~ *typical* monster movies, including *Abbott and Costello Meet the Killer: Boris Karloff*.

ie and *ei*, p. 338

EXERCISE

1. *C*

2. More than seven thousand life-size ~~soldeirs~~ *soldiers* and horses were uncovered in the burial complex of China's first emperor Qin Shihuangdi.

3. As the excavations of the warriors continued, the site grew to the size of approximately four football ~~feilds~~ *fields*.

4. Archaeologists have diligently ~~peiced~~ *pieced* together the crumbled clay figures and have re-created Shihuangdi's army.

5. By examining the terra-cotta figures, archaeologists have learned much about the ~~anceint~~ *ancient* sculpting techniques used during the emperor's time.

6. Can you ~~concieve~~ *conceive* of the amount of work involved in creating the army, which looked so terrifyingly real?

7. I ~~beleive~~ *believe* that in 1980 archaeologists found two horse-drawn, bronze chariots in a side tomb.

8. *C*

9. According to Chinese history, Shihuangdi protected the secret of his terra-cotta army by ~~feindishly~~ *fiendishly* burying alive anyone who knew about the burial complex.

10. Although the emperor was ruthless, he unified China by creating systems for writing, money, transportation, and ~~wieghts~~ *weights* and measures.

–cede, –ceed, and –sede, p. 339

EXERCISE

1. Joel was about to ~~conceed~~ *concede* defeat when his opponent suddenly faltered.

2. *C*

3. To make her kitchen wheelchair-accessible, Melba will ~~procede~~ *proceed* with her plan to lower the countertops and install tilt-out bins and roll-out shelves.

4. The school board will ~~acceed~~ *accede* to the request for additional teaching materials.

5. According to the exercise physiologist, Grandfather's heart rate while exercising should not ~~excede~~ *exceed* 145 beats per minute.

6. A picture and a biography of the author can be found on the ~~preceeding~~ *preceding* page.

7. In the 1898 Treaty of Paris, Spain granted Cuba its freedom, agreed to ~~ceed~~ *cede* Puerto Rico and Guam to the United States, and gave the Philippine Islands to the United States in exchange for $20 million.

8. Because your parents respect my judgment, let me ~~interceed~~ *intercede* on your behalf.

9. At daybreak the valley's inhabitants were relieved to discover that the floodwaters had ~~receeded~~ *receded*.

10. *C*

Prefixes, p. 340

Exercise A

1. override
2. misstate
3. hyperactive
4. reentry [*or* re-entry]
5. dislocate
6. illogical
7. antisocial
8. predate
9. misspell
10. disengage
11. disembark
12. impassive
13. refill
14. dissatisfied
15. predispose
16. refinance
17. immobilize
18. discontinue
19. misspend
20. immeasurable

Exercise B

21. To overcome her ~~irational~~ *irrational* fear of the water, Aunt May has enrolled in a swimming class.

22. Because of the weather, we were forced to ~~depplane~~ *deplane* in Pittsburgh although our destination was Chicago.

23. The Paleolithic Age is the name given to the earliest part of human ~~prehhistory~~ *prehistory*, although the period is also known as the Old Stone Age or the Ice Age.

24. For centuries, humankind has searched the globe for potions that will guarantee ~~imortality~~ *immortality*.

25. The largest human migration in modern history occurred between 1892 and 1954 when twelve million ~~imigrants~~ *immigrants* were processed at Ellis Island.

Suffixes A, p. 341

EXERCISE A

1. generally
2. leanness
3. friendly
4. truthfully
5. emptiness
6. slyly
7. swiftness
8. quickly
9. gentleness
10. joyously
11. openness
12. royally
13. woolly
14. carefully
15. steadily
16. meanness
17. cowardly
18. plainness
19. heaviness
20. busily

EXERCISE B

21. Although it is ~~socially~~ *socially* acceptable for Kuwaiti women to wear European clothes outside the house, they usually wear a traditional *dara'a*, or housecoat, once they get home.

22. Thanks to the valiant efforts of the firefighters, the small child was returned ~~safly~~ *safely* to her mother.

23. Artist Gerardo Tena ~~consistenttly~~ *consistently* wins prizes for his innovative Mata Ortiz pottery.

24. The ~~suddeness~~ *suddenness* of Rosa's arrival ruined our birthday surprise for her.

25. According to Buddhist thought, attaining ~~happyness~~ *happiness* that relates to the mind and the heart requires training.

Suffixes B, p. 342

EXERCISE A

1. housing
2. serenely
3. politeness
4. involvement
5. seizure
6. enforceable
7. lonely
8. tying [*or* tieing]
9. cringing

10. homeless
11. natural
12. accommodation
13. immediately
14. contriteness
15. definitely
16. caring
17. achievement
18. separation
19. requirement
20. advantageous

EXERCISE B

21. After ~~tasteing~~ *tasting* a Senegalese dish of fish and rice called *cheb-ou-jen*, I want to try more of the country's traditional foods.

22. The relations between the seven major ethnic groups of Senegal are, in general, ~~peacful~~ *peaceful*.

23. Since gaining its independence from France in 1960, Senegal has noticed a ~~declineing~~ *declining* economy.

24. How ~~amazeing~~ *amazing* that the Senegalese economy relies almost entirely on one export product: peanuts.

25. One of the most popular forms of ~~amusment~~ *amusement* in Senegal is storytelling, which serves as a valuable vehicle for educating the children.

Suffixes C, p. 343

EXERCISE A

1. bountiful
2. denied
3. compliance
4. industrious
5. conveyed
6. payment
7. dutiful
8. dreariness
9. decayed
10. grayest
11. cageyness
12. comedian
13. annoyed
14. relying
15. harmonious
16. funniest
17. paid
18. deployment
19. brassiness
20. laid

EXERCISE B

21. The counselor told me to check the *Occupational Outlook Handbook* for a description of various jobs, the education required for each, and ~~emploiment~~ *employment* trends.

22. Is this Blackfoot ~~ceremonyal~~ *ceremonial* headdress worn during the Sun Dance?

23. The guest speaker was a ~~dignifyed~~ *dignified* gentleman with a white beard and a twinkle in his eye.

24. Dressed in white satin and lace, the bride ~~carryed~~ *carried* a beautiful bouquet of red roses and calla lilies.

25. Because we camped in an arid climate, Maxine constantly complained about the ~~driness~~ *dryness* of her skin.

Suffixes D, p. 344

EXERCISE A

1. slimmer
2. permitted
3. hottest
4. forgettable
5. difference
6. dripping
7. muddy
8. feeling
9. regretted
10. remittance
11. excelled
12. skimmed
13. treating
14. mopping
15. selecting
16. referring
17. grabbed
18. regrettable
19. deterrence
20. preferable

EXERCISE B

21. Throughout his e-mail message, José made several ~~refferences~~ *references* to his upcoming trip to Guatemala.

22. Balance and muscle movement are ~~controled~~ *controlled* by the part of the brain called the cerebellum.

23. The Wright brothers, the inventors of the first practical airplane, built their first ~~propeler~~ *propeller* in 1903.

24. To gather information for my research project, I ~~scaned~~ *scanned* numerous newspaper and magazine articles.

25. Our community Meals on Wheels program ~~benefitted~~ *benefited* not only the recipients of the meals but also the volunteers who delivered them.

ie and *ei*; *–cede*, *–ceed*, and *–sede*; Prefixes and Suffixes, p. 345

EXERCISE A

1. (truely), propeller, spicier, freight
2. intercede, (ilogical) funniest, noticeable
3. overrated, amusement, gentleness, (procede)
4. (dissappointment) counterfeit, forgettable, ninety
5. paid, steadiness, (couragous) excelled

EXERCISE B

6. A *mosqueta*, created by ~~artisticaly~~ *artistically* ~~combine-ing~~ *combining* gold and pearls, has become a symbol of Panama.

7. Although its origin is ~~mysteryous~~ *mysterious*, the brooch, ~~resembleing~~ *resembling* a flower, was named *mosqueta*—the Spanish name for the white musk roses of the Mediterranean area.

8. Balboa was probably the first ~~foriegner~~ *foreigner* to know of Panama's pearl beds.

9. According to legend, on Balboa's famous trek across the Isthmus of Panama, he made the ~~acquainttance~~ *acquaintance* of a Native American ~~cheif~~ *chief* whose costume ~~consistted~~ *consisted* mainly of pearls.

10. One of the ~~earlyest~~ *earliest* written records of Panamanian pearl jewelry was made in 1821 by a French engineer who was visiting.

11. He tells of women, ~~prouddly~~ *proudly* wearing earrings and combs of gold and pearls, ~~celebrateing~~ *celebrating* Panama's independence from Spain.

12. Although the pearls were ~~plentyful~~ *plentiful*, ~~acquireing~~ *acquiring* the treasures of the deep was not an easy task.

13. In 1938, the red tide—a natural phenomenon caused by a ~~reproduceing~~ *reproducing* organism— ~~destroied~~ *destroyed* Panama's oyster beds and, ~~regretably~~ *regrettably*, the pearl supply.

14. In the 1950's, Panama's production of *mosquetas* was ~~resummed~~ *resumed*, but the coveted ~~peices~~ *pieces* of jewelry were made with cultured pearls imported from Japan.

15. Imported filigree wire was another ~~innoveation~~ *innovation* that changed the creation of the *mosqueta*.

Plurals A, p. 346
EXERCISE A

1. booths
2. dishes
3. observatories
4. histories
5. moustaches
6. pouches
7. subsidies
8. luxuries
9. Thursdays
10. hierarchies
11. missionaries
12. wrenches
13. hermits
14. medleys
15. ambushes
16. Ruizes
17. alloys
18. temptresses
19. minorities
20. phalanxes [*or* phalanges]

EXERCISE B
21. (trenchs), commodities, monkeys, flashes
22. intermediaries, Mondays, (fireflys), foxes
23. monuments, dresses, punches, (theorys)

24. queries, scratches, (seagulles), quizzes
25. sculptresses, (crucifixs), cemeteries, peaches

Plurals B, p. 347
EXERCISE A

1. beliefs
2. scenarios
3. waifs
4. tomatoes
5. sheriffs
6. videos
7. carafes
8. pianos
9. hairdos
10. loaves
11. reefs
12. sopranos [*or* soprani]
13. knives
14. tattoos
15. Calvinos
16. studios
17. hoofs [*or* hooves]
18. echoes
19. stereos
20. innuendoes [*or* innuendos]

EXERCISE B
21. If possible, leave the skins on ~~potatos~~ *potatoes*, for the skin is both nutritious and flavorful.

22. *C*

23. "Two ~~halfs~~ *halves* make a whole," I explained to my little sister, who is curious about fractions.

24. Female bottle-nosed dolphins bear single ~~calfes~~ *calves*, which swim and breathe minutes after birth.

25. At the beginning of this song, the ~~altoes~~ *altos* harmonize beautifully.

Plurals C, p. 348
EXERCISE A

1. languages, ~~ditchs~~ *ditches*, quizzes, torpedoes
2. ~~academys~~ *academies*, essays, tornadoes, prescriptions
3. carafes, strategies, cameos, ~~rooves~~ *roofs*
4. headdresses, studios, ~~technicalitys~~ *technicalities*, trenches
5. strawberries, ~~ranchs~~ *ranches*, hairdos, midwives
6. democracies, assessments, ~~tabooes~~ *taboos*, classes
7. ~~ratioes~~ *ratios*, kidneys, lives, sorceresses
8. hooves, stereos, ~~sphinxs~~ *sphinxes*, sororities

9. syringes, anthologies, ~~videoes~~ *videos*, sheriffs

10. Tuesdays, ~~symphonys~~ *symphonies*, echoes, loaves

EXERCISE B *Some answers may vary.*

11. The curtain opened slowly to reveal three grand ~~pianoes~~ *pianos* and two ~~celloes~~ *cellos* but no performers.

12. Topped with fresh garlic and lemon zest, my favorite casserole contains thin layers of ~~potatos~~ *potatoes*, spinach, and ~~tomatos~~ *tomatoes*.

13. Place the ~~trophys~~ *trophies* on these ~~shelfs~~ *shelves*.

14. Does Robert Tree Cody Red Cedar Whistle play flute ~~soloes~~ *solos* on the CD *White Buffalo*?

15. Hoping their ~~enemys~~ *enemies* were retreating, the soldiers could hear the receding ~~echos~~ *echoes* of gunfire.

16. The grass clippings, ~~leafs~~ *leaves*, and dead ~~branchs~~ *branches* can be added to the compost pile.

17. In honor of our country's ~~heros~~ *heroes*, how many ~~monumentes~~ *monuments* have been erected in Washington, D.C.?

18. Unpacking the ~~boxs~~ *boxes* in the attic, we found ~~photoes~~ *photos* depicting Grandmother's childhood in Japan.

19. The ~~missionarys~~ *missionaries* convinced the warring ~~chieves~~ *chiefs* to put aside their ~~knifes~~ *knives* and spears and to communicate peacefully.

20. I enjoy the contemporary ~~songes~~ *songs* of Sergio and Odair Assad, ~~virtuosoes~~ *virtuosos* of the classical guitar.

Plurals D, p. 349

EXERCISE A

1. mice
2. women
3. sheep
4. Vietnamese
5. scissors
6. bass [*or* basses]

7. teeth
8. trout [*or* trouts]
9. corps
10. Swiss
11. shrimp [*or* shrimps]
12. politics
13. salmon [*or* salmons]
14. gentlemen
15. oxen
16. chassis
17. species
18. Sioux
19. moose
20. aircraft

EXERCISE B

21. To practice his addition skills, my little brother rolls three ~~dices~~ *dice* and calculates the sum.

22. *C* [*or* reindeers]

23. Although ~~squashes~~ *squash* are not usually eaten raw, the word *squash* is derived from the Narragansett Indian word *asquutasquash*, meaning "that which is eaten raw."

24. More than three hundred ~~childs~~ *children* will compete in our region's Special Olympics this year.

25. For the fruit salad we will need pears, strawberries, ~~grapefruits~~ *grapefruit*, bananas, and apples.

Plurals E, p. 350

EXERCISE A

1. ladybugs
2. choirmasters
3. dogcatchers
4. general assemblies
5. passers-by
6. disc jockeys
7. firefighters

8. chiefs of staff

9. charge accounts

10. air bags

11. justices of the peace

12. forty-five-year-olds

13. chambers of commerce

14. chaise lounges

15. post offices

16. commanders in chief

17. gearboxes

18. chief executive officers

19. dockworkers

20. letters of advice

EXERCISE B

21. The bride is designing the gowns that her
maids of honor
~~maid of honors~~ will wear in the wedding.

22. What kinds of prizes will the contest's
runners-up
~~runner-ups~~ receive?

23. In June my *brothers-in-law* ~~brother-in-laws~~ are traveling to
Jamaica to attend the Fisherman's Festival.

24. *C*

25. *C*

Plurals F, p. 351

EXERCISE A

1. alumni

2. bases

3. apexes [*or* apices]

4. phenomena [*or* phenomenons]

5. millenniums [*or* millennia]

6. larvae [*or* larvas]

7. seraphs [*or* seraphim]

8. vertebrae [*or* vertebras]

9. fibulae [*or* fibulas]

10. mediums [*or* media]

11. alumnae

12. radiuses [*or* radii]

13. chateaux [*or* chateaus]

14. focuses [*or* foci]

15. antennae [*or* antennas]

16. curricula [*or* curriculums]

17. ampullae

18. colloquia [*or* colloquiums]

19. bacilli

20. octopuses [*or* octopi *or* octopodes]

EXERCISE B

21. Using tables of contents and ~~index~~ *indexes [or indices]* can
facilitate the research process.

22. *C* [*or* dicta]

23. *Algae* ~~Algaes~~ serve a vital function in an eco-
system, but they can deplete the oxygen
supply and can block light from plant life.

24. Is it necessary to memorize the molecular
formulae [or formulas]
~~formulaes~~ for tomorrow's test?

25. *C* [*or* cactuses]

Plurals G, p. 352

EXERCISE

1. 6s [*or* 6's]

2. *i*'s

3. *and*s [*or* *and*'s]

4. 1990s [*or* 1990's]

5. *u*'s

6. $s [*or* $'s]

7. *goodbyes* [*or* *goodbye*'s]

8. 3s [*or* 3's]

9. *yous* [*or* *you*'s]

10. Gs [*or* G's]

Plurals H, p. 353

EXERCISE A

1. midshipmen

2. kickstands

3. 7s [*or* 7's]

4. tableaus [*or* tableaux]

5. bills of sale

6. *and*s [*or* *and*'s]

7. Portuguese

8. parentheses

9. Fs [*or* F's]

10. lice

EXERCISE B

11. Two North American ~~grouses~~ *grouse*, the blue grouse and the spruce grouse, are sometimes called "fool hens" because their fearlessness makes them easy to hunt.

12. Between the ages of six and twelve, humans generally lose their twenty deciduous, or baby, ~~tooths~~ *teeth*.

13. Although my family owns six ~~alarms clock~~ *alarm clocks*, we still overslept this morning!

14. Most of the ~~passer-bys~~ *passers-by* stopped to examine the vendor's wares.

15. C

16. C

17. Coincidentally, my two sisters' ~~mother-in-laws~~ *mothers-in-law* were born on the same day.

18. Although the ~~Swisses~~ *Swiss* in the exchange student program speak English, their native language is German.

19. Through several family ~~crisises~~ *crises*, Sue has managed to keep her sense of humor.

20. Between the ~~vertebraes~~ *vertebrae [or vertebras]* are intervertebral disks, which permit various movements of the spinal column.

Numbers, p. 354

EXERCISE

1. The name of our club, which has ~~35~~ *thirty-five* members, is the Seattle Sherlockian Society.

2. So that everyone has a copy of the by-laws, I made 40 ~~5-page~~ *five-page* booklets. [or ~~40~~ *forty* 5-page]

3. Through research we discovered that we are not alone in our fascination for Sherlock Holmes; approximately ~~7~~ *seven* Sherlockian societies exist in the San Francisco Bay area alone.

4. Because time was limited, we were able to visit only ~~15~~ *fifteen* Web sites dedicated to Sherlock Holmes, but many more exist.

5. Several members of our club plan to attend a Sherlockian conference in Chicago, Illinois, tentatively scheduled for July ~~fifteenth~~ *15*, 2003.

6. Holmes's creator, Sir Arthur Conan Doyle, was born in Edinburgh in ~~eighteen hundred fifty-nine~~ *1859*.

7. Conan Doyle wrote ~~4~~ *four* novels and fifty-six short stories featuring Sherlock Holmes.

8. C [or 221B]

9. On the ~~1st~~ *first* floor of the museum, visitors can see the study—made famous by Doyle's stories—overlooking Baker Street.

10. Tonight at ~~eight thirty~~ *8:30* P.M. my favorite Sherlock Holmes movie, *The Hound of the Baskervilles*, is playing on television.

Words Often Confused A, p. 355

EXERCISE

1. already
2. all together
3. assure
4. born
5. all right
6. brake
7. altar
8. ensure
9. all ready
10. break

Words Often Confused B, p. 356

EXERCISE

1. desert; course
2. course; capital
3. compliment; dessert
4. cloths; coarse
5. capitol; consul
6. choose; clothes
7. counselor; complement
8. counsel; clothes
9. coarse; capital
10. council's; course

Words Often Confused C, p. 357
EXERCISE

1. lead; formally
2. its; loose
3. led; morale
4. Formerly; miners
5. losing; latter
6. lead; minor
7. It's; moral
8. Later; lead
9. led; its
10. moral; lose

Words Often Confused D, p. 358
Exercise

1. stationery; personnel
2. plane; pieces
3. past; principal's
4. personal; peace
5. passed; quiet
6. stationary; quite
7. plain; peace
8. stationary; principal
9. principle; quite
10. stationary; plane

Words Often Confused E, p. 359
EXERCISE

1. than
2. too
3. whose
4. their
5. Who's
6. you're
7. wasted
8. Two
9. waist
10. There

Review A: Spelling Rules, p. 360
EXERCISE A

1. unknown
2. glorious
3. serviceable
4. enduring
5. really
6. kindliness
7. trueness
8. bluely
9. skimming
10. slyness

Exercise B

11. sons-in-law
12. spoonfuls
13. tomatoes
14. radios
15. symphonies
16. 3s [*or* 3's]
17. mixes
18. alumni
19. leaves
20. species

EXERCISE C

21. Tanzania is not dominated by one ~~cheif~~ *chief* ethnic group; the estimated 120 black tribal groups generally live in peace.
22. When the interruptions cease, you can ~~procede~~ *proceed* with your presentation.
23. The vocabulary test includes 20 ~~5-syllable~~ *five-syllable* words. [*or* ~~20~~ *twenty* 5-syllable]
24. ~~15~~ *Fifteen* of my friends and family members will attend the Cinco de Mayo festival with me.
25. At the ~~hieght~~ *height* of his popularity, this author wrote at least one book per year.

Review B: Words Often Confused, p. 361
EXERCISE

1. lose
2. complimented
3. desert
4. led
5. than
6. stationery
7. morale
8. past
9. minor
10. all ready
11. later
12. all together
13. whose
14. counselor
15. formerly
16. plane
17. waste
18. personnel
19. clothes
20. break

Review C: Spelling and Words Often Confused, p. 362
EXERCISE A

1. Is there a ~~possibillity~~ *possibility* that you can ~~interceed~~ *intercede* on my behalf?
2. My ~~freinds' ilogical arguement~~ *friends' illogical argument* seemed comical to those of us witnessing it.

3. Inside the ~~buryed~~ *buried* wooden box we found several jeweled ~~knifes~~ *knives*.

4. The American Indian Movement, supported by many modern Sioux, has ~~activly~~ *actively* protested government treatment of Native Americans since the 1960s.

5. ~~6 justice of the peaces~~ *Six justices of the peace* attended the seminar.

6. Is it ~~socialy accepttable~~ *socially acceptable* for the family's ~~hier~~ *heir* to travel abroad?

7. ~~Conceeding~~ *Conceding* defeat, the ~~immpassive~~ *impassive* warriors laid down their ~~sheilds~~ *shields*.

8. The ~~boxs~~ *boxes* in the basement were filled with ~~photoes~~ *photos* of my ancestors.

9. ~~Childs~~ *Children* in the small farming community ~~merryly~~ *merrily* celebrated the ~~1st~~ *first* day of spring.

10. Because the water spot on the ~~cieling~~ *ceiling* is barely ~~noticable~~ *noticeable*, repainting the whole room seems ~~unecessary~~ *unnecessary*.

EXERCISE B

11. dessert; complements

12. borne; clothes

13. all together; capitol

14. formerly; desert

15. It's; desert

16. cloths; its

17. Who's; capital

18. you're; already

19. counsel; moral

20. principal; led

Review D: Spelling and Words Often Confused, p. 363

EXERCISE

1. All ~~12 soldeirs~~ *twelve soldiers* should remain ~~stationery~~ *stationary* until dismissed.

2. Although we ~~stompped~~ *stomped* our feet, the ~~deers~~ *deer [or C]* ~~proceded~~ *proceeded* to eat ~~you're~~ *your* flowers.

3. Congress ~~past~~ *passed* a bill to ~~upphold~~ *uphold* the ~~principal~~ *principle* of civil rights.

4. ~~Whose~~ *Who's* been chosen to ~~reveiw~~ *review* the ~~bill of sales~~ *bills of sale*?

5. Given the choice of ~~runing~~ *running* a mile or doing calisthenics, I choose the ~~later~~ *latter*.

6. If he continues to ~~loose wieght~~ *lose weight*, his ~~clotheing~~ *clothing* will not fit.

7. ~~1st your~~ *First you're* a junior and then a senior.

8. Annie's home ~~videoes~~ *videos* ~~actualy~~ *actually* look ~~professionnal~~ *professional*.

9. Of ~~coarse~~ *course*, I appreciate a sincere ~~complement~~ *compliment*.

10. Our school ~~councilor~~ *counselor* owns two dance ~~studioes~~ *studios*.

11. ~~Sillyness~~ *Silliness* seemed ~~innappropriate~~ *inappropriate* in the ~~principle's~~ *principal's* office.

12. Will both sopranos ~~conceed~~ *concede* to singing ~~soloes~~ *solos* tonight?

13. I ~~beleive~~ *believe* we got ~~their~~ *there* at ~~5 o'clock~~ *five o'clock*, but I'm not positive.

14. After checking the ~~indexes~~ *indices [or C]* of several ~~anthologys~~ *anthologies*, I found the poem.

15. Both ~~runner-ups~~ *runners-up* ~~immediatly~~ *immediately* demanded a rematch.

16. I've ~~all ready~~ *already* ~~unnpacked~~ *unpacked* 6 ~~20-pound~~ *twenty-pound* boxes. [or 6 20-pound]

17. The ~~chieves~~ *chiefs* looked splendid in ~~thier~~ *their* colorful headdresses.

18. I ~~ensure~~ *assure* you the performance ~~exceded~~ *exceeded* our expectations.

19. ~~Its~~ *It's* too early to go ~~shoping~~ *shopping*; most of the stores are still closed.

20. You ~~inncorrectly~~ *incorrectly* spelled *Venezuela* with ~~4 es~~ *four e's*.

Language and Sentence Skills Practice Answer Key

Proofreading Application: Memo, p. 364

SUBJECT: Office Procedures

~~14~~ *Fourteen* interns will be ~~joinning~~ *joining* RGT, Inc., this summer. RGT's ~~personal~~ *personnel* office has asked me to outline procedures that will help to ~~insure~~ *ensure* that you have a rewarding experience. (Of ~~coarse,~~ *course,* your ~~imediate~~ *immediate* supervisor will give you additional instructions specific to your job.)

(1) Dress ~~appropriatly.~~ *appropriately.* Your ~~cloths~~ *clothes* and general appearance are a part of RGT's public image. Please refrain from wearing attire that might be ~~unprofessionnal.~~ *unprofessional.*

(2) You will spend a great deal of time in the resource room, either copying documents or returning ~~reffernce~~ *reference* materials to the ~~shelfs.~~ *shelves.* If ~~you're~~ *your* task is the ~~later,~~ *latter,* please follow the system of organization used in the resource room. The ~~one thousand five hundred~~ *1,500* books and other documents there are used by hundreds of employees; the ~~principle~~ *principal* deterrent to employees' efficient use of time is the incorrect shelving of materials.

(3) Any calls that you ~~recieve~~ *receive* should be ~~loged~~ *logged* and counted ~~dayly~~ *daily* so that you can turn in a weekly total to your supervisor.

If you can follow these simple procedures, ~~than~~ *then* you will find, as I have, that RGT is a truly satisfying place to work.

Literary Model: Short Story, pp. 365–66

EXERCISE A

For each of the following items, the student should show at least one of the following possible answers.

1. regretted, predecessor
2. waited, replacing, red-faced
3. leisurely
4. verger, vicar, predecessor
5. home, red-faced
6. forties
7. marble, chancel
8. clergyman
9. red-faced
10. leisurely

EXERCISE B

1. *Responses will vary. A sample response is given.* The rule "When adding a prefix, do not change the spelling of the original word" was easiest for me to learn because it is intuitive and requires no changes to be made.

2. *Responses will vary. A sample response is given.* The rules about *ie* and *ei* were hard for me to learn because I'm always confusing words with those letters in them.

EXERCISE C

Responses will vary. A sample response is given.

I would like to nominate Lamont Beaulieu for the Keys to the City Award. This young man has made an altogether outstanding contribution to the maintenance of parks in our area. Leading the Green City Team, he has borne many of the responsibilities of organization and implementation. One way to compliment Mr. Beaulieu for his enthusiasm, which boosts everyone's morale, is to present him with this annual award. We know he will continue to lead well.

EXERCISE D

Responses will vary. A sample response is given.

Lamont Beaulieu was born to have a positive impact on his community.

Writing Application: Instructions, p. 367

Writing Applications are designed to provide students immediate composition practice in using key concepts taught in each chapter of the *Language and Sentence Skills Practice* booklet. You may wish to evaluate student responses to these assignments as you do any other writing that students produce. To save grading time, however, you may want to use the following scoring rubric.

Scoring Rubric

The instructions include three homonyms, spelled correctly.

1   2   3   4   5

The instructions are clear and written so that ten- and twelve-year-olds can follow them.

1   2   3   4   5

The instructions are organized by some recognizable pattern—room by room, for example.

1   2   3   4   5

The assignment is relatively free of errors in grammar, usage, mechanics, and spelling.

1   2   3   4   5

Total Score _____

5 = highest; 1 = lowest

Choices: Investigating Common Errors, p. 368

Choices activities are designed to extend and enrich students' understanding of grammar, usage, and mechanics and to take learners beyond traditional classroom instruction. To use the Choices worksheet, have each student pick an activity that interests him or her. In some cases, you may wish to assign an activity to a particular student or group of students. You may also want to request that students get your approval for the activities they choose. Establish guidelines for what constitutes successful completion of an activity. Then, help students plan how they will share their work with the rest of the class.

Choices activities can be scored with a pass-fail grade or treated as bonus-point projects. Those activities that require students to research or create a certain number of items might be graded in a traditional manner.

Sentence Fragments and Run-on Sentences A, p. 369

EXERCISE

1. The executive power shall be vested in a President of the United States of America, he shall hold his office during the term of four years.

2. The Senate of the United States shall be composed of two Senators from each state, and each Senator shall have one vote.

3. In order to form a more perfect union, do ordain and establish this Constitution for the United States of America.

4. All bills for raising revenue shall originate in the House of Representatives, the Senate may propose or concur with amendments as on other bills.

5. The right of citizens of the United States to vote shall not be denied or abridged by the United States or by any State on account of race, color, or previous condition of servitude.

6. The removal of the President from office or of his death or resignation, the Vice-President to become President.

7. The right of citizens of the United States, who are eighteen years of age or older, to vote.

8. He shall have power, by and with the advice and consent of the Senate, to make treaties.

9. Abridging the freedom of speech, or of the press.

10. New states may be admitted by the Congress into this union, no new state shall be formed or erected within the jurisdiction of any other state.

Sentence Fragments and Run-on Sentences B, p. 370

EXERCISE

1. F	6. S
2. F	7. R
3. S	8. F
4. R	9. F
5. F	10. S

Revised paragraphs may vary. A sample revision is given.

In Egypt, one such clash was brought on by Amenhotep IV, the pharaoh who ruled from about 1379 B.C. to 1362 B.C. He angered the polytheistic priests by teaching the existence of only one god, the sun, symbolized by a sun disk called the Aton. Amenhotep even changed his name to Akhenaton to honor the Aton. He moved the capital to Tell el Amarna from Thebes, where the nobles and priests had become powerful. Egyptian wealth no longer poured in to the priests at the great temple of Thebes. A fierce political struggle broke out between Akhenaton and priests and nobles who worshiped many gods. The pharaoh gradually learned that orders cannot change religious beliefs; when he died, the clash between church and state ended. His successor, Tutankhamen, proved his willingness to revert to the old system of beliefs. Well known today, Tutankhamen, whose life-sized gold funeral mask was discovered in his tomb in 1922, died at age eighteen. Nevertheless, he ruled long enough to move Egypt's capital city back to Thebes.

Subject-Verb Agreement A, p. 371

EXERCISE A

1. sings	6. have
2. Is	7. Doesn't
3. do	8. makes
4. is	9. there's
5. has	10. seems

EXERCISE B

11. Cass and Trina don't like cafeteria food, so each of them ~~bring~~ *brings* a lunch from home.

12. C

13. For almost three years, the two of them ~~has~~ *have* eaten lunch together nearly every day.

14. There ~~are~~ *is* a little grove of trees outside the door of the cafeteria.

15. Many students in the senior class ~~prefers~~ *prefer* to eat outside when the weather is pleasant.

Subject-Verb Agreement B, p. 372

EXERCISE A

1. has	6. C
2. turns	7. has
3. remains	8. needs
4. Does	9. march
5. volunteer	10. is

EXERCISE B

11. Did you tell me (he) ~~try~~ *tries* to read at least one book a week?

12. Many (students) in the senior class ~~partici-pates~~ *participate* in community service projects.

13. Has Julie told everyone what time the (movie) begins?

14. Less than (twenty percent) of the eligible voters ~~has~~ *have* an opinion about that subject.

15. (Soup and sandwich) ~~are~~ *is* the lunch special at that restaurant today.

Pronoun-Antecedent Agreement A, p. 373

EXERCISE A

1. (One) of the girls who attended the meeting has given me a copy of (their, *her*) notes.

2. (Officers) of the student council will conduct an orientation session for (its, *their*) successors.

3. In (*their*, its) excitement about the lopsided victory, the (crowd) cheered and shouted for at least twenty minutes after the game ended.

4. Relations between the (United States) and (their, *its*) neighbors to the north and south have not always been cordial.

5. (Anyone) who wants to help decorate the senior class's float for the homecoming parade should put (their, *his or her*) name and phone number on this list.

6. (Marcus,) (Sam,) and (Cody) knew that (he, *they*) would do well on the final exam.

7. I've shown Simone and Nelda how to do these problems, but now the (girls) need to try to do them (herself, *themselves*).

Language and Sentence Skills Practice Answer Key

8. My (grandmother) and (Aunt Louisa), who have never flown on an airplane, are taking (*their, her*) first flight next week.

9. Either the (hedgehog) or the (opossum) rolls (*themselves, itself*) up in a ball when threatened.

10. Neither (Sam) nor (Zack) remembered to write down (*his, their*) Social Security number.

EXERCISE B

11. Each part of the country seems to have their *its* own regional legends and folklore.

12. *C*

13. *C*

14. Clarence, along with two other students, is planning to work to year after their *his* graduation.

15. Despite what their mother told them, two of the little girls forgot to wear her *their* boots today.

Pronoun-Antecedent Agreement B, p. 374

EXERCISE A

1. The yearbook (staff) surprised their *its [or C]* sponsor by dedicating the yearbook to her.

2. During the class picnic, (some) of the girls decided to have her *their* picture taken.

3. Either (Marcus) or (Alex) can lend you his *C* notes.

4. Over (75 percent) of the tickets have been sold already, most of it *them* to parents.

5. Does everyone who owns a (dog) understand that they *it* must be kept on a leash at all times?

EXERCISE B

6. Over a third of the tomato plants died because we forgot to water them.

7. Each finalist will have to pay his or her own airfare and other expenses.

8. Not one of the boys in that family has to be reminded to make his bed in the morning before breakfast.

9. Every member of the graduating class should congratulate himself or herself for having passed his or her final exams.

10. Nobody likes to be reminded about his or her faults or shortcomings.

Pronoun Forms A, p. 375

EXERCISE A

1. she		6. she
2. me		7. Who
3. he		8. us
4. they		9. he
5. whom		10. We

EXERCISE B

11. I think Diana dances much more gracefully than her. *she*

12. Two of the bassoon players, Martina and him, *he* have been selected to play in the city's student orchestra.

13. The librarian gave the reading list to whomever *whoever* wanted a copy.

14. Mr. Cantu gave my brother and I a ride to *me* the store this afternoon.

15. *C*

16. My friends and me are going fishing this *I* weekend.

17. The children who put up the signs about a lost puppy are them. *they*

18. Do you have the list of people who we are *whom* inviting to the ceremony?

19. *C*

20. The committee assignments were made by Samantha, who is the president of the club, and he. *him*

Pronoun Forms B, p. 376

EXERCISE

1. he—S	11. we—S
2. us—OP	12. her—DO
3. him—A	13. they—PN
4. him—DO	14. her—OP
5. Who—S	15. them—IO
6. him—IO	16. I—PN
7. he—PN	17. us—OP
8. them—DO	18. She—S
9. her—IO	19. us—OP
10. them—OP	20. him—DO

Clear Pronoun Reference A, p. 377

EXERCISE

Answers will vary. Sample responses are given.

1. When the boy blew out all the candles with one breath, all the children cheered.

2. One of the dams on the creek had a small crack, but that crack was not enough to cause the flood.

3. That our family's farm was affected by the drought in the 1930s ought to be obvious from this photograph.

4. Cassie and her grandmother talked for an hour on the phone, but Cassie forgot to tell her about the missing puppy.

5. Shawn enjoys going out in the ski boat, although he hasn't been able to stay up on the skis very long yet.

6. The instructions say that you should never use this cleaning fluid near an open flame.

7. I prefer that the wait staff bring the soup or salad before the main course.

8. Even though we waited in line at the ticket window for hours, we weren't able to get a ticket.

9. Cassie was happy that the dog returned home before Cassie had a chance to put up the notices or place an ad in the newspaper.

10. When the second sailboat rounded the buoy and sped toward the finish line, the race became exciting.

Clear Pronoun Reference B, p. 378

EXERCISE

Answers may vary. Sample responses are given.

1. I love the poetry of Dylan Thomas, but I haven't read all his poems.

2. One dictionary source says that the two spellings are equally accepted.

3. When we saw Antoinette's slides of Costa Rica, we all wanted to go there.

4. Roberto and his father agreed on the strategy Roberto should use.

5. Your sprints are not very fast today, probably due to your injury.

6. I have enjoyed reading all of his fiction, but the book I liked best was a mystery.

7. Of all the instruments she played, she enjoyed either piano or guitar the most, and she practiced piano regularly.

8. When you see Francine and Teresa this afternoon, be sure to tell Francine how much I enjoyed her singing as well as Teresa's accompaniment.

9. The contest between Mac and Colin was over when Colin spelled the word *pterodactyl* correctly.

10. Whenever the children did their chores without being asked, their mother was enormously pleased.

Verb Forms A, p. 379

EXERCISE A

1. ~~Builded~~ *Built* in the early 1970s, the opera house in Sydney, Australia, stands out in the city's harbor.

2. The Woolworth Building in New York City has ~~rose~~ *risen* 792 feet straight up since 1913.

3. When Calgary, Canada, became the 1988 winter Olympics location, special buildings were ~~constructing~~ *constructed*.

4. Some people have said that the Taj Mahal is the most beautiful building they have ever ~~seed~~ *seen*.

5. Countless visitors have _took_ (taken) a tour of the Louvre in Paris.

6. Surely you _payed_ (paid) a visit to Notre Dame while in France.

7. The great pyramids of Egypt seem to have _standed_ (stood) since the beginning of time.

8. Tourists who have _went_ (gone) to China would speak of the Great Wall.

9. Have you also _heared_ (heard) of Hadrian's Wall, which the Romans built between what is now England and Scotland?

10. For many years visitors have _get_ (gotten [or got]) tours of the Empire State Building in New York City.

EXERCISE B

11. forgotten [or forgot]
12. dived [or dove]
13. drank
14. forgiven
15. froze

Verb Forms B, p. 380

EXERCISE

1. I am sure that unkind remark _hurted_ (hurt) her feelings.

2. The hose must have _froze_ (frozen) and burst during last week's cold weather.

3. Someone his age really should have _knowed_ (known) better.

4. After the witness had been _swore_ (sworn) in, the defense attorney _begun_ (began) questioning her.

5. He had had the shoes so long that he had _wore_ (worn) holes in the soles.

6. The driver who had barely avoided an accident was clearly _shook_ (shaken).

7. Students, please turn your tests over and _pass_ (past) them forward; time has _ran_ (run) out.

8. I would have _wrote_ (written) a longer essay, but I simply _forget_ (forgot) some of the names of the people.

9. By the time the rest of the decorating committee _shown_ (showed) up, we had already _blowed_ (blown) up most of the balloons.

10. The sweater _shrunk_ (shrank) to half its former size because she had _throwed_ (thrown) it into the dryer with the rest of the clothes.

11. C

12. She has _arose_ (arisen) before dawn every day this month.

13. He seems to have _became_ (become) more confident of his abilities during the past year.

14. The old book had _laid_ (lain) on a shelf in a dark corner of the library for many years.

15. Although she hadn't _seed_ (seen) her friend for several years, she _find_ (found) that they still had much in common.

16. He _lay_ (laid) the book down on the arm of the couch, took off his glasses, and closed his eyes for a few minutes.

17. The little boy _knowed_ (knew) he should not have _did_ (done) that.

18. Either I have _leaved_ (left) my keys somewhere, or they have _fell_ (fallen) out of my pocket.

19. C

20. For many years, those two brothers _fight_ (fought) and argued, but now they _got_ (get) along.

Verb Tense, p. 381

EXERCISE A

Revisions may vary. A sample revision is given.

[1] Some composers, such as Dmitri Shostakovitch (1906–1975) of Russia, wrote traditional symphonies of four distinct movements. [2] After 1945, serious musicians accepted the innovative sounds of synthesizers and other

experimental instruments. [3] Composers also allowed musicians a greater role in determining the sound of a piece. [4] African American contributions to contemporary music included rhythm and blues and soul music. [5] The rhythms of Latin America have had a growing and appreciative audience in recent times.

EXERCISE B

6. will have received

7. fixes

8. have done

9. C

10. arrives

Comparative and Superlative Forms of Modifiers, p. 382

EXERCISE A

1. I was able to finish the paper more quicklyer *more quickly* because I had organized my research notes.

2. The diamond in her ring is smaller but *more brilliant* brilliant than the one in her mother's ring.

3. Did you enjoy the movie or the dinner afterward most? *more*

4. Of all the grandchildren, Robert is the one with the darker hair. *darkest*

5. If I hadn't felt so badly, I would have done *bad* best on the test. *better*

EXERCISE B

Answers may vary. Sample responses are given.

6. Is it harder to attend school or to work a fifteen-hour day?

7. If you had lived in England earlier than 1819, you wouldn't have had any more choice than any other British child. [or If you had lived in England earlier than 1819, you would have had no more choice than any other British child.]

8. The Factory Act of 1819 addressed some of the worst conditions; children less than nine years old couldn't work in the cotton mills any more.

9. Children at least nine years old but younger than eighteen couldn't be made to work more than twelve hours a day in the textile factories.

10. For a longer time than the textiles industry, mines were still allowed to employ boys under ten years old, as well as girls and women.

Misplaced and Dangling Modifiers A, p. 383

EXERCISE

Answers will vary. Sample responses are given.

1. In the laboratory, Dr. Ortiz pioneered treatment for unusual viral infections.

2. Unhappy with dormitory costs, Sonia chose to live at home.

3. Before touring the U.S. Capitol, they stopped first at the National Gallery of Art.

4. Few students on their way to school pay attention to billboards.

5. With the old bike wobbling and squeaking on every turn, John made slow progress.

6. Everyone wants to see the historically interesting Declaration of Independence.

7. The principal promised to announce the results by Friday.

8. After viewing a documentary on African wildlife, I am interested in the possibility of travel.

9. At a garage sale Sulima found a trumpet that only has one small dent.

10. To comprehend the principles of calculus, students should have a background in algebra.

Misplaced and Dangling Modifiers B, p. 384

EXERCISE

Answers may vary. Sample responses are given.

1. The mother was clearly embarrassed by her child's kicking and screaming.

2. While we waited for the bus in the rain, all the traffic lights went out at the intersection.

3. To cook a complete dinner for twenty guests, you must first plan carefully.

4. Because it was raining and dreary outside, we weren't able to go to the game.

5. The Legislature welcomed its new member, recently elected by the voters of our district.

6. The woman was dismayed to realize that she had forgotten to take the package that she had wrapped so carefully to the post office.

7. The boys watched the pelicans swooping and diving toward the water.

8. I forgot how to do only this kind of problem, but all the others were easy.

9. After placing a classified ad in the newspaper, we received many phone calls about the job.

10. The parks and recreation department has set aside an area where people are allowed to walk their dogs without leashes.

Correct Use of Modifiers, p. 385

EXERCISE

Answers may vary. Sample responses are given.

1. The little girl realized she couldn't climb high enough to get her kite, twisted and snarled in the branches of the tree.

2. At the art museum I saw some of the most remarkable paintings I've ever seen.

3. Don't you know how to fold laundry any better than that?

4. As Melissa's sister was walking to the corner to mail a letter, a lost puppy came up to her and wagged its tail.

5. Too exhausted from hours of cleaning out the garage, we no longer found the movie so attractive.

6. Although he looks better than he did yesterday, I'm sure he still doesn't feel very well.

7. Her gymnastics routine was more difficult than Maxine's, but Maxine's was executed more carefully.

8. Remind Alex that, when he finishes his homework, he should meet us at the basketball court.

9. To the pilots flying at an altitude of twenty-seven thousand feet, the sunset on the clouds was truly beautiful.

10. Mark won the competition because he worked harder than anyone else.

Standard Usage A, p. 386

EXERCISE A

1. The trees have ~~less~~ *fewer* leaves than they did even a few days ago.

2. The <u>reason</u> Jerome couldn't come with us <u>is</u> ~~because~~ *that* he couldn't find his shoes.

3. Kris thought the comedian's jokes were ~~kind of~~ *somewhat [or rather]* juvenile.

4. Although the car was ~~ensured~~ *insured*, the company wouldn't pay for the broken windshield.

5. When I went to visit her at the hospital, I <u>took</u> *C* her a bouquet of flowers.

6. As Cole <u>accepted</u> *C* the award, the audience stood and clapped for him.

7. I hope her comment wasn't an ~~illusion~~ *allusion* to my new haircut.

8. Greta and ~~myself~~ *I* will take responsibility for organizing the canned food drive.

9. I felt so ~~nauseous~~ *nauseated* all morning that I was sure I had caught the flu.

10. Clayton got these diagrams ~~off~~ *from* a Web site.

EXERCISE B

Answers may vary. Sample responses are given.

11. Finally, her anxiety began to ease somewhat, and she began to feel rather better about herself.

12. I read in the newspaper that some people will try to clean up the creek on Saturday.

13. Those golden retrievers, which belong to the Campbells, are gentle, well-behaved dogs.

14. We hope that this week our history teacher won't act as though we don't have any other homework except what she assigns.

15. You're much more generous than I would have been in that situation.

Standard Usage B, p. 387

EXERCISE

Answers may vary. Sample responses are given.

Dear Gabriela,

  [1] It's been rather a long time since I wrote you, so I thought I would try to catch you up on recent events in my life. **[2]** The reason I haven't written is that I've had a lot of homework this semester. **[3]** In every class except for chemistry, the teachers assign so much work that I have hardly any time for myself. **[4]** They act as if we don't have anything else to do. **[5]** Yesterday, I was supposed to finish a paper, then work on my science project, and start drafting a speech that I have to give in class next week. **[6]** I hope all this hard work will have an effect on my grades this year!

  [7] I hope you're doing well at your new school and that you're taking fewer classes than you did here. **[8]** I'd like to call you sometime, but we're likely to run up a huge phone bill. **[9]** Maybe we could meet somewhere this summer. **[10]** Until then, I guess we'll just have to adapt to the situation as well as we can. Take care.

Your friend,

Carolyn

Standard Usage C, p. 388

EXERCISE A

1. You may recall that Benjamin Franklin
   invented
   ~~discovered~~ bifocals.

2. Winston Churchill is one of the most
   famous
   ~~notorious~~ heroes of England.

3. Clarence has ~~less~~ *fewer* college options than his brother Charles.

4. Some of the Girl Scouts are ~~liable~~ *likely* to knock on your door next week.

5. That ~~type~~ *type of* movie often gives Bernice nightmares.

6. The teacher reacted ~~like~~ *as if* Clarence turned his work in late all the time.

7. The final exam in Biology II was ~~alot~~ *a lot [or much]* easier than I expected it to be.

8. Charles ~~borrowed~~ *lent* me his bicycle because mine had a flat tire.

9. On Saturday morning, ~~don't~~ *doesn't* he have to mow the lawn, bundle the newspapers, wash the car, give the dog a bath, ~~and etc.~~ *etc.*?

10. Frankly, they ought to ~~of~~ *have* done it ~~theirselves~~ *themselves*.

EXERCISE B

  [11] Perhaps I shouldn't ~~of~~ *have* been so confident that I could look after my toddler cousin and study for the economics test at the same time. **[12]** ~~Somewheres~~ *Somewhere* I got the notion that the younger a child is, the less mischief he can get into. **[13]** Little Danny ~~didn't hardly look~~ *hardly looked* at the teddy bear I had ~~taken~~ *brought* him before he attempted to eat the pages of my textbook. **[14]** ~~Beside~~ *Besides* that, he grabbed my highlighter and proceeded to create some original hieroglyphics on the living room wall. **[15]** You may have guessed that I had to ~~leave~~ *let* my studies go until I had no other responsibilities.

Capitalization A, p. 389

EXERCISE A

1. The resolution passed by the student council of (J)efferson (C)ounty (H)igh (S)chool read: "(R)esolved: (T)hat the student council supports an increase in the length of the lunch period from fifteen to thirty minutes."

2. On (F)riday, some of us are going to (E)l (M)ercado, a (T)ex-(M)ex restaurant, to celebrate Matthew's eighteenth birthday.

3. The (G)lobe (T)heatre, where many of (S)hakespeare's plays were first performed, was in (L)ondon, not in (S)tratford-on-(A)von.

4. Many people are unaware that the continent of (n)orth (a)merica includes not only the (u)nited (s)tates (except for (h)awaii), but also (c)anada and (m)exico.

5. How many doctors are members of the (a)merican (m)edical (a)ssociation ((ama))?

EXERCISE B

6. Born in (d)ublin, (i)reland, on (n)ovember 30, 1667, and educated at (t)rinity (c)ollege, the young (s)wift became known in (l)ondon as a skillful writer of political and religious essays.

7. *Gulliver's (t)ravels,* (s)wift's greatest satire, was originally published in 1726 under the title *(t)ravels into (s)everal (r)emote (n)ations of the (w)orld.*

8. The book's (H)ero, (l)emuel (g)ulliver, travels to such strange lands as (l)illiput, where the tiny people are always at war.

9. In another (L)and, (g)ulliver finds much to admire in the (h)ouyhnhnms, a race of decent and reasonable (H)orses.

10. (S)oon, (g)ulliver realizes that the seemingly virtuous (h)ouyhnhnms can barely tolerate the other race on the island, the (y)ahoos.

Capitalization B, p. 390

EXERCISE A

1. (m)any of my friends think that (j)ane (a)usten's books must be tedious, but I thought (E)mma was a really funny novel.

2. Are we all going to (g)randma and (g)randpa (c)ook's house during spring break?

3. (t)heir house is on the (a)tlantic coast, not far from (o)cean (c)ity, (m)aryland.

4. My mother's family emigrated from (c)ounty (m)ayo, (i)reland, during the (g)reat (f)amine of the 1840s, which was caused by the complete failure of the potato crop.

5. Maria introduced her friends to her great-grandmother, (S)ra. (a)lvarez, who was born in (m)exico early in the twentieth century.

EXERCISE B

[6] Both opposing forces, Republicans and Nationalists, were responsible for the deaths of many civilians. **[7]** The right-wing (r)epublicans were aided by (g)ermany and (i)taly, while the (n)ationalists were helped by the (S)oviet (u)nion and a group of volunteers from fifty (N)ations, called the (i)nternational (b)rigade. **[8]** Intellectuals and artists were in special danger. **[9]** Among the nonmilitary casualties was Federico García (l)orca, whose literary efforts had already made him known around the (W)orld. **[10]** One of (S)pain's most important modern writers, he was both a poet and a playwright. **[11]** His play *The (h)ouse (O)f Bernarda (a)lba* dealt with suffering under a dictatorship. **[12]** His collection *(g)ypsy (b)allads* also won him popular acclaim. **[13]** The future dictator of Spain, (g)en. Francisco Franco, began his uprising not long after the poetry collection's publication. **[14]** Betrayed while hiding at a friend's house, (l)orca was arrested and briefly imprisoned at (g)ranada. **[15]** Tragically, the gifted (W)riter Lorca died at the hands of his political enemies on (a)ugust 18, 1936.

Commas A, p. 391

EXERCISE *Optional commas are underlined.*

1. Ladies and gentlemen, please join me in welcoming our guest speaker, Derek Creighton-Jones, who really needs no further introduction.

2. No, thank you, I never buy anything from a telephone salesperson.

3. Sharon and Randy can set up the tables, and Ron can start blowing up the balloons.

4. The original Library of Congress, established in 1800 under President John Adams, lost its collection when the U.S. Capitol was burned by the British in 1814.

5. President Jefferson, then retired, offered his personal library, which he had been collecting for fifty years, as a replacement.

6. After years of renovation, the beautifully restored Jefferson Building of the Library of Congress reopened to the public on May 1, 1997.

7. This coming weekend, we plan to scrape down the woodwork, patch a few little holes in the walls, and choose the paint color.

8. Coach Randall and the Physical Education Department director, Dr. Etheridge, have agreed on the schedule of practices.

9. Although many of my relatives live in the area around Des Moines, Iowa, my mother and father were both born in Illinois, she in Cairo and he in Chicago.

10. Please be sure to bring your scripts to the first rehearsal, which has been scheduled to begin promptly at 4:00 P.M., Thursday, January 17.

Commas B, p. 392
EXERCISE

1. Late in the spring, perhaps as late as May 15, the school board will dedicate the new school.

2. Chloe, who was named after her aunt, prefers to be called by her middle name, Ann.

3. According to this flier, the parade starts at the intersection of Broad Street and Elm Avenue, proceeds along Broad Street to city hall, and ends at the civic center.

4. "Nicholas," his father said, pointing to the billboard, "there's the playoff schedule."

5. Many old recipes, my mother told us, are less specific than the recipes in modern cookbooks.

6. In my notes, I've recorded that the first sprouts appeared on April 12, 2002, and the first bloom appeared on June 1.

7. Uh-oh, I finished the homework, but I forgot to put it in my backpack this morning.

8. The rehearsal ran late, past ten o'clock, so all of us feel a little sleepy today.

9. I was so tired that the cheerful chirping of the birds, which I usually enjoy, was annoying.

10. The loud, plaid pattern of his coat clashed with the gray pinstriped fabric of his trousers.

11. Framed and hung carefully above the fireplace, the portrait was truly impressive.

12. By the way, I hope you heard that the meeting we scheduled for Tuesday afternoon has been postponed until Thursday.

13. You should address the letter to Dr. Keith Inman, Director of Admissions, Chataway College, 1112 College Street, Chataway, NH 02011.

14. My uncle's dogs, Lucy and Linus, are purebred longhaired Chihuahuas.

15. Beverly likes broccoli and green beans, but for some reason, she never eats salads.

16. That boy's name is Michel, not Michael.

Language and Sentence Skills Practice Answer Key   **149**

17. Did you have Ms. Rocha for biology or Mr. Price͵ the same teacher͵ my brother had?

18. My little cousin's favorite book͵ *Goodnight Moon͵* has been read so many times͵ that the pages are falling out.

19. Unless one of the candidates͵ receives a clear majority͵ a runoff election will be held.

20. He's not in class this afternoon͵ because he had an appointment͵ I think͵ with the dentist.

Semicolons and Colons, p. 393
EXERCISE
Answers for items 5, 6, and 7 may vary.

1. Every morning he looked for signs of rain͵ every afternoon the sun baked the soil a little more.

2. Your application package should contain the <u>following</u>, two completed copies of the application form͵ your essay, double-spaced and neatly typed͵ three letters of recommendation, preferably from teachers or former employers͵ and a self-addressed, stamped envelope.

3. This week's rehearsals have been scheduled as <u>follows</u>, <u>4</u> 30 P.M. on Monday, Tuesday, and Wednesday͵ <u>6</u> 30 on Thursday͵ and <u>6</u> 00 on Friday.

4. This is exactly what the instructions <u>say</u>, Insert bolt A as shown on figure 2-C.

5. Michael is slightly older than his twin <u>brother</u>, Tom was born at <u>4</u> 39 P.M., five minutes later than Michael.

6. My cousin Taylor is a talented <u>athlete</u>, he plays on both the football and baseball teams, runs three miles almost every day, and swims at least twice a week.

7. We have to be at the station by <u>6</u> 15͵ the train leaves at <u>6</u> 30.

8. To fulfill the district's minimum requirements for graduation, you will need these <u>credits</u>, four years of English, three years of math, three years of science, and three years of social studies.

9. Electives in fine and performing arts are also required, as are computer science courses͵ two years of a foreign language are strongly recommended.

10. Despite their efforts to decipher the old map, they could not locate the buried treasure͵ perhaps, after all, it would remain forever hidden.

Quotation Marks with Other Punctuation A, p. 394
EXERCISE

[1] "Sure͵ no problem. [2] What kind of problems are they?"

[3] "Oh͵" Teresa said͵ "just some problems converting fractions to decimals. [4] I don't think I understood Ms. Minot's explanation very well. [5] I think she said͵ 'Divide everything by ten͵' or maybe she said͵ 'Multiply everything by ten͵' or maybe—oh͵ I just don't know!"

[6] "Well, I doubt she said any of those things͵ but let me show you. [7] Get me a piece of paper and a pencil͵ please." [8] Teresa ran from the room and came back with the items.

[9] "I don't suppose you could͵ well͵ just do one or two or maybe even four or five of these problems͵ could you?"

[10] "Teresa͵" sighed Reggie͵ barely suppressing a laugh͵ "how do you think that would help you learn to convert fractions to decimals?"

Copyright © by Holt, Rinehart and Winston. All rights reserved.

Quotation Marks with Other Punctuation B, p. 395

EXERCISE A

1. Martin's father took his glasses off, wiped his eyes, and said,_I don't know whether to laugh or cry about that.

2. _Are we supposed to read all of Chapter 16, The Cradle of Civilization_tonight?_Crystal asked.

3. _We certainly are_answered Cleo_but it's only thirty pages long.

4. Kim asked_Did I just make this up, or did Ms. Simpson really say_No homework tomorrow?

5. Isn't_Maria_one of the best known songs from *West Side Story*?

EXERCISE B

6. "Who's that?" Sun Mi wanted to know.

7. "Charles Drew, who was a surgeon," Clint said, "saved many lives in the early part of the century by networking blood banks."

8. Sun Mi asked, "Will that information help us get started on the Black History Month project?"

9. "Yes," Clint said, "but not just because he's an accomplished African American. Read this."

10. "Wow!" Sun Mi exclaimed. "It was only after Dr. Drew proved there was no scientific basis for labeling blood plasma according to ethnicity that the practice ceased in 1945."

Apostrophes, p. 396

EXERCISE

1. They should_ve been able to complete the assignment in an hour_s time.

2. This Friday_s game will probably be rained out; we_ll have to play a makeup game next week.

3. She_d be better off if she_d listened to her mother and father_s advice.

4. The Smiths_farm is in a neighboring county, near Zeke_s grandmother_s place.

5. I_d like to eat at Joe_s Family Restaurant tonight; they_re famous for their chicken and dumplings.

6. Our buses will leave from the south parking lot at four o_clock, and we_ll return from the theater by ten o_clock tonight.

7. We_ll be the class of_02.

8. Last winter_s big snowstorm badly damaged the barn_s roof.

9. If you order the special, you_ll be sure to get your money_s worth.

10. Did you hear that everyone_s bikes were smashed when the bus backed into the school_s bike rack?

11. Cecily_s parents_business is located near the People_s Drugstore on Main Street.

12. This teddy bear_s fur is torn and it_s missing an eye.

13. What_s the address of the girl whose grandmother_s photograph was published in the paper?

14. After a few minutes_rest, she_ll attempt the afternoon_s most difficult dive.

15. Cass_s distress was apparent to all of us.

16. Each member_s vote counts the same; no one_s vote is more important than anyone else_s.

17. Who's going to wake me up at four o'clock in the morning so that I'll be at the airport on time?

18. Isn't Al's painting style quite a bit different from everyone else's?

19. This week it's Dan and Felicia's turn to clean out the mice's cage.

20. The yearbook staff's photograph was mislabeled, much to Mr. Gomez's chagrin.

All Marks of Punctuation Review A, p. 397

Answers may vary slightly.

1. This first slide—could someone please get the lights?—is of the waterfall near our campsite.

2. I don't think I want to go to that store anymore; caveat emptor is written above the doorway.

3. "Oh, my," laughed Cecil. "That means 'Let the buyer beware.'"

4. How many of you have already read John Steinbeck's novel The Grapes of Wrath?

5. My great-grandfather was one of the Oklahomans who migrated to California during the Dustbowl of the 1930's.

6. Please do not bring any of the following items to camp: expensive jewelry, CD players, cellular telephones, or pagers.

7. I wish you could have seen his face—I almost burst out laughing!—when he realized it was a surprise party.

8. Nash, who is older than Neil, is a left-handed writer, but he paints with his right hand.

9. The Thirty Years' War (1618–1648), which began as a civil war, eventually involved most of Europe.

10. "No, no, no, a thousand times no!" yelled the hot-tempered conductor. "You'll have to do that part again, sopranos!"

All Marks of Punctuation Review B, p. 398

Answers may vary slightly.

May 2, 2003

[1] Dear Dr. Lebowitz:

[2] I'm writing to thank you, first of all, for speaking to senior class members planning to attend Prairie Tech U next fall. [3] In my opinion, the best talk was yours. [4] Your final comment about learning from our failures as well as from our successes (I've experienced a few of both) was appreciated. [5] What an inspirational speaker you are!

[6] I have, of course, another reason for writing: I am interested in knowing whether freshman leaders have been selected yet. [7] My application for one of the positions should have reached your office by the March 31, 12:00 P.M. deadline. [8] I realize both that there were many applicants and that you're quite busy, but I am hoping to find out before I complete the student loan process. [9] I knew the first time I read about the position in your booklet, "What Awaits You at Prairie Tech U," that I would enjoy taking on the extra duties. I look forward to hearing from your office.

[10] Sincerely,

Booker Williams

Spelling A, p. 399

1. judgment
2. cross-training
3. approval
4. conceited, reference
5. mischievous
6. concedes, weird
7. downhill
8. C
9. videos
10. development, supersede

EXERCISE B

11. As the group of runners stumbleed *stumbled* toward the finish line, their exhaustion was apparent.

12. The awkward silence was more than noticable *noticeable*; it was embarasing *embarrassing*.

13. The stubborness *stubbornness* of the superintendent had certainly been a factor in the rebelion *rebellion*.

14. C

15. C

16. This anonymous letter, accordding *according* to the police sergeant, is unmistakeably *unmistakably* the work of a disgruntled former employee.

17. The regulators' responsibility is to protect the innocent from the unnscrupulous *unscrupulous*.

18. C

19. There is no concievable *conceivable* reason this endeavor could fail.

20. C

Spelling B, p. 400

EXERCISE A

1. The choir director expects the sopranoes *sopranos* and the altoes *altos* to know they're *their* parts by Wednesday.

2. His father, who was an alumni *alumnus* of the university, interceeded *interceded* with the dean.

3. The attornies *attorneys* general of several states met to discuss the settlement yesterday.

4. Tornados *Tornadoes [or C]* have been seen in the area during the past few hours.

5. 27 *Twenty-seven* students signed up for the calculus class.

6. C [or Z's; 3's]

7. Your assignment is to read pages two hundred fifty-seven *257* through two hundred ninety-five *295*.

8. The number of bookshelfs *bookshelves* in this library is insufficeint *insufficient*.

9. Unfortunatly *Unfortunately*, the accident that occured *occurred* last night was unavoidable.

10. The international financeir *financier* apparently considered the law no hindrance to his activitys *activities*.

EXERCISE B

11. thieves
12. libraries
13. editors in chief
14. waltzes
15. Hernandezes
16. cameos
17. runners-up
18. phenomena [or phenomenons]
19. 1970s [or 1970's]
20. feet
21. cherubim [or cherubs]
22. DVDs [or DVD's]
23. trash
24. Sandys
25. ancestries
26. foxes
27. theories
28. cacti [or cactuses]
29. i's
30. radios

Words Often Confused, p. 401

EXERCISE A

1. borne
2. complement
3. counsel
4. latter
5. past
6. minor
7. Who's
8. led
9. personnel
10. desert

EXERCISE B

11. I can't describe the affect *effect* the defeat had on the team's moral *morale*.

12. As soon as their *they're* finished talking to the career councilor *counselor*, we'll join them for refreshments.

13. One of the fundamental principals *principles* of our democracy is the right of citizens to choose their representatives.

14. Jeff had all ready *already* ensured *assured* his father that he would have the breaks *brakes* adjusted.

15. The venture capitol *capital* firm has borne most of the company's financial losses.

16. C

17. I had to go to the stationary [*stationery*] store because I needed a single, large peace [*piece*] of a certain kind of paper.

18. Are you quite sure that one of you're [*your*] fillings is lose [*loose*]?

19. If my plain [*plane*] leaves at four o'clock, than [*then*] we need to leave for the airport by half past two.

20. When I past [*passed*] her the ball, she wasn't quiet [*quite*] ready.

Spelling and Words Often Confused, p. 402
EXERCISE

[1] February 10, 2003 [*C*]

To: Ms. Carol Varner

[2] From: Senior Class Counsel [*Council*]

[3] Subject: Status of Courtyard Landscaping Project [*C*]

[4] At it's [*its*] first meeting last fall, the representatives of the senior class voted to landscape the courtyard outside the cafeteria as our classes [*class's*] gift to the school. [5] Spring, of coarse [*course*], is just around the corner, and we want to make every concieveable [*conceivable*] effort to finish the project by May. [6] Our goals, as you know, are to beautify our surrounddings [*surroundings*], to camouflage some of the unssightly [*unsightly*] chain-link fence, and to lower noise levels. [7] The echoes of a hundred voices bounce off the brick walls and must be irritating for the counsilors [*counselors*] who's [*whose*] offices overlook the courtyard.

[8] We have added compost to the soil in the planters and beds, and replaced the sundial that had fallen off it's [*its*] pedestal. [9] We beleive [*believe*] the small trees, shrubs, and flowers we have chosen will compliment [*complement*] the building's design and colors. [10] Some of the students have familiarized themselfs [*themselves*] with the plants that grow best in our region; none of the plants should require more then [*than*] routine maintenance. [11] The planting will begin next Wednesday after school and will last until 6 [*six*] o'clock or latter [*later*]. [12] All together [*Altogether*], we expect forty or fifty volunteers to work on the project. [13] With hard work and a minimum amount of capitol [*capital*], we will transform our "dessert" [*desert*] into a lush garden. [14] It will certainly be a more pleasant and pieceful [*peaceful*] place then [*than*] it is now.

[15] As we have discused [*discussed*] in the passed [*past*], we'd like to hold a dedication ceremony early in May. [16] We'd like to invite both you and Mr. Raymond, the principle [*principal*], to speak at the dedicateion [*dedication*]. [17] Also, we all want you to know how much we've appreciated your council [*counsel*] and your fundraising expertise. [18] Thank's [*Thanks*] for all you're [*your*] help. [19] The class is also grateful to the PTA. [*C*]

[20] We twelvth [*twelfth*] graders—the Class of 03 [*'03*]— are all ready [*already*] looking foreword [*forward*] to the time when we can revisit our courtyard as alumnea [*alumni*]!

Review A: Usage, p. 403
EXERCISE A

1. C

2. Humphrey Bogart, along with Ingrid Bergman, increased their [*his*] fame in a film story set in Casablanca, Morocco.

3. The Trail of Tears refer [*refers*] to the route of the Cherokee people on their forced march to a reservation west of the Mississippi in the 1830s.

4. *Heart of Darkness*, a novel well known among Joseph Conrad's works, concern [*concerns*] the search for a corrupt adventurer in the interior of Africa.

5. For his and her *(their)* science project, Alice and Casey tested several hundred students.

EXERCISE B

Answers may vary. Sample responses are given.

6. Long, low, and lonesome, the whistle of a faraway train pierced the night.

7. Covered with dirt and scratches from their struggle through the underbrush, the weary hikers were refreshed by the cool waters of the creek.

8. The screenwriter adapted the novel better than any other writer.

9. The class met the visiting professor, recently arrived from Denmark.

10. You would hardly recognize him if you saw him; he's as tall as his brother now.

Review B: Mechanics, p. 404

EXERCISE A

Answers may vary slightly.

1. I'd really like to have a big salad tonight. Please bring these items from the store: romaine lettuce, tomatoes, a red onion, and two cucumbers.

2. Last Wednesday afternoon—I believe it was Wednesday, but it may have been Tuesday—the faculty met with the principal and discussed plans for the new wing.

3. The Gomezes' cat's name is Mr. Tibbs.

4. Our journey's end finally in sight, we sighed with relief.

5. According to the police report, the victim of the hit-and-run accident told the officer that he (the victim) doesn't remember what happened.

6. Cecilia likes to read mysteries. I told her she should try the novels of P. D. James, including *An Unsuitable Job for a Woman*.

7. "Let me see," said the birdwatcher. "My book says that bird is called a two-toed, red-feathered, purple-spotted something or other."

8. "Oh, Grandma, what big teeth you have!" cried the little girl in the red, hooded cape.

9. My father still can recite Tennyson's poem "The Charge of the Light Brigade," which he memorized when he was an eighth-grader.

10. Embarrassed, Nick picked up the note cards he had dropped on the floor and said, "OK, um, let me see where I was. . . . Oh, here's my place!"

Review C: Usage and Mechanics, p. 405

EXERCISE

Answers may vary slightly.

[1] On saturday night, november 28, 1942, that situation began to change. [2] Fire breaked *(broke)* out in the cocoanut grove, a huge, popular nightclub in boston. of the nearly 1 *(one)* thousand people packed into the club, more than 400 *(four hundred)* died, and hundreds more were injured. [3] recent medical breakthroughs helped save many lives; the victims were given blood plasma injections (the technology for separateing *(separating)* plasma was only four years old at the time), and to combat infection, sulfadiazine, one of the sulfa drugs discovered in the 1930s and 1940s *(or 1930's)(or 1940's)*, was administered.

[4] Sulfa drugs, however, couldn't combat infection from Staphylococcus aureus, a bacteria *(bacterium)* that often infected burn wounds and skin grafts. at the time, most burn patients who got a staph *(or "staph")* infection died. [5] the drug that could fight staph infections was penicillin, discovered by british scientist alexander fleming in 1928, but it was hard to manufacture, and only a small supply existed, reserved for the use of the u.s. military forces. [6] An emergency supply of penicillin was driven from the production facility of the drug's manufacturer, merck & co., inc., in new jersey, three hundred sixty-eight *(368)* miles to the massachusetts general hospital in boston.

[7] The survival of the cocoanut grove fire's victims focused national attention on the new "wonder drug." [8] Penicillin seemed to work

miracles, stopping infections that ~~formally~~ _formerly_ killed
~~there~~ _their_ victims and ~~cureing~~ _curing_ pneumonia and
blood infections. **[9]** by 1945, however,
fleming, penicillin's ~~inventor,~~ _discoverer_ was warning
against the overuse of the drug, for he had
~~all ready~~ _already_ been able to grow ~~bacteriums~~ _bacteria_ that
were ~~resistent~~ _resistant_ to penicillin. **[10]** in fact, fleming
predicted that, as people started to take peni-
cillin at home rather than in the hospital, more
drug-resistant bacteria would develop. fleming
was worried that many people wouldn't take
the drug properly.

Proofreading Application: E-mail, p. 406
Revisions may vary slightly. A sample revision is
given.

TO: customerservice@discsbymail.com

SUBJECT: Unacceptable Service

To Whom It May Concern:

About four months ago I received your
glossy advertisement to join your Discs-by-Mail
Club, the offer seemed very attractive. Almost
too good to be true. Now I realize it was too
good to be true.

I sent you my first order the same day your
advertisement arrived, the three CDs I had
ordered showed up in my mailbox _ten_ days
later, Than the delivery time stated on your
agreement. The next month only two of the
four CDs that arrived were ones I had requested, I had to go to the trouble of mailing the two
Frank Sinatra CDs back to you.

To make me a satisfied customer, At this
point, the only thing you can do is cancel my
club membership.

Sincerely,

Lajos Bartok

Literary Model: Drama, pp. 407–408

EXERCISE A

Common Sentence Error	Revision
1. double negative	haven't done anything
2. adjective where adverb needed	talk in a more genteel manner
3. adjective where adverb needed	speak sensibly
4. incorrect past form	before I came, I did
5. objective case for nominative	She that (_or_ who)
6. incorrect past form	I did
7. double negative	don't care for anything
8. double negative	don't want any gold or any
9. lack of subject/ verb agreement	why ladies are
10. double negative	don't ever want to see

EXERCISE B
Answers will vary. A sample response is given.
Shaw might have wanted to show that intelligence, ambition, and a sense of fair play don't
rise and fall with the perfection of speech
conventions.

EXERCISE C
Answers will vary. A sample response is given.
Vendor: I come for a job in your flower shop, I
does, Miss.

Liza: I see. Have you any experience selling
flowers?

Vendor: What do you call the likes of these in
this here basket?

Liza: Yes, of course. You do well in your trade
then?

Vendor: Never had no complaints to speak of,
though my feet's givin' me the dickens.

Liza: I wonder if you'd like a part-time job learning to bundle and arrange the flowers before they're put on the floor?

Vendor: You wouldn't want me takin' on no gentlemen buyers out in the shop, I take it.

Liza: Why don't we see how you do? If you learn the trade, we'll teach you to communicate with the customers. What do you say?

Exercise D

Answers will vary. A sample response is given.

In friendly e-mail communication it is sometimes fun to spice up a message with informal or nonstandard usage. Using *ain't*, for example, provides emphasis or tone sometimes. On the other hand, whenever I'm communicating with a supervisor on the job I use my standard English and a formal tone. Even a brief message to a college official or employer should be free of slang and nonstandard usage. My private journal is written in any style that pleases me at the time!

Writing Application: Newsletter, p. 409

Writing Applications are designed to provide students immediate composition practice in using key concepts taught in each chapter of the *Language and Sentence Skills Practice* booklet. You may wish to evaluate student responses to these assignments as you do any other writing that students produce. To save grading time, however, you may want to use the following scoring rubric.

Scoring Rubric

The explanation uses ten indefinite pronouns with correct agreement.

1   2   3   4   5

The explanation of the ceremony is clear and adequate.

1   2   3   4   5

The explanation's tone and diction inspire confidence.

1   2   3   4   5

The assignment is relatively free of errors in usage and mechanics.

1   2   3   4   5

Total Score _____

5 = highest; 1 = lowest

Chapter 17: Writing Clear Sentences, pp. 411–32

Selecting Appropriate Conjunctions, pp. 411–12

EXERCISE A

Answers will vary. Sample answers follow.

1. and
2. consequently,
3. however,
4. therefore,
5. and
6. Hence,
7. neither . . . nor
8. Nevertheless,
9. but
10. Both . . . and

EXERCISE B

Answers will vary. Sample answers follow.

11. however,
12. and
13. Because
14. neither . . . nor
15. Nevertheless,
16. consequently,
17. as well as
18. but | however,
19. but
20. therefore, | and

Selecting Appropriate Subordinating Conjunctions, pp. 413–14

EXERCISE A

Answers will vary. Sample answers follow.

1. Before
2. When
3. Although
4. Even though
5. Because
6. As
7. so that
8. Despite
9. while
10. Although

EXERCISE B

Answers will vary. Sample answers follow.

11. While
12. so that
13. Since
14. even though
15. Because
16. because
17. when
18. As
19. So that
20. Though

Revising Sentences by Inserting Adverb Clauses, pp. 415–16

EXERCISE A

Answers will vary. Sample answers follow.

1. When they first begin, most music students find that playing the piano is not as easy as it looks.
2. Understanding the notes can be difficult if a student cannot read music well.
3. Many of the exercises can be repetitive while a student is first learning to play.
4. Even though they may learn to play quite well, most piano students will not become concert pianists.
5. Concert grand pianos are the most melodic, whereas a used practice piano may not carry a tune as well.
6. Good coordination is necessary for playing the piano whenever a piece of music is technically difficult.
7. Since the pianist does not press down directly on the strings, playing the piano is probably easier than playing a violin or a cello.
8. Most pianists practice for several hours before a recital so that they can perform well.
9. Most amateur pianists feel a sense of accomplishment after they have finished a successful performance.
10. Some people find that playing the piano is an excellent mood brightener despite the hard work required to play well.

Answers will vary. Sample answers follow.

11. Some people devote several hours a week to fitness workouts, whereas others have no time to exercise.

12. If you use your imagination, including exercise in your lifestyle does not require sacrificing hours of time.

13. Instead of taking the elevator, climb the stairs so that you can build exercise into your daily routine.

14. As you enter a parking lot, look for a parking place that requires you to walk some distance to the building.

15. Parking at the extreme edge of the parking lot can be advantageous since you get some exercise and save your car some dents and scrapes.

16. Although you may need to adapt your schedule to allow for the additonal time, try walking briskly or bicycling to school or work.

17. You will hardly notice the extra minutes that exercise takes out of your day unless you are unusually hard-pressed for time.

18. Though you may not be aware of it, dancing is one of the best forms of aerobic exercise.

19. Along with exercise, you may want to experiment with some dietary changes while you increase your activity level.

20. After you use these methods for a few months, you may notice increased muscle tone and higher energy levels.

Subordinating Ideas by Using Adjective Clauses, pp. 417–18

EXERCISE A

Answers will vary. Sample answers follow.

1. Basketball, which was not well known until 1946, is a popular sport today.

2. The Harlem Globetrotters team, which consisted of former African American college stars, helped make basketball a successful spectator sport.

3. The Globetrotters, who got their start in 1926, won fans by touring all over the world.

4. Basketball games that helped the Globetrotters establish themselves internationally were flashy and comical.

5. The Globetrotters, who defeated almost all other teams until the 1950s, continue to thrill and amuse their audiences.

6. In 1946, the Basketball Association of America, which was responding to the demands of basketball fans, began staging professional games.

7. The fans, many of whom bought tickets for every game, wanted to see their favorite college players continue as professionals.

8. In California, where Stanford University players perfected the jump shot, college basketball was as popular as it was on the East Coast.

9. In 1949, the Basketball Association of America, which was a league that played in mid-size cities in the Midwest, merged with the National Basketball Association (NBA).

10. NBA superstars, who are well rewarded for their talent, have become wealthy celebrities.

EXERCISE B

Answers will vary. Sample answers follow.

11. Europeans, who once thought mountains were too dangerous to ascend, did not climb tall peaks until the late 1700s.

12. Mont Blanc, which is Europe's highest peak, was first reached by Swiss climbers in 1786.

13. Mountain climbing tools and clothing that were once quite awkward are now sophisticated.

14. Early climbers, who needed protection from cold and snow, wore bulky, heavy clothing.

15. Contemporary climbers, who are not weighed down by heavy attire, wear thin layers of special weather-resistant clothing.

Correcting Faulty Coordination, pp. 419–20

EXERCISE A

Answers will vary. Sample answers follow.

1. *When* Syrians began arriving in the United States around 1900, ~~and~~ most needed to find employment as soon as possible.

2. Some Syrians accepted jobs in factories, ~~and~~ *while* many became peddlers traveling the country.

3. Women peddled ~~also, and they peddled~~ in order to make money and raise the standard of living.

4. Sometimes women were more successful at peddling than men, ~~and~~ *because* people trusted the female peddlers more easily than their male counterparts.

5. The peddlers got their start by finding a Syrian supplier, ~~and~~ *whom* someone else recommended ~~the supplier~~.

6. *When* Peddlers were successful, ~~and~~ they became suppliers.

7. Sometimes the peddlers joined together *to* ~~and they~~ formed communities.

8. *When* The peddlers traveled long distances, ~~and~~ they carr*ying* heavy packs.

9. They traveled to faraway places, ~~and~~ *where* people wanted their goods.

10. *Although* ~~The~~ Syrians succeeded in business as peddlers, ~~and~~ department stores threatened their livelihood.

EXERCISE B

Answers will vary. Sample answers follow.

11. Transcendentalism was a philosophical and literary movement, ~~and it~~ *that* flourished in New England in the mid-1800s.

12. The chief source of transcendentalist ideology was a book called *Critique of Pure Reason*, ~~and this book was~~ written by the German philosopher Immanuel Kant.

13. An innovative educator who based his philosophy on transcendentalist theory was Bronson Alcott, ~~and he was the~~ father of Louisa May Alcott, author of *Little Women*.

14. *Because* The movement was idealistic and visionary, ~~and~~ it attracted the attention of many famous authors.

15. However, the most famous proponent of transcendentalism was Ralph Waldo Emerson, ~~and he was~~ an essayist, poet, and lecturer.

16. Some transcendentalists *who* wanted to create independent communes; ~~and they~~ disliked the conventional stereotyping of male and female roles in society.

17. The transcendentalists created two communities, ~~and these communities~~ *that* were utopian, or idealistic.

18. Brook Farm, *which* required all residents to work and share profits equally, ~~and it~~ was only briefly successful as a transcendentalist community.

19. Most American literature courses include *Nature* and "Self-Reliance"; ~~these works were~~ written by Emerson.

20. Students may search the Internet; ~~the Internet~~ *which* contains information on literary movements.

Correcting Faulty Parallelism, pp. 421–22

EXERCISE A

Answers will vary. Sample answers follow.

1. The country of South Africa has ~~no~~ *neither* navigable rivers ~~and does not have~~ *nor* high mountain ranges ~~either~~.

2. In most of South Africa, finding hardwood forests is as difficult as ~~to~~ find^(ing) abundant rainfall.

3. To increase their water supply, South Africans have built dams, developed water projects, dug wells, and ration~~ing~^(ed) water.

4. During the summer, tropical air masses move south, causing thunderstorms, scattering hail, and trigger^(ing) dangerous lightning.

5. Important geographical facts about South Africa include that most of the country has an elevation of 3,000 to 6,500 feet above sea level, that it is^(has) bordered^(ing it) on three sides ~~by the~~ ⟨ocean⟩, and ~~having~~ ^(that it has) only sporadic rainfall.

6. The Atlantic Ocean's cold Benguela Current causes both fog and low~~ers the~~^(y) temperatures on the West Coast.

7. C

8. The ingenuity of the South African people is evident in the fact that they built these dams to supply drinking water and ^(to) provid~~ing~^(e) hydroelectric power.

9. A class project can be an opportunity to learn about the strengths ^(and ingenuity) of a foreign country ~~and learning about the ingenuity that it has~~^(y).

10. C

EXERCISE B
Answers will vary. Sample answers follow.

11. (tr) Are you most interested in the personal lives or in the ⟨activities⟩ ~~that were~~^(y) political of early American leaders?

12. During her oral report on James Madison, Tamorra quoted from his speeches and ~~was~~^(y) describ~~ing~^(ed) his political stance.

13. James Madison is important to history both as the Father of the Constitution and ~~being~~^(as) the fourth president of the United States.

14. Madison participated in the Constitutional Convention of 1787, where his role in designing the system of checks and balances was as significant as his part ~~to~~^(in) create^(ing) the U.S. federal system.

15. Like his close friend Thomas Jefferson, Madison decided to oppose a national bank not only to thwart the growth of manufacturing, but ^(also to) supporting^(y) a strong central government.

16. As a member of the Virginia assembly, Madison not only supported Jefferson's appeal for the separation of church and state but also confront^(ed)~~ing~~ the skilled orator Patrick Henry on the issue.

17. Drafting the Bill of Rights demonstrated both Madison's eloquence and ~~that he~~^(y) ^(his) respected^(y for) democratic principles.

18. Jefferson asked Madison to be secretary of state not only because of their friendship but also ^(because of) ~~Jefferson recognized~~^(y) Madison's ability.

19. As secretary of state, Madison supported the Embargo Act of 1807, which failed both because U.S. merchants ignored it and ^(because) loss of trade damaged the economy.

20. During Madison's first administration as president, rising nationalism became as strong a reason for supporting the War of 1812 as ~~to~~^(y) stop^(ping) the destruction of free trade.

Review A: Revising Paragraphs for Clarity, pp. 423–24

EXERCISE A

Answers will vary. Sample answers follow.

The first tissue cells, called earlywood, are big, remain relatively far apart, and have thin walls. However, the latewood cells, formed later in the tree's development, are small, appear close together, and have thick walls. In most cases, the light earlywood and dark latewood of trees create distinct rings that are visible to the naked eye. Ring growth and appearance are influenced both by soil variations and by atmospheric conditions.

The most extensive American tree-ring record, which is almost 8,700 years, is held by the bristlecone pine. Approximately 7,300 years of rings have been identified in the wood of some buried oaks in Europe.

Archaeologists examine tree rings either to determine dates of events and objects or to analyze changing environments. Tree-ring science, called dendrochronology, has been used to pinpoint the dates of everything from wooden artworks to forest fires. The Laboratory of Tree-Ring Research established at the University of Arizona, Tucson, is the largest in the world.

EXERCISE B

Answers will vary. Sample answers follow.

Ancient Greeks had imaginative theories about geological phenomena. The Greek philosopher Aristotle, for example, believed not only that minerals were produced when the earth breathed but also that the earth was round.

Ancient Romans had creative theories about volcanic smoke and eruptions. They thought that an active volcano on Vulcano, an island in the Tyrrhenian Sea, was the home of a god. (It is likely that the word *volcano* is derived from the name of this island.) Vulcan was the Roman god both of metalworking and of fire. According to myth, Vulcan was the gods' blacksmith. The Romans believed that Vulcan's forge produced smoke and that this smoke drifted from the crater of the volcano. When the volcano exploded, the Romans thought that Vulcan was hammering on his blacksmith's anvil.

Fossils inspired imaginative theories, too. Herodotus, the Greek historian, had unusual ideas about fossilized shells that he discovered embedded in Egyptian limestone. The fossils, he guessed, were actually lentils that had been dropped by the slaves who constructed the pyramids.

Revising to Eliminate Fragments, pp. 425–26

EXERCISE A

Answers will vary. Sample answers follow.

1. Snakes never blink. And seem unable to close their staring eyes.

2. Actually, snakes' eyes are always closed. Because their lower, transparent eyelids are permanently raised.

3. Snakes look through this thin lower eyelid, Which is fused to a piece of skin that used to be an upper eyelid.

4. Oddly enough, snakes' eyes are permanently focused. On objects in the distance.

5. To see items that are nearby, These creatures must contract the lenses of their eyes forward.

6. Snakes are lacking ears. Protruding that e from their bodies.

7. Having no eardrums, Snakes are unable to hear the way human beings do.

8. Snakes' inner ears process vibrations. that Traveling through the ground.

9. A snake darts its tongue in and out. To gather minute amounts of chemicals in the air.

10. *C*

EXERCISE B
Answers will vary. Sample answers follow.

11. Pauli Murray, an African American, was not only a biographer. But also a historian, poet, priest, teacher, lawyer, and activist.

12. Murray was orphaned at three, *was* Being raised in her grandparents' home by an aunt.

13. Murray's aunt, a teacher, taught her to read and write, And Murray's grandparents provided strong role models.

14. For example, Murray's grandfather was a Civil War veteran, Helped establish one of the original schools for free African Americans in Virginia and North Carolina.

15. C

16. Murray earned degrees from several colleges and became a teacher. Even though Harvard University had rejected her because she was female.

17. Working as a lawyer, Murray fought for civil rights and for the right of women to attend graduate school.

18. In 1977, Murray became a priest of the Episcopal Church, The first African American woman to do so.

19. C

20. Murray emphasized the use of imagination to confront and cope with trauma. Also stressing the integration of spiritual and social values.

Revising Run-on Sentences, pp. 427–28

EXERCISE A
Answers will vary. Sample answers follow.

1. There are about 150 species of octopus they live in seas all over the world.

2. Some octopuses live at the bottom of the sea, *but* others prefer being near the water's surface.

3. Typically an octopus measures between one and two feet in length however a few types grow to as long as thirty feet.

4. An octopus uses the suction cups on its tentacles to move across the ocean floor, it can also expel water and move by propulsion.

5. This sea creature has a beak resembling that of a parrot after biting its prey, the octopus injects it with poisonous saliva.

6. If a hard shell protects the prey, an octopus can drill into it, to bore a hole, an octopus uses its radula, a hard structure that resembles a tongue.

7. An octopus can eject ink if it feels threat- *, and* ened the ink temporarily retains the shape of the octopus and distracts the enemy.

8. The soft body of an octopus looks like an *; however* empty sack, it contains a sophisticated brain and nervous system.

9. Octopus eyes resemble those of vertebrates each has a movable lens, retina, cornea, and iris.

10. The octopus is intelligent, scientific experimentation has shown that this mollusk uses its complex brain and optical systems to learn.

EXERCISE B
Answers will vary. Sample answers follow.

11. Snow consists of miniature crystals made of ice snowflakes are created when these fragments of frozen water adhere to each other.

12. If the temperature exceeds −40°F, a snow crystal needs a foreign particle to act as a nucleus, without a nucleus, the crystal cannot form.

Language and Sentence Skills Practice Answer Key

13. Usually, nuclei are particles of sea salt or minerals。less frequently, nuclei are particles of automobile and industry exhaust.

14. Snow crystals always have a symmetrical six-sided structure, *; nevertheless* they exist in an apparently limitless range of forms.

15. There are seven different kinds of snow crystal shapes, *and* they all are incredibly beautiful.

16. One type of snow crystal looks like a perfectly formed glass column with a cap on each end, it could have been designed by an architect.

17. Another kind of snow crystal resembles a pansy blossom, *however,* it is more precisely formed than a flower.

18. A snow crystal's shape is largely determined by the temperature when it was formed, *but* it is also slightly influenced by humidity.

19. The size of snow crystals is affected by the amount of moisture in the air, large crystals are formed when the humidity is high.

20. The beauty of snow crystals makes them an appealing subject for photography。several fine collections of pictures have been published.

Correcting Unnecessary Shifts in Subject, Tense, and Voice, pp. 429–30

EXERCISE A
Answers will vary. Sample answers follow.

1. German pianist Clara Schumann was an unusual child because she *did* is not speaking until she was eight years old.

2. Taught to play the piano by her father, Clara perform*ed*s her first concert at age nine in 1828.

3. His daughter became one of the most famous pianists in history and also *was* is known as a gifted composer.

4. Clara often traveled to new cities and play*ed*s concerts.

5. She wrote almost two dozen pieces for piano, and often one of them was performed by her at each of her concerts. *(tr)* — *ing*

6. After she married composer Robert Schumann, *Clara stopped composing* ~~new works were no longer composed by Clara.~~

7. C

8. Robert die*d*s when Clara was thirty-seven, so she began a full-time concert career to support her family.

9. Clara's performing career, which lasted for sixty years, *was* is longer and more accomplished than that of any of her male peers.

10. C

EXERCISE B
Answers will vary. Sample answers follow.

11. C

12. Johnson saved money from part-time jobs and fled to New York, where *he began* art school ~~was begun.~~

13. Johnson saved his wages from odd jobs in New York and won scholarships, and then *he used* the money ~~was used~~ to travel to Paris.

14. Thereafter, he usually avoided the United States and lived abroad because *he* it was thought that African Americans had a better life there.

15. Johnson evenually settled in Denmark, where *he married* a Danish weaver named Holcha Krake ~~was married to him.~~

16. C

17. Krake coordinated joint exhibits of their art and ~~was~~ supporting^ed the couple with profits from the sale of her weavings.

18. Johnson liked to paint at a Danish fishing village, ~~and~~ where he attracted who people enjoyed watching him dance while he worked.

19. He painted peaceful scenes of small-town life and active city street scenes, but he also depicts^ed historical events, such as the 1943 riots in Harlem.

20. Johnson was a popular, but not a famous, artist—one of his paintings ~~is~~ was shown in 1940 at the New York World's Fair.

Review B: Revising Paragraphs for Clarity, pp. 431–32

EXERCISE A

Answers will vary.

The writer Carl Sandburg did not have an easy childhood. The mattress on which he was born was stuffed with corn husks. As a youth, Sandburg was thrown in jail twice—once for riding on a freight train without paying and another time for swimming naked in a pond.

Sandburg held a variety of jobs, ranging from firefighter to traveling salesperson. He did not have much money, but he often bought books instead of food. Finally, he married and began to work at a series of newspaper jobs. Late at night, he wrote poetry.

Among Sandburg's many prizes for his poetry were two Pulitzers. He was interviewed on almost every major television talk show. However, he was happiest when schools were named for him. When Sandburg died at eighty-nine, he was famous worldwide. "Fog" and "Chicago" are just two of his many well-known poems.

EXERCISE B

Answers will vary.

Mary Shelley's mother was the author of *A Vindication of the Rights of Women*, and her father was an influential philosopher. Mary wrote stories as a young child. At sixteen, she met Percy Bysshe Shelley, a young poet whom she later married.

During a visit to Geneva, Switzerland, Mary wrote a short story that was later expanded to a novel. She named the novel *Frankenstein; or, The Modern Prometheus*. It is one of the most famous horror stories of all time; almost everyone is familiar with this bizarre tale of scientific experimentation gone awry.

When Percy Shelley drowned at sea in 1822, Mary occupied herself with educating their child, promoting her husband's poetry, keeping a journal, corresponding, and writing novels. Many critics believe that her best work is not *Frankenstein*, but a book called *The Last Man*. This futuristic novel relates the story of how all of humanity is destroyed by a devastating plague.

Chapter 18: Combining Sentences, pp. 433–48

Inserting Adjectives, Adverbs, and Prepositional Phrases, pp. 433–34

EXERCISE A

Answers will vary. Sample answers follow.

1. Jamila has collected her observations and posted them. ~~The observations are~~ of the falcons. ~~Her observations are~~ on her own Web site.

2. The peregrine falcon is a bird whose population is declining. It displays characteristics of a typical bird. ~~The number of falcons is decreasing~~ across the United States, Europe, and Asia.

3. The peregrine falcon adapts to *various* climates. ~~These climates vary.~~ It adapts quickly.

(tr) 4. The falcon is a bird of prey. ~~Its feathers are~~ *with* bluish gray. ~~It has~~ *and* a short, curved, notched beak.

5. The falcon hunts *and kills diverse* animals. ~~It kills animals~~ by swooping down on them. ~~The animals are diverse.~~

6. The falcon dives on its prey and kills it. ~~It kills the prey~~ by the force of the impact. ~~The prey is~~ unsuspecting.

7. Peregrine falcons often inhabit areas where smaller birds are plentiful. ~~The areas are open and rocky.~~ ~~The areas are~~ near water.

8. Peregrine falcons also like to nest in cities. ~~Peregrine falcons like nesting in large cities.~~ ~~They like nesting~~ on high skyscrapers.

9. The falcons like cities ~~for a good reason.~~ It's because of the supply of pigeons. ~~The supply of pigeons is~~ abundant.

10. Falconry is a sport *that* ~~Falconry~~ involves training birds of prey to hunt game. ~~These birds are~~ strong and swift.

EXERCISE B

Answers will vary. Sample answers follow.

11. New deposits of sediment continue to build on top of the rocks. ~~This occurs~~ throughout the canyon. ~~The rocks have many layers.~~

12. Colca Canyon is a *deep* fissure in *southern* Peru. ~~It is in southern Peru. Colca Canyon is a deep fissure.~~

13. *Amazingly,* Colca Canyon is deeper than the Grand Canyon. ~~The Grand Canyon is~~ in Arizona. ~~The depth of Colca Canyon is amazing.~~

14. Made by the Colca River, the canyon is the deepest on the planet *in a lengthy process over thousands of years*. ~~The process was lengthy. In fact, it took many thousands of years.~~

15. The canyon walls consist of *layers of spectacular* rocks. ~~The rocks are layered. The rocks are spectacular.~~

16. The sediment shaped the rocks into *enormous, multicolored* folds. ~~The folds are enormous. They also have many different colors.~~

17. Many of the rock layers are *sedimentary* ~~old~~. They are 100 to 160 million years old. ~~They were formed from sediment.~~

18. *Adventurous* People can glimpse the sedimentary rock formations. ~~The people are adventurous.~~ ~~The formations can be seen~~ as they paddle kayaks down the *choppy* river. ~~The river is choppy.~~

19. Colca Canyon continues to deepen. ~~The deepening of the canyon is gradual.~~ *ly* It deepens because of constant erosion.

20. College geology professors teach their students. ~~They tell students~~ about Colca Canyon and rock formations. ~~The other rock formations are~~ in other locations.

Using Participial and Absolute Phrases, pp. 435–36

EXERCISE A

Answers will vary. Sample answers follow.

1. Nationally known for her lectures, Janet Harmon Bragg also wrote newspaper columns.

2. Encouraging her African American audiences, Bragg urged them to become aviators.

3. Making stunt flights across America, Bessie Coleman showed courage early in her career.

4. Discouraged by rejection from an American aviation school, Coleman went to France for her flight training.

5. In 1921, she was issued a pilot's license allowing her to fly all over the world.

6. Her global fame assured, Coleman was the first American to receive this type of license.

7. Coleman, returning to America soon afterward, began an aviation school.

8. Making impressive exhibition stunt flights, Coleman attempted to inspire other African Americans to become pilots.

9. Advertisements appealing to audiences of that time promised that she would be seen in motion pictures.

10. Attracting attention, Coleman's flights were significant because she was the only African American female pilot of the period.

EXERCISE B

Answers will vary. Sample answers follow.

11. Created about 2000 B.C., the *Epic of Gilgamesh* is one of the most significant epics.

12. Containing parts of ancient myths, *The Epic of Gilgamesh* is similar to the *Odyssey*.

13. Audiences, loving the legend of Gilgamesh, have enjoyed this epic for thousands of years.

14. Gods and goddesses' concocting many strange adventures for him, the life of Gilgamesh was filled with danger and excitement.

15. Watched by a fire-breathing monster, Gilgamesh chopped down a tree in a sacred forest.

16. Enraged by the king's bold act, the monster charged at Gilgamesh.

17. The monster, blinded by gusts of hot wind, stopped his assault.

18. Obsessed with discovering the secret of immortality, Gilgamesh never reached his goal.

19. The gods and goddesses keeping this secret, Gilgamesh did, however, manage to find an herb that would restore his youth.

20. Accepting his mortality and vulnerability, the king eventually returned home and died.

Using Appositive Phrases, pp. 437–38

EXERCISE A

Answers will vary. Sample answers follow.

1. Octavio Paz's poems contain images of his Indian past and of the Mexican landscape. His poems are lyrical pieces that express his loneliness.

2. In 1933, Octavio Paz published his first book of poems at age nineteen. Paz was a Mexican poet, social critic, and essayist.

3. His most respected long poem was written about the planet Venus. The piece is called *Salamandra*.

4. He was a multitalented author, Paz is famous for not only his poetry but also his prose.

5. One of his prose works is taught in literature courses all over the world. It is a book titled *The Labyrinth of Solitude*.

6. Another of his prose works addresses the history of Mexico and of the world. Paz called this text *Itinerario*.

Language and Sentence Skills Practice Answer Key

7. Paz won the world's highest literary honor in 1990. ~~He was awarded~~ the Nobel Prize in literature.

8. ~~Paz was~~ a career diplomat. ~~He~~ spent twenty-five years at posts in the diplomatic service.

9. Paz was committed to fighting social injustice. He died in 1998.

10. Paz's literary work is an inspiration to writers who follow in his footsteps. ~~His work~~ is frequently studied in college courses.

EXERCISE B

Answers will vary. Sample answers follow.

11. The kidney keeps a constant balance between water and dissolved chemicals in most animals. It is the main organ for filtering waste matter.

12. The human kidney contains about a million micro-organs. ~~The kidney is~~ a remarkably complex organ.

13. Nephrons manufacture about 1.5 quarts of urine every day. ~~They are~~ micro-organs.

14. ~~A glomerulus is~~ a snarled clump of capillaries. Blood passes into a nephron through a glomerulus.

15. The blood's plasma is filtered through the glomerulus and a surrounding pocket. ~~This pocket is~~ Bowman's capsule.

16. ~~The tubule is~~ a tube-like structure that has a network of capillaries on its walls. The resulting water and dissolved materials end up in a tubule.

17. Capillaries are tiny blood vessels. ~~The capillaries~~ reabsorb any substances that the body needs.

18. ~~The water balance is~~ a delicate monitoring system. The body's water balance determines how much liquid is reabsorbed.

19. Urine is the only substance left in the tubule after reabsorption is complete. ~~This~~ liquid consists of waste products.

20. A urinalysis is often included as part of a physical health exam. ~~This is~~ a chemical analysis of the urine.

Review A: Revising a Passage by Combining Sentences, pp. 439–40

EXERCISE A

Answers will vary.

When an opossum is threatened, it expertly pretends to be dead. The opossum curling into a ball, many predators assume it is dead. It contorts its face into a frozen, deathlike grimace and sticks its tongue out. Remaining completely still, it keeps its eyes wide open in order to respond instantly if necessary.

On the other hand, lizards that encounter a predator usually scamper away rapidly. However, sometimes a predator catches a lizard. Most lizard species drop their tails in this circumstance. The predator, confused by the tail, is so distracted that the lizard has time to run away.

EXERCISE B

Answers will vary.

These Ice Age homes, some over 20,000 years old, represent the oldest human architecture on the planet. By using radiocarbon dating, scientists have concluded that the houses were constructed in eastern Europe between 14,000 and 25,000 years ago. At that time, eastern Europe was like the Arctic—treeless, windy, and extremely cold. Because wood was not available, Ice Age people built their houses from enormous mammoth bones, using considerable effort to construct them. Just one mammoth bone can weigh several hundred pounds.

Each house was made of hundreds of tusks and bones arranged in a twenty- to thirty-foot-wide circle. Usually, there was a hearth in the center. Archaeologists believe that the houses were draped with animal skins. A blazing fire in the hearth serving as a source of warmth, the skin and bone roof provided a shelter from the elements.

Coordinating Ideas, pp. 441–42

EXERCISE A

Answers will vary. Sample answers follow.

1. Farmers ∧and ranchers who keep animals depend on the occasional assistance of a local veterinarian. ~~Ranchers who keep animals also depend on the assistance of a veterinarian.~~

2. Farmers depend on veterinarians to maintain the health of their animals, and ~~Veterinarians are also needed~~ to help animals breed and give birth.

3. Veterinary medicine was practiced in Babylonia ∧and Egypt in 2000 B.C. ~~It also was practiced in Egypt then.~~

4. In this region, people considered many animals sacred and therefore untouchable, consequently ∧Veterinary science was often based on observation alone.

5. About 1000 B.C., the Greeks adopted veterinary medicine as a science that involved ∧both experimentation, and observation ~~They also involved observation as part of this science.~~

6. For 1,300 years following the collapse of the Roman Empire, the medical care of horses, and other animals was left to the horseshoers. ~~The medical care of other animals was also left to the horseshoers.~~

7. Veterinary medicine was introduced in colleges in the eighteenth century, and ~~It was~~ practiced on cattle.

8. Today veterinarians must earn the doctor of veterinary medicine (DVM) degree, They

receive it after they successfully complete the course work in physical and biological sciences.

9. Veterinarians must earn a degree in order to practice. ~~They must~~ and also obtain a license ~~in order to practice.~~

10. Like medical doctors, veterinarians may perform surgery on animals if necessary, and ~~They~~ also administer and prescribe medicine.

EXERCISE B

Answers will vary. Sample answers follow.

11. Teresa has recently learned about white dwarfs, and ~~She~~ knows that they were once stars.

12. The radius of white dwarfs is similar to that of the earth, and ~~Their~~ mass is equal to the sun's.

13. Once a star becomes a white dwarf, its dense matter degenerates, ~~This matter also~~ and ∧loses many of its electrons.

14. A star can remain stable for billions of years, but ~~When~~ its energy source is used up, i begins to die.

15. Helium, and hydrogen ~~an~~ energy sources inside a star, ha been consumed by the time a star become a white dwarf. ~~Hydrogen, another energy source, has also been depleted.~~

16. Sirius is the brightest star that can be seer from Earth, The companion of Sirius is th most recognizable white dwarf.

17. White dwarfs occasionally belong to bina star systems, ~~Many white dwarfs also~~ and ∧display the behavior of a nova, a star whose brightness suddenly increases and then decreases.

Language and Sentence Skills Practice Answer Key

169

18. The ionic energy escapes from the white dwarf over the course of several billion years, *, and* The white dwarf begins to lose its color during this period.

19. White dwarfs are the next-to-last stage in stellar evolution for stars that are less than 1.4 times as massive as the sun. Their average density is 1,000,000 times that of water.

20. The final stage of stellar evolution occurs when the white dwarf becomes an object sometimes called a black dwarf. At this point, the white dwarf is a cold, motionless mass.

Subordinating Ideas, pp. 443–44

Answers will vary. Sample answers follow.

1. My teacher began by explaining the origin of the horses, *which* ~~These horses~~ were brought to North America from Cuba.

2. In Cuba, the Spanish established stock farms, *which* ~~These farms~~ supplied horses to Hernando Cortés for his exploration of Mexico in 1519.

3. American Indians were introduced to a new way of life. ~~This was because~~ *when* the Spanish colonists brought the horse to the southwest in the late sixteenth century.

4. *Because* The Navajos lived in the southwest, The *y* ~~Navajos~~ were the first American Indians to have horses.

5. *As* Escaped Spanish horses roamed northward, Other American Indian groups captured and trained the *m* ~~horses~~.

6. The Plains Indians soon adapted to this new form of transportation. ~~The Plains Indians~~ *who* had been farmers and village dwellers.

7. The horse revolutionized the hunting of buffalo, *which* ~~Buffalo~~ soon became the mainstay of the Plains Indians' lives.

8. *Because of* The horse ~~changed something,~~ The Plains Indians became nomadic, following the buffalo and developing a new style of warfare.

9. The new way of life drew new groups of people to the plains, *where* ~~The people~~ *y* could live ~~there~~ more profitably.

10. Early cavalry officers frequently acknowledged the expert riding skills of their opponents. The *who* officers fought the Plains Indians in the 1800s.

Answers will vary. Sample answers follow.

11. *When* Calinda heard about Nawal el Saadawi in a literature class, She decided to write her term paper on this admirable woman.

12. *After* Calinda reviewed her notes from class, She found more information in the library.

13. Nawal el Saadawi is a famous writer, *who* ~~She~~ lives in Egypt.

14. Many of her books have been translated from Arabic into English. ~~They~~ *which* are widely read.

15. Her novel *Woman at Point Zero* criticizes *how* ~~something.~~ Restrictions on the lives of some Egyptian women have narrowed the range of options available to them.

16. Her fiction is poetic and elaborate. ~~It is~~ *which* based on complex, lyrical Arabic narratives.

17. *Death of an Ex-Minister and Other Stories* is one of her collections. *that* ~~It~~ contains experiments with diction and narration.

18. *While* El Saadawi's works of sociology and fiction have drawn attention to women's causes. Her travel accounts and political articles have promoted her crusade against the exploitation of women.

19. El Saadawi was put in prison. *because* She expressed her views opposing the social policies of Anwar Sadat's government.

20. Opposition to her determination to improve conditions for women helps to explain *why* something el Saadawi did. She founded the Arab Women's Solidarity Association (AWSA), an international organization for women to fight censorship and repression.

Review B: Coordinating and Subordinating Ideas, pp. 445–46

EXERCISE A
Answers will vary. Sample answers follow)

1. Penguins are such a photogenic bird. *that* Nearly everyone is familiar with their "tuxedo-clad" appearance.

2. *Because* The king penguin has a grayish blue back, a black plume on its head, a white breast, and a yellow band at its throat. A flock of them resembles a group of little men.

3. Penguins are short, flat-footed seabirds. *that* They can stand erect.

4. *Although* Some species of penguins live inland on ancestral nesting grounds. Most prefer the arctic climates and chilly coasts of Antarctica, New Zealand, Australia, Africa, and South America.

5. Penguins in prehistoric times stood as tall as six feet. *but* Today they are much shorter.

6. Emperor penguins are currently the tallest penguins at three and one-half feet. They *which* can weigh as much as eighty pounds.

7. Penguins' short, paddlelike wings don't enable flight. *because* They are fixed at the middle joint.

8. Penguins live most of their lives on land. *and* They do not need to fly because they have few natural predators.

9. Using their wings and feet to propel themselves through the water, penguins can swim as fast as twenty-five miles per hour. *and* They can leap as high as six feet out of the water onto land.

10. Penguins, feeding on squid, fish, and crustaceans, *so they* eat only underwater. They do not know how to eat on land.

EXERCISE B
Answers will vary. Sample answers follow.

11. Among the admissions requirements of many colleges are good high school grades. Colleges may also expect *and* personal recommendations from teachers or employers.

12. The college admissions process requires students to send high school transcripts *and* to prospective colleges and universities. Students send various other materials as well.

13. Students are required to take admissions tests. Two such tests are the American College Test (ACT) and the Scholastic Assessment Test (SAT).

14. *Both* The ACT is a test *and the SAT are* used by colleges and universities to determine whether students meet the standards for admission. The SAT also determines students' eligibility for admission.

15. *Although* Many students submit scores from both the ACT and the SAT. Most United States

colleges and universities require scores from only one of these tests.

16. Students typically take these tests during their junior, *or senior* year of high school. ~~The tests may also be taken during the senior year of high school.~~

17. Both tests are given several times each year, Students can repeat the tests as often as they wish.

18. The ACT has several sections, ~~These sections~~ *or that* include English, mathematics, science, and reading tests.

19. The SAT contains two parts, *however,* Many schools in the United States do not require applicants to take both parts.

20. The ACT is scored on a scale of 1 to 36, *but* SAT I scores and SAT II scores range from 200 to 800.

Review C: Revising a Passage by Combining Sentences, pp. 447–48

EXERCISE A
Answers will vary.

If the teeth in front become worn, a whole row of fresh teeth is directly behind them. As a shark matures, its new teeth are larger than its old ones. During its lifetime, one shark can wear out and replenish thousands of teeth.

Different species of sharks have different types of teeth. Depending on the food a species eats, the size and shape of teeth may vary widely. Tiger sharks, for example, are omnivorous eaters, and their food ranges from turtles to seabirds. Their strong, scale-shaped teeth can crush a turtle's shell or a seabird's bones. A sand tiger shark has curved teeth that are a sharp, deadly snare for squid or fish. The Port Jackson shark has tiny, pointed teeth at the front of its mouth for snatching prey; at the back of its mouth are flat, powerful teeth that can quickly break the shells of mussels and crabs.

EXERCISE B
Answers will vary.

Australia lies on the eastern part of the Indian Ocean. Asia is to the north, and Antarctica and Africa are to the south and the west respectively. The ocean is roughly 6,200 miles from north to south and between 4,000 and 6,000 miles from east to west. It averages about 13,000 feet in depth; however, its greatest depth is 24,442 feet.

Besides its many landmasses, the Indian Ocean contains abundant sea life. Large sea mammals and sea turtles are found throughout the ocean. Sponges, tuna, dolphins, sharks, and crabs also inhabit the waters of the ocean. The most common birds are the albatross and the frigate bird. Inhabiting the Antarctic and African coasts, many species of penguins are among the abundant animal life of the Indian Ocean.

Chapter 19: Improving Sentence Styles, pp. 449–62

Varying Sentence Beginnings, pp. 449–50

EXERCISE

Answers will vary. Sample answers follow.

1. A coldblooded reptile, the American alligator is commonly found in North Carolina, South Carolina, Florida, and along the Gulf Coast of the United States.

2. Although many people find alligators fascinating to watch and study, experts advise these observers to distance themselves from alligators by at least fifteen feet.

3. Occurring in April and May, the principal breeding season for alligators lasts between six and eight weeks.

4. Frequently, alligator nests contain more than two dozen eggs.

5. To keep their eggs above water, female alligators construct their nests carefully.

6. Because alligators do not sit on their eggs to keep them warm, the incubation of the eggs depends on how well the nest is constructed.

7. Linked to the availability of food, a young alligator's growth rate may vary from a few inches to as much as one foot per year.

8. Vulnerable to a variety of natural enemies, young alligators often remain with their mothers for more than two years.

9. Predators known for their ferocity, alligators are carnivores and scavengers.

10. Even though alligators can survive for extended periods without food, their powerful jaws and sharp teeth guarantee that they will seldom be hungry.

Varying Sentence Structure, pp. 451–52

EXERCISE A

Answers will vary. Sample answers follow.

After clearing the leaves and weeds, they pour wine on the ground, bow, and make an offering of three kinds of food: chicken, fish, and pork. To complete the ceremony, they burn incense and paper that represents money.

Retaining some customs from the past, a Chinese American wedding celebration is another significant ritual. The groom's family may send the bride hundreds of moon cakes that are given to friends and relatives. Traditionally, the moon cakes serve as announcements. Written on red paper, wedding invitations are engraved with gold letters.

On the day of the ceremony, the bride may wear a red wedding dress. According to custom, the groom's family provides the banquet; however, the bride's family gives the couple household goods, furniture, and money.

EXERCISE B

Answers will vary. Sample answers follow.

Saudi Arabia, a country of about eighteen million people, covers most of the Arabian Peninsula in southwestern Asia. Hot and dry, most of Saudi Arabia gets less than four inches of rain each year. Because scant rainfall and hot temperatures persist during most of the year, very little vegetation grows in Saudi Arabia. The country is ruled by a monarch, or king, whose power is absolute, but the king often consults his Council of Ministers. The Saudi legal system is based on Islam, the religion founded by Mohammed in A.D. 622. Islamic law prescribes a strict code of behavior and governs courts as well as family life. The power and prestige of Saudi Arabia come from two sources: The country has great oil wealth, and it is the site of two of the holiest cities of Islam—Mecca and Medina.

Review A: Varying Sentence Beginnings and Structure, pp. 453–54

EXERCISE A

Answers will vary. Sample answers follow.

Many people think that Mozart is the greatest composer who ever lived. When he was only four years old, Mozart began writing original compositions, and he learned to play the violin. At age six he toured Europe, playing for royalty, famous musicians, and ordinary people. Soon Mozart began to write large compositions; he created symphonies at age eight, and he wrote an opera when he was eleven. While composing, he liked to wear ruffled, embroidered, velvet jackets, a tiny golden sword, and an apron that protected his fancy outfit from ink stains. Not surprisingly, he was obsessed with his appearance when he was an adult too. He saw a barber often and wore luxurious clothes. Because many clients gave him trinkets as payment instead of cash, Mozart was constantly in debt. Often ill, he was too thin and had yellow skin scarred by smallpox blisters. Suffering from malnutrition and kidney failure, Mozart died when he was only thirty-five.

EXERCISE B
Answers will vary. Sample answers follow.

When O'Keeffe's husband, the famous photographer Alfred Stieglitz, died, she was fifty-nine years old. Moving again to New Mexico, O'Keeffe spent the rest of her life there. She lived in an adobe home with a spectacular view of the nearby cliffs. Although O'Keeffe spent much of her time painting the scenery, she also pursued other activities. Athletic and curious, she rode horses in the moonlight, observed the ceremonies of American Indians, and went river rafting. O'Keeffe gathered bones that she found while hiking and depicted them in her paintings. Moreover, her neighbors thought she was strange and were afraid of her. However, others appreciated her generosity to the community. She donated money to local institutions, including an elementary school and a recreation center.

Revising Wordy Sentences, pp. 455–56
EXERCISE A
Unnecessary words and commas are crossed out. Answers will vary. Sample answers follow.

1. Have you heard of the Acoma ~~American Indians~~, who are American Indians living in New Mexico?

2. Many experts debate ~~and argue~~ that the Acoma pueblo, or village, is the oldest constantly occupied, ~~inhabited~~ settlement in the United States.

3. Centuries before Coronado ~~arrived in and~~ explored the Southwest, the Acoma

American Indians had been living ~~for hundreds of years~~ in their Sky City.

4. From an immense, ~~huge~~ plain west of Albuquerque rises a mesa made of sandstone, ~~which is stone made of sand~~.

5. The Acoma pueblo is ~~located above and~~ on top of that mesa, which is approximately ~~about~~ 7,000 feet in elevation.

6. From a distance ~~far away~~ it is hard to see the two hundred or more adobe buildings ~~made of mud and straw~~.

7. These homes are also constructed with wooden beams ~~made from trees,~~ and flat, ~~level~~ stones.

8. The American Indians grow ~~and raise~~ beans, squash, and maize in fields beneath, ~~or under,~~ the mesa.

9. C

10. Today the church of San Esteban Rey, built ~~and constructed~~ in the 1600s, towers high above ~~the rest of~~ the pueblo.

EXERCISE B
Unnecessary words and commas are crossed out. Answers will vary. Sample answers follow.

11. King Louis XIV, ~~a king~~ of France, ruled ~~as king~~ in the seventeenth and early eighteenth centuries.

12. Louis XIV reigned for over seventy years, ~~seventy-two, to be exact~~.

13. Louis was an absolute monarch, meaning that he ~~was a monarch who~~ had final political authority ~~over everything and everybody~~ in ~~his own country of~~ France.

14. Having received an education that prepared him well for leadership, Louis proclaimed that he himself would be his

own chief minister, ~~instead of appointing someone else to that office~~.

15. C

16. Because he wished to become the most powerful ruler in Europe, Louis fought four wars ~~so that he would be recognized as the dominant king in Europe.~~

17. In the War of the Spanish Succession, Louis hoped to preserve the right of his grandson Philip to be king of Spain ~~and ruler of that entire country.~~

18. ~~One of the things that~~ Louis is remembered for ~~is~~ building ~~the fact that he built~~ the palace of Versailles, where he lived in splendor with his court.

19. C

20. ~~In the early years of the eighteenth century,~~ Louis' reign of seventy-two years ended with his death in 1715.

Revising a Wordy Paragraph, pp. 457–58
EXERCISE A
Answers will vary. Sample answers follow.

Many icebergs and glaciers contain caves ~~that are~~ created ~~and made~~ by ice that melts ~~into water~~ and then *re*freezes ~~hard~~. When water enters cracks in the earth ~~and seeps into them~~, earthquake caves are sometimes formed. The ~~sides, or~~ walls of volcanoes can contain lava caves, which are forged when an inner layer of lava flows ~~as a liquid~~ and an upper layer of lava ~~becomes solid~~ *solidifies*. Sea caves, such as the famous ~~and well-known~~ Blue Grotto in Italy, might take centuries to form; waves slam into ~~the bases of~~ cliffs ~~for hundreds of years~~, gradually carving away the rock. Underground caves are created in two ~~different~~ ways. Both ~~of~~

~~the methods~~ involv*ing* water. In the first method, an underground stream ~~deep beneath the earth~~ moves through rock fissures; slowly, the water erodes the rock and makes a ~~hollow~~ cave. In the second method, water filters through limestone, dissolving minerals. This process creates not only a cave, but also stalagmites, stalactites, and other ~~beautiful,~~ exquisite rock formations.

EXERCISE B
Answers will vary. Sample answers follow.

Humpback whales, which migrate ~~and travel~~ through that area, sing beautiful, ~~involved, and~~ complex melodies. The whales' songs range from six to thirty minutes ~~a half hour~~ in length. Some whales link ~~many~~ songs ~~together~~ into one continuous performance ~~and it lasts~~ *sing* for hours ~~on end~~. Originally, scientists ~~at first~~ thought the humpbacks' noises were erratic, ~~not conforming to a regular pattern~~. However, after recording, studying, and analyzing the songs, scientists discovered ~~that there was~~ a distinct, clear pattern ~~in evidence~~. Each song has several themes, and these themes contain phrases. Even though the ~~humpback~~ whales' songs are various lengths, the songs inevitably include the same ~~identical~~ number of phrases in a theme. As they repeat a phrase ~~over and over again~~, the whales change it a little bit until, after numerous repetitions, the concluding ~~and last~~ phrase is completely distinct from the initial one.

Revising Sentences Through Reduction, pp. 459–60
EXERCISE A
Answers will vary. Sample answers follow.

1. This army of clay soldiers was discovered in 1974, *when* ~~at which time~~ workers were ~~engaged in~~ digging a well.

2. The Terracotta Army consists of more than seven thousand men ~~who are made of~~ clay, ~~and that clay was~~ fired.

3. The sculptures, ~~which are~~ life-size, were supposed to guard the first emperor of China *when* ~~in the event that~~ he died.

4. *Although* ~~Despite the fact that~~ so many warriors were produced, each one is ~~an individual who is~~ unique.

5. For example, the soldiers, ~~who are all~~ standing, have facial expressions ~~that~~ differ*ing* and styles of beard ~~that~~ var*ious*.

6. ~~The fact that~~ there is even transportation; more than one hundred war chariots and approximately six hundred clay horses ~~that are designed~~ *wait* to carry some of the warriors.

7. *Because* ~~Due to the fact that~~ they are leaders, the generals *are muscular* ~~possess muscles that are big~~ and ~~have a build that is heavy~~ *heavily* *t* .

8. *If* ~~In the event that~~ an enemy ~~were to~~ overc*a*me the troops, the emperor's burial mound, ~~which is nearby,~~ remained protected ~~by means of~~ booby traps.

9. When archaeologists excavate sites such as the Terracotta Army, we can learn more about peoples ~~that lived in the past~~ and their cultures ~~that they had~~.

10. Archaeology may be work ~~that is~~ dirty, but it is also ~~work that is~~ rewarding.

EXERCISE B

Answers will vary. Sample answers follow.

11. ~~Due to the fact that~~ Anderson ~~had been~~ interested in flying since he was a boy, ~~he~~ *Anderson* borrowed money to buy his first airplane.

12. Anderson then ~~very shortly thereafter~~ taught himself to fly.

13. Anderson*'s* *became* ~~becoming~~ chief flight instructor ~~and flight trainer~~ of the first ~~and original~~ African American military pilot group ~~was the result~~ *for* ~~of~~ two reasons.

14. He earned outstanding flight credentials and ~~he met and~~ favorably impressed First Lady Eleanor Roosevelt, ~~who was~~ influential.

15. Anderson's project was called the Tuskegee Experiment, ~~a sort of testing program~~.

16. The Tuskegee Experiment took place ~~at the school of the same name~~ Tuskegee Institute in Alabama; ~~that was at a time~~ when no African Americans had ever been trained as military pilots.

17. ~~The fact is that it was~~ the Roosevelt Administration ~~that~~ started the Tuskegee Experiment.

18. It was Roosevelt's successor ~~and the next president~~, Harry Truman, who used Anderson's successful program to bring an end to sanctioned racial discrimination in the military.

19. Among Anderson's ~~many~~ famous ~~and notable~~ students at Tuskegee were General Benjamin O. Davis, Jr.; General Daniel "Chappie" James, Jr.; *and* Colonel Herbert Carter; ~~and other well-known Tuskegee~~ pilots who distinguished themselves in military careers.

20. Chief Anderson *died* ~~lived~~ ~~until the last decade of the twentieth century; the fact is that it was~~ in 1996 ~~that he died~~.

Review B: Revising a Paragraph by Reducing Wordiness, pp. 461–62

EXERCISE A

Answers will vary. Sample answers follow.

Because Singer's family often did not have the money for food, he had no toys when he was a child. Consequently, he amused himself by reading so that he could forget his difficulties. As he became a young man, Singer confronted an even greater problem—anti-Jewish sentiment was increasing dangerously in Europe. To escape what would be called the Holocaust, he immigrated to the United States when he was thirty-one. When the Nazis came into power, many of Singer's friends and family were killed, and most of Warsaw was destroyed. Devotedly, Singer recreated the Warsaw of his childhood through his writing. He wrote in Yiddish, an increasingly neglected combination of Russian, Slavic, and German that uses the Hebrew alphabet. Singer wrote novels, short stories, children's books, and other works, eventually winning the Nobel Prize in literature.

EXERCISE B

Answers will vary. Sample answers follow.

Monarch butterflies deposit their eggs on poisonous milkweed leaves. Emerging, the caterpillars eat the deadly plants without suffering any ill effects. Because few other animals can tolerate it, the milkweed ensures a steady supply of nourishment for the caterpillars. By ingesting the poison, the caterpillars also make themselves toxic to enemies. Another example of this unusual practice is the South American scarlet macaw, which consumes poisonous fruits and seeds. To counteract the poison, the macaw eats a clay, kaolin, that absorbs the toxins, preventing any harm to the bird. Chimpanzees also eat fruit with poisonous seeds but avoid illness or death. Because these animals have muscular lips, they can eat around the toxic seeds. While eating, the woolly monkeys of the Amazon are similarly careful. These monkeys feed on poisonous trees, but they eat only new leaves whose toxins are in low concentrations.

Language and Sentence Skills Practice Answer Key

Resources, pp. 463–64

Manuscript Form, pp. 463–64

Students should have transferred information given in the exercise to the appropriate lines on the model page.